名家精彩演讲系列丛书

英汉双语同步对照

U0604694

改变世界的力量
诺贝尔奖大师演讲精选

成应翠　韩彦芳　主编

NOBEL

 北京航空航天大学出版社
BEIHANG UNIVERSITY PRESS

图书在版编目（CIP）数据

改变世界的力量：诺贝尔奖大师演讲精选：英汉对照 / 成应翠，韩彦芳主编 . -- 北京：北京航空航天大学出版社，2017.3

ISBN 978-7-5124-1045-9

Ⅰ.①改… Ⅱ.①成… ②韩… Ⅲ.①英语－汉语－对照读物②演讲－世界－选集 Ⅳ.① H319.4：I

中国版本图书馆 CIP 数据核字（2017）第 002519 号

改变世界的力量：诺贝尔奖大师演讲精选

主　　编　　成应翠　韩彦芳

责任编辑　　江小珍

*

北京航空航天大学出版社出版发行

北京市海淀区学院路 37 号（邮编 100191）　http://www.buaapress.com.cn

发行部电话：(010)82317024　传真：(010)82328026

读者信箱：bhpress@263.net　邮购电话：(010)82316936

北京艺堂印刷有限公司印装　各地书店经销

*

开本：710×960　1/16　印张：15.75　字数：343 千字

2017 年 3 月第 1 版　2017 年 3 月第 1 次印刷

ISBN 978-7-5124-1045-9　定价：39.80 元

本书编委会

主　编：成应翠　韩彦芳

编委会成员（排名不分先后）：

前言

诺贝尔奖，自 1901 年设立之日起，便举世瞩目，如今虽已历经百年，却光芒依旧。每年的 12 月，诺贝尔奖都会对"一年来对人类做出最大贡献的人"进行嘉奖，这些获奖大师是人类杰出思想的代表，是推动人类进步的动力，是改变世界的导师。

"如果心灵世界不随之进步，那么不断增长的物质力量只能招致更多的危难⋯⋯"

——美国黑人运动领袖马丁·路德·金诺贝尔和平奖演讲词

"我们承认压迫始终存在，而我们也会继续为公平正义奋斗。我们承认堕落很难对付，但仍为尊严奋斗⋯⋯"

——美国首位黑人总统奥巴马诺贝尔和平奖演讲词

"对一个人的伤害就是伤害所有人，因此只有一起行动才能维护正义和人类共同的尊严⋯⋯"

——南非国父曼德拉诺贝尔和平奖演讲词

"一个作家必须要有一块属于自己的领地。一个人在日常生活中应该谦卑退让，但在文学创作中，必须颐指气使，独断专行⋯⋯"

——中国籍作家莫言诺贝尔文学奖演讲词

透过大师们的获奖演讲，你可以走进他们的内心世界，近距离地和大师们来一次跨越时空的心灵对话，感受他们探索未知、追求真理的勇气。一篇篇获奖演讲就像是一场场直抵灵魂的精神洗礼，为你打开通往另一个更广阔世界的大门，鉴于此，我们将这些充满智慧与激情的文字汇集成了一本《改变世界的力量：诺贝尔奖大师演讲精选》。

本书精选了历年来最有影响力的诺贝尔奖大师获奖演讲，内容涵盖"文学的力量：创作让理想闪光的诺贝尔奖大师演讲"、"独立的人格：以卓越思想启迪人生的诺贝尔奖大师演讲"、"共建未来世界：捍卫人类家园的诺贝尔奖大师演讲"以及"和平的使者：点燃和平希望的诺贝尔奖大师演讲"。翻开本书，你能近距离感受诺贝尔奖大师的崇高人格和语言风采：从美国文坛硬汉欧内斯特·海明威的诺贝尔文学奖获奖演讲中，你可以对理想的写作有更深刻的认识；从第一个获得诺贝尔文学奖的中国籍作家莫言的演讲中，你可以了解到作家创作的初衷和动力；从带领联合国跨越两个世纪的秘书长科菲·安南的诺贝尔和平奖获奖演讲中，你能体会到他为人类共同的美好未来所做出的不懈努力⋯⋯

翻开本书，原汁原味的英文、精准流畅的译文、贴心细致的讲解，会带给你强烈的心灵震撼和美妙的语言享受。本书有着让你拿起来就放不下的几大特色：

✓ 诺贝尔奖大师演讲词表达地道、用词精妙，最适合跟读、效仿、反复精听

本书所选演讲是诺贝尔奖大师思想的延伸和智慧的结晶，其表达地道、用词精准，适合模仿学习。跟诺贝尔奖大师学演讲，能让经典好英文不知不觉"潜入"你的大脑，使你的英语表达能力迅速提升！

✓ 品读诺贝尔奖大师演讲，追随大师足迹，接受灵魂洗礼，活出完美人生

与诺贝尔奖大师面对面，汲取榜样的正能量。诺贝尔奖大师像一座精神的灯塔，照亮人们前行之路。诺贝尔奖大师的演讲是极具智慧的精神食粮，给人一种心灵的启迪。

✓ 诺贝尔奖大师速写，让你快速了解诺贝尔奖大师最亮丽的风采

书中每篇演讲前都特别提供了"名家速览"这个板块，可以帮助你提前领略到诺贝尔奖大师的风采。另外，本板块还提供了对相应演讲的简要介绍，让你在阅读时能心中有数，轻松实现英语阅读零压力！

✓ 全面合理的板块设置

名家速览→演讲现场→精美译文→演讲关键词→精华佳句，是你最贴心的私房笔记！它们使得本书的学习功能更强大，保证每一篇英语演讲都可以真正实现360度"无死角"的英语学习！

诺贝尔奖大师演讲有着非凡的语言力量，或慷慨激昂，或轻松幽默，或质朴真诚，或意义深远。翻开本书，你不仅能感受到诺贝尔奖大师的语言魅力，还能学习到最地道的英语表达和丰富的文化知识。本书是广大在校大学生、英语爱好者及社会各阶层人士提高英语水平的理想之选。就让本书带你收获智慧财富，帮助你拓宽思想格局，扩充生命价值吧！

编　者
2017 年春于北京

ontents
目 录

Chapter 2　独立的人格：以卓越思想启迪人生的诺贝尔奖大师演讲

Chapter 3　共建未来世界：捍卫人类家园的诺贝尔奖大师演讲

Chapter 4　和平的使者：点燃和平希望的诺贝尔奖大师演讲

文学的力量：创作让理想闪光的诺贝尔奖大师演讲

Speech 1

Writing, a Lonely Life
写作，孤寂的生涯

—Speech by Ernest Hemingway for the Nobel Prize in Literature in 1954
——美国文坛硬汉欧内斯特·海明威 1954 年诺贝尔文学奖获奖演讲

 名家速览 About the Author

诺贝尔奖大师	欧内斯特·海明威
奖 项 归 属	诺贝尔文学奖
获 奖 理 由	因为他精通于叙事艺术——突出地表现在其著作《老人与海》之中；同时也因为他对当代文体风格之影响。
获 奖 作 品	《老人与海》
相关演讲链接	海明威在第二次美国作家大会上的发言——作家与战斗

欧内斯特·海明威（Ernest Hemingway，1899—1961），美国著名小说家，战地记者，1899 年 7 月 21 日出生于美国伊利诺伊州芝加哥市郊区奥克帕克的一个医生家庭，父亲酷爱打猎、钓鱼等户外活动，母亲喜爱文学。海明威作为战地记者参加了第一次世界大战并在战争中受伤，康复后作为加拿大多伦多《星报》的记者常驻巴黎，一面当记者，一面写小说，在近 10 年的时间里出版了《太阳照常升起》等许多作品，1928 年离开巴黎，在美国的佛罗里达州和古巴过着宁静的田园生活，1929 年出版的长篇小说《永别了，武器》被称为"迷惘的一代"文学的最佳作品。1937—1938 年海明威以战地记者的身份奔波于西班牙内战前线，第二次世界大战期间作为记者随军行动并参加了解放巴黎的战斗，于 1940 年发表了以西班牙内战为背景的反法西斯主义的长篇小说《丧钟为谁而鸣》，1952 年发表中篇小说《老人与海》，并于 1954 年获得诺贝尔文学奖。本文是海明威诺贝尔文学奖的获奖演讲，当年由于他本人疾病缠身无法出席颁奖典礼，因而这篇演讲词是由美国驻瑞典大使代读的，其中谈及了海明威本人对获奖和理想的写作的看法。

文学的力量：创作让理想闪光的诺贝尔奖大师演讲

演讲现场
Speech Script

精美译文
Suggested Translation

1 Having no *facility* ① for speech-making and no command of *oratory* ② nor any domination of *rhetoric* ③, I wish to thank the administrators of the generosity of Alfred Nobel for this Prize.

2 No writer who knows the great writers who did not receive the Prize can accept it other than with *humility* ④. There is no need to list these writers. Everyone here may make his own list according to his knowledge and his conscience.

3 It would be impossible for me to ask the Ambassador of my country to read a speech in which a writer said all of the things which are in his heart. Things may not be immediately *discernible* ⑤ in what a man writes, and in this sometimes he is fortunate; but eventually they are quite clear and by these and the degree of *alchemy* ⑥ that he possesses he will endure or be forgotten.

4 Writing, at its best, is a lonely life. Organizations for writers *palliate* ⑦ the writer's loneliness but I doubt if they improve his writing. He grows in public *stature* ⑧ as he sheds his loneliness and often his work deteriorates. For he

1 我不擅演讲，也不懂修辞，只能在此感谢诺贝尔奖委员会慷慨授予我这项荣誉。

2 任何作家，当他知道那么多伟大的作家都没有得奖时，都不可能心安理得地接受这个奖项。也没有必要在此一一列举这些没获奖的作家了，因为每个人都会根据自己的理解和良知，列出自己心中的名单。

3 请我国大使代读这篇演讲，还要讲尽我心中无限事，这几乎是不可能的。作家写的东西可能不会那么快就被人理解，在这一点上，有些作家很幸运；但是最终他们会得到理解的，而且作家点石成金的能力大小会决定他们是不朽还是被遗忘。

4 写作处于巅峰状态时，是一种孤独的生涯。作家参与的一些组织固然能缓解这种孤独，但能否提高其写作就另当别论了。通常在公众的关注和吹捧之下，他会摆脱孤独，但他

① facility [fə'sɪlɪtɪ] *n.* 技巧，技艺，灵巧

② oratory ['ɒrətərɪ] *n.* 演讲术，雄辩

③ rhetoric ['retərɪk] *n.* 运用语言的技能；花言巧语

④ humility [hju(:)'mɪlɪtɪ] *n.* 谦卑，谦逊

⑤ discernible [dɪ'sɜːnəbl] *adj.* 可辨别的；可识别的

⑥ alchemy ['ælkɪmɪ] *n.* 点金术；魔力

⑦ palliate ['pælɪeɪt] *vt.* 减轻；掩饰 如：palliate a crime/disease 减轻罪行 / 疾病

⑧ stature ['stætʃə] *n.* 尊重

does his work alone and if he is a good enough writer he must face eternity, or the lack of it, each day.

5 For a true writer each book should be a new beginning where he tries again for something that is beyond *attainment* [9]. He should always try for something that has never been done or that others have tried and failed. Then sometimes, with great luck, he will succeed.

6 How simple the writing of literature would be if it were only necessary to write in another way what has been well written. It is because we have had such great writers in the past that a writer is driven far out past where he can go, out to where no one can help him.

7 I have spoken too long for a writer. A writer should write what he has to say and not speak it. Again I thank you.

的作品也会随之流于平庸。而一个在孤寂中工作的作家，如果他又确实不同凡响，那他就必须每天面对永恒或者缺乏永恒的状况。

5 对一个真正的作家来说，每一部作品都是一个新的开始，都将是对以往能力的超越。他要不断尝试别人没做过的事，或者别人未能成功的事。这样，他才可能成功。

6 如果只是换种方式去诠释别人的作品，那文学创作该是多么简单啊。我们已经有那么多伟大的作家，正是如此，现在的写作者才要远离他们，去一个没有人能帮忙的地方创作。

7 作为一个作家，我已经说得够多了。一个作家有话要说，他应该去写作，而不是口头表达。所以，再次感谢你们。

演讲关键词 Practical Expressions

1. to have no facility for speech-making 不擅演讲
2. to have no domination of rhetoric 不懂修辞
3. a lonely life 孤独生涯
4. accept... other than with humility 心安理得地接受……
5. shed loneliness 摆脱孤独
6. work deteriorates 作品流于平庸

⑨ attainment [ə'teɪnmənt] n. 成就；学识；达到 如：a man of high attainments 有很高造诣的人

文学的力量：创作让理想闪光的诺贝尔奖大师演讲

1. Writing, at its best, is a lonely life.

　写作处于巅峰状态时，是一种孤独的生涯。

2. A writer should write what he has to say and not speak it.

　一个作家有话要说，他应该去写作，而不是口头表达。

 诺贝尔奖背后的那些趣事

意外得奖后的疯狂

　　对获奖者来说，诺贝尔奖的到来常常是出人意料、让人喜出望外的。

　　2002 年诺贝尔经济学奖颁给了丹尼尔·卡尼曼和弗农·史密斯，以表彰他们在心理和实验经济学研究方面做出了开创性工作。

　　然而，卡尼曼却认为自己是一名心理学家而非经济学家。他 1934 年出生于以色列，1961 年获得美国加利福尼亚大学伯克利分校博士学位。他在以色列希伯来大学、加拿大不列颠哥伦比亚大学和美国加利福尼亚大学伯克利分校三所学校都拥有教授头衔。自 1993 年以来，他一直在普林斯顿大学教书，是该大学第 3 位获得诺贝尔奖的教授。2002 年 10 月 9 日，他得知自己获奖的消息后，十分激动，竟把自己反锁在屋里，后来来庆贺的人们不得不破窗而入。

Speech 2
Chinese Novel（1）
中国小说（1）

—Speech by Pearl Buck for the Nobel Prize in Literature in 1938
——唯一同时获得普利策奖和诺贝尔奖的女作家赛珍珠 1938 年诺贝尔文学奖获奖演讲

名家速览 About the Author

诺贝尔奖大师	赛珍珠（珀尔·布克）
奖 项 归 属	诺贝尔文学奖
获 奖 理 由	因为她对中国农民生活真实而丰富的史诗般的描述，以及她自传性质的杰作。
获 奖 作 品	《大地》
相关演讲链接	中国抗日战争爆发后，赛珍珠在美国发表一系列抗战演讲

赛珍珠（1892 年 6 月 26 日—1973 年 3 月 6 日）是一位美国女作家。她出生后四个月就被身为传教士的父母带到了中国，从此在中国镇江长大成人。成年后，赛珍珠回到了美国，开始用英语创作。她以中国农村为题材的小说《大地》1932 年在美国获普利策奖，又于 1938 年获诺贝尔文学奖。她成为美国第一位获诺贝尔文学奖的女作家。回到美国后，她一方面积极投身妇女权利和少数民族权利运动，另一方面努力写作，创作出大量反映亚洲尤其是中国文化的作品。赛珍珠在中国生活了近 40 年，她把中文称为"第一语言"，把镇江称为"中国故乡"。在中国期间，她曾任教于金陵大学（今南京大学），教授外文和教育学等课程，她的丈夫布克也在该校教授农业技术和农场管理，他们平时居住在金陵大学的一栋小楼内，至今南京大学还留有赛珍珠夫妇当年的故居。许多中国知名文化人士，如林语堂、徐志摩、梅兰芳、胡适、老舍等人，都曾是她家的座上客。本篇演讲选自赛珍珠的诺贝尔文学奖获奖演讲，文中她详细讲述了中国小说的发展史和自己对中国小说的欣赏态度，以及她在中国所受的有关小说创作的教育。

文学的力量：创作让理想闪光的诺贝尔奖大师演讲

演讲现场
Speech Script

精美译文
Suggested Translation

1 Members of the Swedish Academy, Ladies and Gentlemen,

2 When I came to consider what I should say today it seemed that it would be wrong not to speak of China. And this is none the less true because I am an American by birth and by *ancestry* ① and though I live now in my own country and shall live there, since there I belong. But it is the Chinese and not the American novel which has shaped my own efforts in writing. My earliest knowledge of story, of how to tell and write stories, came to me in China. It would be *ingratitude* ② on my part not to recognize this today. And yet it would be presumptuous to speak before you on the subject of the Chinese novel for a reason wholly personal. There is another reason why I feel that I may properly do so. It is that I believe the Chinese novel has an illumination for the Western novel and for the Western novelist.

3 When I say Chinese novel, I mean the *indigenous* ③ Chinese novel, and not that *hybrid* ④ product, the novels of modern Chinese writers who have been too strongly under foreign influence while they were yet ignorant of the riches of their own country.

1 尊敬的瑞典学院的成员们，女士们、先生们：

2 当我思考着今天要说些什么的时候，我发觉不谈谈中国小说似乎是不对的。千真万确，尽管我出生在美国，在血缘上也是美国人，我现在应该，也确实居住在我自己的祖国——美国，因为我属于那里，但是在写小说上给我启蒙、促使我开始努力写作的是中国的而非美国的小说。我最初学到的有关故事的知识，以及讲故事、写故事的方法都来自于中国。所以，如果我今天在这里不讲讲这些，那就是忘恩负义。然而，仅仅因个人原因而在你们面前大谈中国小说又太冒昧。所以，其实还有另一个原因让我觉得应该这样做。那就是我相信中国小说对西方小说和西方的小说家具有启发意义。

3 我所说的中国小说指的是地地道道的本土小说，并不是现代中国小说家那些混血的作品。现代中国小说家们都深受外国的影响，对自己本国的财富却浑然不知。

---

① ancestry ['ænsɪstrɪ] *n.* 血统，家族　如：be of good ancestry 出身名门

② ingratitude [ɪn'grætɪtjuːd] *n.* 忘恩负义　如：ingratitude to one's parents 对父母不孝

③ indigenous [ɪn'dɪdʒɪnəs] *adj.* 本土的　如：Indians were the indigenous inhabitants of America. 印第安人是美洲的土著居民。

④ hybrid ['haɪbrɪd] *adj.* 混合的，混血的　如：hybrid animals 杂交动物

4 The novel in China was never an art and was never so considered, nor did any Chinese novelist think of himself as an artist. The Chinese novel its history, its scope, its place in the life of the people, so vital a place, must be viewed in the strong light of this one fact. It is a fact no doubt strange to you, a company of modern Western scholars who today so generously recognize the novel.

5 But in China art and the novel have always been widely separated. There, literature as an art was the exclusive property of the scholars, an art they made and made for each other according to their own rules, and they found no place in it for the novel. And they held a powerful place, those Chinese scholars. Philosophy and religion and letters and literature, by arbitrary classical rules, they possessed them all, for they alone possessed the means of learning, since they alone knew how to read and write. They were powerful enough to be feared even by emperors, so that emperors devised a way of keeping them enslaved by their own learning, and made the official examinations the only means to political advancement, those incredibly difficult examinations which ate up a man's whole life and thought in preparing for them, and kept him too busy with memorizing and copying the dead and classical past to see the present and its wrongs. In that past the scholars found their rules of art. But the novel was not there, and they did not see it being created before their eyes, for the people created the novel, and what living people were doing did not interest

4 在中国，小说从来都不是艺术，不受尊重，也没有任何中国小说家认为自己是艺术家。因此中国小说的历史性、它的视角、它在人们生活中的地位——如此重要的地位，都要从这个角度来看待。对于你们这些直到今天才慷慨认可中国小说的现代西方文人来说，这无疑会是一个奇怪的事实。

5 在中国，艺术和小说一直以来都是分离的。作为艺术的文学是文人们独有的资产，他们即兴创作，互相应和。但是在文学里，没有小说的位置。中国的文人享有很重要的地位。按照一些专制的古典规则，这些中国文人独断地享有所有哲学、宗教、文字和文学，就因为他们独自霸占着学习机会，只有他们能读会写。就连皇帝也怕他们，所以皇帝创造了一种用文人们自己的学识来约束他们的办法——使官方考试成为在政治上晋升的唯一途径。对于那些难得不可思议的考试，文人们常常要穷尽一生，忙着记忆复制过去那些死板的经典，以古鉴今，借古讽今。那时候文人有自己的艺术规则。但小说不在其中，他们也没有亲眼见到过小说；因为小说来自普通民众，而人民做的事不会使那些视文学为艺术的人感兴趣。如果文人忽视人民，反过来，人民就会讥笑文人。他们拿这些文人们开了无数玩笑，其中一个是这样的：有一天一群野兽相约到山上捕猎。他

those who thought of literature as an art. If scholars ignored the people, however, the people, in turn, laughed at the scholars. They made innumerable jokes about them, of which this is a fair sample: One day a company of wild beasts met on a hillside for a hunt. They bargained with each other to go out and hunt all day and meet again at the end of the day to share what they had killed. At the end of the day, only the tiger returned with nothing. When he was asked how this happened he replied very **disconsolately** [5], "At dawn I met a schoolboy, but he was, I feared, too **callow** [6] for your tastes. I met no more until noon, when I found a priest. But I let him go, knowing him to be full of nothing but wind. The day went on and I grew desperate, for I passed no one. Then as dark came on I found a scholar. But I knew there was no use in bringing him back since he would be so dry and hard that he would break our teeth if we tried them on him."

6 The scholar as a class has long been a figure of fun for the Chinese people. He is frequently to be found in their novels, and always he is the same, as indeed he is in life, for a long study of the same dead classics and their formal composition has really made all Chinese scholars look alike, as well as think alike. We have no class to parallel him in the West—individuals, perhaps, only. But in China he was a class. Here he is, composite, as the people see him: a small shrunken figure with a bulging forehead, a pursed

们商量好各自出去狩猎一天，一天结束时回来一起分享收获。天黑汇合时，只有老虎两手空空。大家就问他这是怎么回事，他悲伤地回答："黎明时，我见到了一个学生，但我担心他太嫩了，不合你们的口味。直到中午我才碰上了一个牧师，但也放了他，因为他除了还有一口气瘦得什么都没有了。又过了好久，后来我几近绝望，因为什么都没捕到。到黄昏的时候，我碰上一位文人。但我知道带他回来也没有用，因为他又干又硬，想吃他都硌牙。"

6 文人阶级在中国一直是人们取笑的对象。他们在小说里经常出现，而且形象都一样，永远都在死读经典，他们的文章千篇一律，思想也都大致相似。在西方没有任何一个阶级和中国的文人相似，也许相像的只有一些个人。但是在中国，他们是一个阶级，就像人们看到的那样，是一个整体的形象：身材矮小，前额突出，两腮瘦削，鼻子又尖又短，一双小眼睛隐藏在眼镜后面，一副学究的

⑤ disconsolately [dɪsˈkɒnsəlɪtlɪ] *adv.* 悲伤地，郁闷地

⑥ callow [ˈkæləʊ] *adj.* 嫩的，羽毛未长满的　如：a callow youth 乳臭未干的年轻人

mouth, a nose at once snub and pointed, small inconspicuous eyes behind spectacles, a high *pedantic* [7] voice, always announcing rules that do not matter to anyone but himself, a boundless self-conceit, a complete scorn not only of the common people but of all other scholars, a figure in long shabby robes, moving with a swaying *haughty* [8] walk, when he moved at all. He was not to be seen except at literary gatherings, for most of the time he spent reading dead literature and trying to write more like it. He hated anything fresh or original, for he could not catalogue it into any of the styles he knew. If he could not catalogue it, he was sure it was not great, and he was confident that only he was right. If he said, "Here is art", he was convinced it was not to be found anywhere else, for what he did not recognize did not exist. And as he could never catalogue the novel into what he called literature, so for him it did not exist as literature.

7　Yao Ding, one of the greatest of Chinese literary critics, in 1776 enumerated the kinds of writing which comprise the whole of literature. They are essays, government commentaries, biographies, epitaphs, epigrams, poetry, funeral *eulogies* [9], and histories. No novels, you perceive, although by that date the Chinese novel had already reached its glorious height, after

腔调，总是在强调一些只适用于自己的规矩，自命不凡，对普通人和其他文人极尽嘲讽，一身破败长袍，走起路来左右摇摆，傲慢无边。只有在文人的聚会上才能见到他们的影子，平时根本看不到他们，因为大多数时候他们都在埋头死读经书，努力使自己写得与之相像。他们憎恶一切新颖原创的东西，因为这些东西没法归入任何他所知道的风格中。对于没法归类的东西，他就认为一定不是好东西，而且还很自信只有自己是对的。如果他说，"这就是艺术"，那就说明别的地方不可能找到艺术了，因为他不承认的东西根本不可能存在。因为他无法将小说归入任何一类他知道的文学，所以对他来说小说就不是文学。

7　1776 年，中国最伟大的文学评论家之一——姚鼐列举了文学的所有写作类型，包括散文、官方评论文、传记、碑文、格言警句、诗歌、悼词和史料记载。你看，没有小说（尽管经历了民间几个世纪的发展之后，当时中国小说的发展已经达到了顶峰）。除此之外，1772 年伟大的乾

---

⑦　pedantic [pɪ'dæntɪk] *adj.* 学究式的，卖弄学问的　如：a pedantic attention to details 学究式地注意细枝末节

⑧　haughty ['hɔːtɪ] *adj.* 傲慢自大的　如：A haughty girl is always unpopular at school. 骄傲的女孩子在学校常常不受欢迎。

⑨　eulogy ['juːlədʒɪ] *n.* 颂词，赞词　如：funeral eulogy 挽歌，祭词

centuries of development among the common Chinese people. Nor does that vast compilation of Chinese literature, *Ssu Ku Chuen Shu*, made in 1772 by the order of the great Emperor Ch'ien Lung, contain the novel in the encyclopedia of its literature proper.

8 No, happily for the Chinese novel, it was not considered by the scholars as literature. Happily, too, for the novelist! Man and book, they were free from the criticisms of those scholars and their requirements of art, their techniques of expression and their talk of literary significances and all that discussion of what is and is not art, as if art were an absolute and not the changing thing it is, fluctuating even within decades! The Chinese novel was free. It grew as it liked out of its own soil, the common people, nurtured by that heartiest of sunshine, popular approval, and untouched by the cold and frosty winds of the scholar's art. Emily Dickinson, an American poet, once wrote, "Nature is a haunted house, but art is a house that tries to be haunted." "Nature," she said,

"Is what we see,

Nature is what we know

But have no art to say—

So impatient our wisdom is,

To her simplicity."

9 No, if the Chinese scholars ever knew of the growth of the novel, it was only to ignore it the more **ostentatiously** [10]. Sometimes, unfortunately, they found themselves driven to take notice, because youthful emperors found

隆皇帝下令编纂卷帙浩繁的《四库全书》中也没有小说的影子。

8 不，幸亏小说没有被中国文人当作文学。这对中国小说和小说家来说都是一大幸事！这样无论是作品还是人都可以免受文人关于艺术的批判和要求了。小说家不用顾忌表达技巧、文学的意义以及所有关于什么是艺术的讨论，好像艺术是绝对的，不是一个随着时代变化的事物。中国的小说是自由的。它生长于平民中间，受大众喜闻乐见，享受着最热诚的阳光般的支持，并未遭受文人们艺术之风的摧残。美国诗人艾米丽·狄金森曾写道："自然是令人魂牵梦绕的，而艺术只是努力让人记住。"她说："自然

是我们所见，

是我们所知，

而我们的智慧在自然的朴实面前显得那么急躁。"

9 不，如果中国文人知道了小说的发展，他们会更加明目张胆地忽视它。不幸的是，有时文人们发现他们被迫无奈去注意到小说，因为年轻的皇帝认为小说读起来赏心悦目。

---

[10] ostentatiously [ˌɒsten'teɪʃəslɪ] *adv.* 招摇地，故意地

novels pleasant to read. Then these poor scholars were hard put to it. But they discovered the phrase "social significance", and they wrote long literary treatises to prove that a novel was not a novel but a document of social significance. Social significance is a term recently discovered by the most modern of literary young men and women in the United States, but the old scholars of China knew it a thousand years ago, when they, too, demanded that the novel should have social significance, if it were to be recognized as an art.

10 But for the most part the old Chinese scholar reasoned thus about the novel:

Literature is art.

All art has social significance.

This book has no social significance.

Therefore it is not literature.

And so the novel in China was not literature.

11 In such a school was I trained. I grew up believing that the novel has nothing to do with pure literature. So I was taught by scholars. The art of literature, so I was taught, is something devised by men of learning. Out of the brains of scholars came rules to control the rush of genius, that wild fountain which has its source in deepest life. Genius, great or less, is the spring, and art is the sculptured shape, classical or modern, into which the waters must be forced, if scholars and critics were to be served. But the people of China did not so serve. The waters of the genius of story gushed out as they would, however the natural rocks allowed and the trees persuaded, and only

这些可怜的文人们可陷入了困境。但是他们发现了一个叫做"社会意义"的词语，于是他们就写长篇大论的文学评论去证明小说其实不是小说，只是具有社会意义的文献。"社会意义"这个词，是美国现代最年轻的文艺青年男女最近才发现的，但是中国古代的文人们早在一千年前就已经知道了。当时他们就要求，要承认小说是艺术，那它就必须具有社会意义。

10 但是大多数中国古代文人是这样推论小说的：

文学是艺术。

所有的艺术都具有社会意义。

而这本书不具备社会意义。

所以它就不是文学。

因此中国的小说就不是文学作品。

11 我就是在这样一所学校接受的训练。我接受的教养让我一直认为小说和纯粹的文学不沾边。所以我的老师们都是文人。我所接受的文学教育都是被有学问的人改编过的。文人的脑子里产生出约束灵感的规则，而扎根于生活的灵感就像一眼不羁的野泉。天才，或多或少，都是清泉，而艺术，不论古今，都是有固定形态的雕像，泉水必须注入雕像中才能被文人和评论家所用。但是中国的普通人并不这样利用。小说家的灵感像泉水一样随心所欲地喷涌，不管条件多么优厚，周围的山石树木怎样邀请，最

common people came and drank and found rest and pleasure.

终都只有平民百姓过来饮水休憩、寻找欢乐。

12 For the novel in China was the peculiar product of the common people. And it was solely their property. The very language of the novel was their own language, and not the classical Wen-li, which was the language of literature and the scholars. Wen-li bore somewhat the same resemblance to the language of the people as the ancient English of Chaucer does to the English of today, although ironically enough, at one time Wen-li, too, was a ***vernacular***[11]. But the scholars never kept pace with the living, changing speech of the people. They clung to an old vernacular until they had made it classic, while the running language of the people went on and left them far behind. Chinese novels, then, are in the "Pei Hua", or simple talk, of the people, and this in itself was offensive to the old scholars because it resulted in a style so full of easy flow and readability that it had no technique of expression in it, the scholars said.

12 中国的小说是民间的独特产物，是只属于普通大众的瑰宝。小说的语言是他们自己的日常语言，不是文学作品和文人学者用的“文理”。“文理”跟普通大众的语言的关系，就像是乔叟时代的古英语跟现代英语的关系。但讽刺的是，“文理”曾经也是地方语言。但是中国的文人从来不与活生生的、变化着的语言保持同步，他们紧紧抓住古语不放，使之成为经典，而人民的活语言不断发展，将其远远抛在后面。当时中国的小说确实是用“白话文”写的，是人民容易懂的语言。这就冒犯了那些老学究们，因为小说的风格简单流畅，可读性强，对他们来说是没有表达技巧可言的。

13 I should pause to make an exception of certain scholars who came to China from India, bearing as their gift a new religion, Buddhism. In the West, Puritanism was for a long time the enemy of the novel. But in the Orient the Buddhists were wiser. When they came into China, they found literature already remote from the people and dying under the formalism of that period known in history as the Six Dynasties. The professional men of literature were even then

13 我应该暂停一下，讲一种例外的情况。一些印度人来华，带来了新的宗教——佛教。在西方，相当长一段时间内，清教主义是小说的大敌。但是在东方，佛教徒则更智慧。来到中国之后，他们发现文学已经脱离大众，在历史上所谓六朝的形式主义的风气下，文学几近死亡。那些专业文人不注重作品内容，只关注形式，一味追求文章和诗歌语言形式

⑪ vernacular [və'nækjʊlə] *n.* 白话　如：a vernacular poet 白话诗人

absorbed not so much in what they had to say as in pairing into couplets the characters of their essays and their poems, and already they scorned all writing which did not conform to their own rules. Into this confined literary atmosphere came the Buddhist translators with their great treasures of the freed spirit. Some of them were Indian, but some were Chinese. They said frankly that their aim was not to conform to the ideas of style of the literary men, but to make clear and simple to common people what they had to teach. They put their religious teachings into the common language, the language which the novel used, and because the people loved story, they took story and made it a means of teaching. The preface of *Fah Shu Ching*, one of the most famous of Buddhist books, says, "When giving the words of gods, these words should be given forth simply." This might be taken as the sole literary creed of the Chinese novelist, to whom, indeed, gods were men and men were gods.

14 For the Chinese novel was written primarily to amuse the common people. And when I say amuse I do not mean only to make them laugh, though laughter is also one of the aims of the Chinese novel. I mean amusement in the sense of absorbing and occupying the whole attention of the mind. I mean enlightening that mind by pictures of life and what that life means. I mean encouraging the spirit not by rule-of-thumb talk about art, but by stories about the people in every age, and thus presenting to people simply themselves. Even the Buddhists who came to tell

上的对仗，讽刺所有不符合他们规则的文字。在这种百般约束的文学氛围中来了一群满怀自由精神的佛经翻译者。有些是印度人，有些则是中国人。他们直率地说，他们的目的不是迎合当时的文体规则，而是给普通民众简单清晰地讲解他们的教义。他们用普通语言，小说的语言来讲述宗教义理，因为人们喜欢故事，他们就用讲故事的方式传教。著名的佛教著作《梵书》的前言写道："传播神的思想时，要使用简单的语言。"这可以说是中国小说唯一的文学信条了，对他们来说，人民就是神，神就是人民。

14 中国小说的写作目的主要是取悦大众。我说的"取悦"并不单指使大家发笑，尽管制造笑声也是中国小说的一个目的。我所说的"取悦"是指吸引人们的注意力，抓住人们的心；是指通过生活图景和生活的意义来启迪心灵；是指通过讲述各个年龄段的故事来提升精神境界，展现给人民真正的自己，而非用艺术规则颐指气使。就连来传教的佛教徒都发现，如果普通民众看到神也是通过和他们一样的人来发挥作用，他们就能更好

about gods found that people understood gods better if they saw them working through ordinary folk like themselves.

15 But the real reason why the Chinese novel was written in the vernacular was because the common people could not read and write and the novel had to be written so that when it was read aloud it could be understood by persons who could communicate only through spoken words. In a village of two hundred souls perhaps only one man could read. And on holidays or in the evening when the work was done he read aloud to the people from some story. The rise of the Chinese novel began in just this simple fashion. After a while people took up a collection of pennies in somebody's cap or in a farm wife's bowl because the reader needed tea to wet his throat, or perhaps to pay him for time he would otherwise have spent at his silk loom or his rush weaving. If the collections grew big enough he gave up some of his regular work and became a professional storyteller. And the stories he read were the beginnings of novels. There were not many such stories written down, not nearly enough to last year in and year out for people who had by nature, as the Chinese have, a strong love for dramatic story. So the storyteller began to increase his stock. He searched the dry annals of the history which the scholars had written, and with his fertile imagination, enriched by long acquaintance with common people, he clothed long-dead figures with new flesh and made them live again; he found stories of court life and

地理解教义。

15 但是中国小说用白话文写作，是因为普通人不会读写，所以写作语言必须是读出来能让那些只会用口语交流的人都能听懂的话。在一个200人的村子里可能只有一个人会阅读。逢年过节或晚上农活忙完的时候，他就大声地将一些故事读给大家听。中国小说就是在这样简单的方式下成长起来的。读了一阵子之后人们就会在某人的帽子里或者农妇的碗里放一些钱给读小说的人，因为读小说的人需要喝茶润润嗓子，或者补偿他本来可以去织布或编席子的时间。如果凑的钱足够多，他就会放弃一些日常工作，成为一名职业讲故事者。那些他读过的故事就是最初的小说。但是这些故事写下来的并不多，还不够维持一年，因为中国人天性就爱戏剧性的故事。于是说书人就开始增加他的库存。他查阅文人写的枯燥的编年史，通过自己常年与普通大众打交道而培养的丰富想象力加以润色，就能把死去很久的人说得有血有肉，栩栩如生。他讲宫廷生活，讲明争暗斗，讲皇帝那些败家亡国的宠姜们。在他走乡串巷的过程中，他若听到新奇的故事也会记录下来。人们把自己的经历告诉他，他就把这些经历写下来给别人看。说书人对故事加以修饰润色，但不使用文学语言，因为人们不

intrigue and names of imperial favorites who had brought dynasties to ruin; he found, as he traveled from village to village, strange tales from his own times which he wrote down when he heard them. People told him of experiences they had had and he wrote these down, too, for other people. And he embellished them, but not with literary turns and phrases, for the people cared nothing for these. No, he kept his audiences always in mind and he found that the style which they loved best was one which flowed easily along, clearly and simply, in the short words which they themselves used every day, with no other technique than occasional bits of description, only enough to give vividness to a place or a person, and never enough to delay the story. Nothing must delay the story. Story was what they wanted.

16 And when I say story, I do not mean mere pointless activity, not crude action alone. The Chinese are too mature for that. They have always demanded of their novel character above all else. *Shui Hu Chuan* they have considered one of their three greatest novels, not primarily because it is full of the flash and fire of action, but because it portrays so distinctly one hundred and eight characters that each is to be seen separate from the others. Often I have heard it said of that novel in tones of delight, "When anyone of the hundred and eight begins to speak, we do not need to be told his name. By the way the words come from his mouth we know who he is." Vividness of character portrayal, then, is the first quality which the Chinese people have demanded of their

关心那些。不，事实上他一直将听众放在心上。他发现人们最喜爱的风格是：文风流畅，思路清晰简洁，用日常所用的简短语言，除了偶尔为了生动描述一个地方或一个人时稍加修饰外没有任何其他技巧，而这些修饰也绝不会拖延整个故事。没有什么能拖延故事情节。故事才是他们想要的。

16 我说的故事也不只是无意义的活动，不单是粗糙的故事情节。中国人在这方面已经做得够成熟了。他们对人物塑造的要求高于一切。中国人将《水浒传》视为他们最伟大的三部小说之一，不是因为里面充满了刀光剑影的情节，而是因为它塑造了各不相同的108个人物角色，每个都与众不同，都可以单独来看。我经常听到人们兴高采烈地谈起那部小说："只要那108条好汉任何一个开口说话，我们无须知道他们的名字，从他们说话的方式就能知道他是谁。"对人物的生动刻画是中国人对小说的第一要求，其次，要通过人物本身的行为和语言来刻画人物，而不是靠作者

novels, and after it, that such portrayal shall be by the character's own action and words rather than by the author's explanation.

17 Curiously enough, while the novel was beginning thus humbly in teahouses, in villages and lowly city streets out of stories told to the common people by a common and unlearned man among them, in imperial palaces it was beginning, too, and in much the same unlearned fashion. It was an old custom of emperors, particularly if the dynasty were a foreign one, to employ persons called "imperial ears", whose only duty was to come and go among the people in the streets of cities and villages and to sit among them in teahouses, disguised in common clothes and listen to what was talked about there. The original purpose of this was, of course, to hear of any discontent among the emperor's subjects, and more especially to find out if discontents were rising to the shape of those rebellions which preceded the fall of every dynasty.

18 But emperors were very human and they were not often learned scholars. More often, indeed, they were only spoiled and willful men. The "imperial ears" had opportunity to hear all sorts of strange and interesting stories, and they found that their royal masters were more frequently interested in these stories than they were in politics. So when they came back to make their reports, they flattered the emperor and sought to gain favor by telling him what he liked to hear, shut up as he was in the Forbidden City, away from life. They told him the strange and

的解释。

17 相当令人好奇的是，当小说从民间茶馆、村庄和卑贱的城市街头故事中悄然兴起，由没什么学识修养的普通人讲给平民百姓听的同时，它也以同样缺少文学修养的方式在宫廷开始发展起来。古时候的皇帝，尤其是异族皇帝，有一个习惯：雇佣"耳目"出入城乡街头小巷，接近平民百姓，同他们一起坐茶馆，化装成平民，监听他们的谈话。这么做的最初目的当然是皇帝为了听取民众对当朝的不满，尤其是要看看不满之声有没有到可能引发叛乱的程度，毕竟这样的事每朝每代都有发生。

18 但是皇帝们是很人道的，而且他们也不都是学识修养很高的文人。事实上，通常他们都被惯坏了，也很任性。皇帝的"耳目"有机会听到各种奇怪有趣的故事，他们发现他们的皇帝主子对这些故事比对政治更感兴趣。于是当他们回来报告时，就会奉承皇帝，挑整日待在紫禁城、远离民间生活的皇帝喜欢听的话说，以此来得些好处。他们将这些自由的普通人奇怪而有趣的故事讲给皇帝听，后来他们开始拿笔记录这些故事，以

interesting things which common people did, who were free, and after a while they took to writing down what they heard in order to save memory. And I do not doubt that if messengers between the emperor and the people carried stories in one direction, they carried them in the other, too, and to the people they told stories about the emperor and what he said and did, and how he quarrelled with the empress who bore him no sons, and how she intrigued with the chief eunuch to poison the favorite concubine, all of which delighted the Chinese because it proved to them, the most democratic of peoples, that their emperor was after all only a common fellow like themselves and that he, too, had his troubles, though he was the Son of Heaven. Thus there began another important source for the novel that was to develop with such form and force, though still always denied its right to exist by the professional man of letters.

19 From such humble and scattered beginnings, then, came the Chinese novel, written always in the vernacular, and dealing with all which interested the people, with legend and with myth, with love and intrigue, with *brigands* [12] and wars, with everything, indeed, which went to make up the life of the people, high and low.

20 Nor was the novel in China shaped, as it was in the West, by a few great persons. In China the novel has always been more important than the novelist. There has been no Chinese Defoe, no Chinese Fielding or Smollett, no Austin or Brontë

免忘记。我毫不怀疑，皇帝和平民之间的传信者能把故事从一方传递给另一方，也能反过来，将皇帝的故事带给平民。他们给平民讲皇帝都做些什么、说些什么，他如何同不能为他延续后代的皇后争吵，皇后又如何同太监密谋毒害皇帝最宠爱的妃子。所有的这些都能愉悦大众，因为这些向他们证明皇帝是一个和他们一样的普通人，虽然他贵为天子，但他毕竟也有自己的麻烦事。因此，出现了另一种小说的来源，而且这种形式和力量必将得到发展，尽管在专业文人那里它仍然没有存在的权利。

19 中国小说就是这样谦卑而无序地开始的，用白话文写成，写一切能引起人们兴趣的事，这里有传奇、神话、爱情和阴谋，也有强盗和战争，事实上，构成人们或高雅或低俗生活的一切事物都会在小说中出现。

20 中国小说的塑造也和西方不同，不是由几个伟人一蹴而就的。在中国，小说本身永远比写小说的人重要。在中国没有像笛福、费尔丁或斯摩利特这样的人物，也没有奥斯汀、

---

⑫ brigand ['brɪɡənd] *n.* 强盗，土匪

or Dickens or Thackeray, or Meredith or Hardy, any more than Balzac or Flaubert. But there were and are novels as great as the novels in any other country in the world, as great as any could have written, had he been born in China. Who then wrote these novels of China?

21 That is what the modern literary men of China now, centuries too late, are trying to discover. Within the last twenty-five years literary critics, trained in the universities of the West, have begun to discover their own neglected novels. But the novelists who wrote them they cannot discover. Did one man write *Shui Hu Chuan*, or did it grow to its present shape, added to, rearranged, deepened and developed by many minds and many a hand, in different centuries? Who can now tell? They are dead. They lived in their day and wrote what in their day they saw and heard, but of themselves they have told nothing. The author of *The Dream of the Red Chamber* in a far later century says in the preface to his book, "It is not necessary to know the times of Han and T'ang—it is necessary to tell only of my own times."

22 They told of their own times and they lived in a blessed obscurity. They read no reviews of their novels, no treatises as to whether or not what they did was well done according to the rules of scholarship. It did not occur to them that they must reach the high thin air which scholars breathed nor did they consider the stuff of which greatness is made, according to the scholars. They wrote as it pleased them to write and as they were

勃朗特、狄更斯或萨克雷，也没有梅瑞迪斯或哈代，更没有巴尔扎克或福楼拜。但是中国过去和现在都确实有其他国家所有的同样伟大的小说，可以和任何作家的伟大作品相媲美。那么是谁写了中国的小说呢？

21 这也是中国现代文人试图解开的谜——虽然晚了几个世纪。过去25年间接受西方大学教育的文学评论家开始发现他们长久以来忽视的本国小说。但是写这些小说的人已经无从考证了。是一个人写了《水浒传》，还是经过多人几个世纪的补充、修改、深化和发展才有了它今天的样子？现在谁能知道呢？他们已经不在人世了。他们生活在自己的时代，写下了他们的所见所闻，但是却没有留下任何关于自己的信息。《红楼梦》的作者后来在书的前言中写道："不必假借汉唐，只取其事体情理罢了。"

22 他们讲述自己时代的故事，乐于默默无闻。他们没有读过关于自己小说的评论，也没有看过任何论文根据文学的标准来评判他们做得是好是坏。他们不必登高去呼吸文人们的稀薄空气，也不必考虑文人眼中哪些作品能成其伟大。他们写小说是因为高兴，因为能写。他们有时写得好，有时写得并不好，但对这些他们浑然

able. Sometimes they wrote unwittingly well and sometimes unwittingly they wrote not so well. They died in the same happy obscurity and now they are lost in it and not all the scholars of China, gathered too late to do them honor, can raise them up again. They are long past the possibility of literary post-mortems. But what they did remains after them because it is the common people of China who keep alive the great novels, illiterate people who have passed the novel, not so often from hand to hand as from mouth to mouth.

23 In the preface to one of the later editions of *Shui Hu Chuan*, Shih Nai An, an author who had much to do with the making of that novel, writes, "What I speak of I wish people to understand easily. Whether the reader is good or evil, learned or unlearned, anyone can read this book. Whether or not the book is well done is not important enough to cause anyone to worry. Alas, I am born to die. How can I know what those who come after me who read my book will think of it? I cannot even know what I myself, born into another incarnation, will think of it. I do not know if I myself then can even read. Why therefore should I care?"

24 Strangely enough, there were certain scholars who envied the freedom of obscurity, and who, burdened with certain private sorrows which they dared not tell anyone, or who perhaps wanting only a holiday from the weariness of the sort of art they had themselves created, wrote novels, too under assumed and humble names.

不觉。他们最终在这种默默无闻的快乐中死去，现在又在这其中迷失，中国文人觉醒得太晚，已经无法给他们荣誉，也无法提高他们的地位。他们早就错过了事后对其进行文学研究的可能性。但是他们写的东西留了下来，中国的普通大众使这些伟大的小说存活了下来，更多时候目不识丁的人们不是通过书本，而是将其口口相传下来。

23 后来一个版本的《水浒传》前言里，施耐庵——与这本书的成型有很大关系的一位作家——写道："一、心闲试弄，舒卷自恣；二、无贤无愚，无不能读；三、文章得失，小不足悔。呜呼哀哉！吾生有涯，未知吾之后人之读我书者谓何。且未知吾之后身读之谓何，亦未知吾之后身得读此书者乎？吾又安所用其眷念哉！"

24 奇怪的是，有些文人羡慕这种无名的自由，他们有的承受着不敢告人的个人痛苦，有的可能只是想从他们自己创造的令人疲倦的艺术中给自己放个假，他们也开始以假的或者谦卑的名字写小说。写小说的时候他们就把平日的迂腐搁置一旁了，写

And when they did so they put aside *pedantry* ⑬ and wrote as simply and naturally as any common novelist.

25 For the novelist believed that he should not be conscious of techniques. He should write as his material demanded. If a novelist became known for a particular style or technique, to that extent he ceased to be a good novelist and became a literary technician.

的语言也像普通小说家那样简朴自然了。

25 因为小说家认为不能关注技巧。他应该应材料要求而写作。如果一个小说家因一种特定的风格或技巧而出名，那他就不再是一名优秀的小说家，而成为一台文学机器了。

 演讲关键词 Practical Expressions

1. man of letters 作家，学者
2. political advancement 官职晋升
3. common people 人民大众
4. write simply and naturally 写作简朴自然
5. ingratitude 忘恩负义

1. Out of the brains of scholars came rules to control the rush of genius, that wild fountain which has its source in deepest life.

文人的脑子里产生出约束灵感的规则，而扎根于生活的灵感就像一眼不羁的野泉。

2. Nor was the novel in China shaped, as it was in the West, by a few great persons. In China the novel has always been more important than the novelist.

中国小说的塑造也和西方不同，不是由几个伟人一蹴而就的。在中国，小说本身永远比写小说的人重要。

---

⑬ pedantry ['pedəntrɪ] *n.* 迂腐，卖弄学问

功成中年以后

　　世人少年成才者多，但少年能获诺贝尔奖的则少之又少。据统计，诺贝尔文学奖获奖名单里108人的平均年龄居然是64岁！这多少令大家有些瞠目结舌吧，因为这与平日里人们印象中风度翩翩、魅力无限的文艺青年的形象出入太大了。作为史上最年轻的诺贝尔文学奖得主，1907年，年仅42岁的约瑟夫·鲁德亚德·吉卜林凭借世人熟知的《老虎！老虎！》荣登文学之巅。与之形成对比的是2007年诺贝尔文学奖获得者——多丽丝·莱辛。她获奖时已经是88岁高龄，这是她用史诗一样的作品和年华换来的文学桂冠。所以那句"出名要趁早"并不是轻而易举就能做到的！

Speech 3
Chinese Novel（2）
中国小说（2）

—Speech by Pearl Buck for the Nobel Prize in Literature in 1938

——唯一同时获得普利策奖和诺贝尔奖的女作家赛珍珠 1938 年诺贝尔文学
奖获奖演讲

名家速览 About the Author

诺贝尔奖大师	赛珍珠（珀尔·布克）
奖项归属	诺贝尔文学奖
代表作品	《大地三部曲》、《母亲》、《爱国者》
所获主要奖项	1932 年美国普利策奖，1938 年诺贝尔文学奖

赛珍珠在中国的成长经历和对中国的特殊感情奠定了她一生的写作基础。她从小接触中国文学，尤其是中国的小说，这使她看到了不同于西方传统的中国式小说创作方式。她渐渐获得了对中国小说历史的整体把握和对其形象的完整认识。她自己的作品因此不可避免地受到中国历史文化的影响。同时她也发现一个严重的问题：没有一个西方作家从中国文化的角度出发去认识中国小说，他们作品中的中国人无疑是缺乏真实形象的"空中楼阁"。因此，她开始用自己手中的笔描绘自己亲眼所见、亲身体会的中国形象，尤其是中国农村地区的生活状况，传达中国思想和文化，让世界了解中国人民。在诺贝尔获奖演讲时，赛珍珠仍不忘自己的使命，怀着对中国的深厚感情，她发表了这篇热情洋溢、颇具学术意义的演讲，向西方人，乃至整个世界普及了中国小说的特殊发展史和辉煌成就。在叙述中国小说对自己的影响时，她极大地肯定了中国小说扎根平民、写平民的故事、不趋炎附势、不追求艺术形式、脚踏实地的特点。

演讲现场
Speech Script

精美译文
Suggested Translation

1 A good novelist, or so I have been taught in China, should be above all else, that is, natural, unaffected, and so flexible and variable as to be wholly at the command of the material that flows through him. His whole duty is only to sort life as it flows through him, and in the vast fragmentariness of time and space and event to discover essential and inherent order and rhythm and shape. We should never be able, merely by reading pages, to know who wrote them, for when the style of a novelist becomes fixed, that style becomes his prison. The Chinese novelists varied their writing to accompany like music their chosen themes.

2 These Chinese novels are not perfect according to Western standards. They are not always planned from beginning to end, nor are they compact, any more than life is planned or compact. They are often too long, too full of incident, too crowded with character, a *medley*① of fact and fiction as to material, and a medley of romance and realism as to method, so that an impossible event of magic or dream may be described with such exact semblance of detail that one is compelled to belief against all reason. The earliest novels are full of folklore, for the people of those times thought and dreamed in the ways of folklore. But no one can understand the mind of China today who has not read these novels, for

1 一位优秀的小说家——或者说在中国人们是这样教我的——最重要的是"自然"，不矫揉造作，要灵活多变，总是依据脑海中浮现的素材去创作。他的全部职责只是将生活加以整理，审视时间、空间和事件的碎片，从中发现固有的必不可少的秩序、规则和形式。只凭阅读书籍，我们永远不可能知道作者是谁，因为如果一个小说家的风格固定下来，那种风格就会成为他的羁绊。中国小说家的写作就像音乐一样，根据所选的主题变换他们的节奏。

2 根据西方的标准，这些中国小说并不完美。它们没有经过从头到尾的策划，也不像生活那样情节紧凑。通常它们都太长，枝节过多，人物也过于拥挤；素材方面，事实和虚构混杂不清；创作手法上，浪漫主义和现实主义也混为一谈。以至于一个根本不可能发生的魔幻事件或者梦想都可以被描述得准确详细，使人不顾一切地要信以为真。最初的小说包含着大量的民间传说，因为传说就是当时人们思考和梦想的方式。没有读过这些中国小说的人就不可能理解今天中国人的思想，因为这些小说也塑造了当代中国人的思想，民间传说仍然

---

① medley ['medlɪ] *n.* 混杂，混合　如：a medley of flavors 各种味道混合在一起

the novels have shaped the present mind, too, and the folklore persists in spite of all that Chinese diplomats and Western-trained scholars would have us believe to the contrary. The essential mind of China is still that mind of which George Russell wrote when he said of the Irish mind, so strangely akin to the Chinese, "that mind which in its folk imagination believes anything. It creates ships of gold with masts of silver and white cities by the sea and rewards and fairies, and when that vast folk mind turns to politics it is ready to believe anything."

3 Out of this folk mind, turned into stories and crowded with thousands of years of life, grew, literally, the Chinese novel. For these novels changed as they grew. If, as I have said, there are no single names attached beyond question to the great novels of China, it is because no one hand wrote them. From beginning as a mere tale, a story grew through succeeding versions, into a structure built by many hands. I might mention as an example the well-known story, *The White Snake*, or *Pei She Chuan*, first written in the T'ang Dynasty by an unknown author. It was then a tale of the simple supernatural whose hero was a great white snake. In the next version in the following century, the snake has become a vampire woman who is an evil force. But the third version contains a more gentle and human touch. The vampire becomes a faithful wife who aids her husband and gives him a son. The story thus adds not only new character but new quality, and ends not as the supernatural tale it began but as a novel of human

存在，尽管中国的外交官和受过西方教育的学者力图使我们相信并非如此。中国人思想的本质与乔治·罗素所说的爱尔兰人的思想出奇地相似："……这种思想就是民间传说式的想象，认为什么都有可能发生。它创造出金船、银桅杆、海边白色的城市、奖赏和精灵，当这种广泛的民间思想转向政治时，它会随时准备着相信一切。"

3 这种民间思想衍生出充斥着几千年生活的民间故事——也就是中国小说。这些小说一边成长，一边变化。如我所说，毫无疑问这些伟大的中国小说都没有单独的作者，因为他们不是一手写就的。开始只是一个简单的故事，这故事经历了多个版本的演变后在很多双手下才有了现在的结构。拿著名的《白蛇传》来说吧，最初是唐朝一个不知名的作者写的。那时它只是一个主人公为一条白蛇的简单灵异故事。在接下来的一个世纪里，新版本中的白蛇成了一个邪恶的妖女。但是第三版中角色又变得相当温柔、更人性化了。白蛇变成了一个扶持丈夫的忠贞妻子，并且为丈夫生了一个儿子。于是这个故事不仅增加了新人物，而且改变了性质，它不再是开始时的灵异故事，而成为一部关于人类的小说。

beings.

4　So in early periods of Chinese history, many books must be called not so much novels as source books for novels, the sort of books into which Shakespeare, had they been open to him, might have dipped with both hands to bring up pebbles to make into jewels. Many of these books have been lost, since they were not considered valuable. But not all—early stories of Han, written so vigorously that to this day it is said they run like galloping horses, and tales of the troubled dynasties following—not all were lost. Some have persisted. In the Ming Dynasty, in one way or another, many of them were represented in the great collection known as *T'ai P'ing Kuan Shi*, wherein are tales of superstition and religion, of mercy and goodness and reward for evil and well doing, tales of dreams and miracles, of dragons and gods and goddesses and priests, of tigers and foxes and transmigration and resurrection from the dead. Most of these early stories had to do with supernatural events, of gods born of virgins, of men walking as gods, as the Buddhist influence grew strong. There are miracles and allegories, such as the pens of poor scholars bursting into flower, dreams leading men and women into strange and fantastic lands of Gulliver, or the magic wand that floated an altar made of iron. But stories mirrored each age. The stories of Han were vigorous and dealt often with the affairs of the nation, and centered on some great man or hero. Humor was strong in this golden age, a

4　所以在中国历史的早期，很多书都不能叫小说，它们只是小说的素材和源头。如果让莎士比亚去读这种书，他一定会伸出双手从中拾取鹅卵石将之变为珍宝。许多这样的书籍都遗失了，因为人们并不认可其价值。但是并没有全部遗失，汉朝早年的故事就写得生动有力，直到今天人们还认为它们就像奔腾的骏马，随后五代的故事也并没有完全消失。有些还是保留了下来。明朝时，很多这样那样的故事都收集在《太平广记》中，有的写迷信和宗教，有的写乐善好施，善恶有报，有的关于梦想和奇迹，有的写龙写神，写老虎和狐狸，写轮回转世。在佛教日渐强势的影响下，这些早期故事大多数都与超自然事件有关，如处女生神，人走如神等。也有奇迹和寓言故事，例如一个穷书生妙笔生花；梦将人们带到了《格列佛游记》中那样神奇诡异的国度；或者魔棒使一个铁制的祭坛浮在空中。但是故事都是各个时代的写照。汉朝的故事都充满了力量，以某些伟人或英雄为中心，写的都是国家间的大事件。汉朝这个黄金时代还流行幽默，一种生动粗犷、充满活力的幽默。这种幽默在《笑林》的很多故事中都有体现，这些故事可能是收集来的，部分也可能是邯郸淳写的。这段黄金时代消逝之后，故事情境也随

racy ②, *earthy* ③, *lusty* ④ humor, such as was to be found, for instance, in a book of tales entitled *Siao Ling*, presumed to have been collected, if not partly written, by Han Tang Suan. And then the scenes changed, as that golden age faded, though it was never to be forgotten, so that to this day the Chinese like to call themselves sons of Han. With the succeeding weak and corrupt centuries, the very way the stories were written became honeyed and weak, and their subjects slight, or as the Chinese say, "In the days of the Six Dynasties, they wrote of small things, of a woman, a waterfall, or a bird."

5 If the Han Dynasty was golden, then the T'ang Dynasty was silver, and silver were the love stories for which it was famous. It was an age of love, when a thousand stories clustered about the beautiful Yang Kuei Fei and her scarcely less beautiful predecessor in the emperor's favor, Mei Fei. These love stories of T'ang come very near sometimes to fulfilling in their unity and complexity the standards of the Western novel. There are rising action and crisis and dénouement, implicit if not expressed. The Chinese say, "We must read the stories of T'ang, because though they deal with small matters, yet they are written in so moving a manner that the tears come."

6 It is not surprising that most of these love stories deal not with love that ends in marriage or is contained in marriage, but with love outside

之改变了，但是人们并没有忘记它，直到今天中国人都还喜欢称自己为"汉民"。在接下来屡弱而腐败的几个世纪间，故事的写作方式也变得柔情蜜意，虚弱不堪，题材狭小，就像中国人说的："六朝时期，人们写的都是琐事，女人、瀑布或者小鸟等。"

5 如果说汉朝是黄金时代，那么唐朝就是白银时代了——因其爱情故事而闻名的白银时代。这是一个爱情的时代，杨贵妃和她之前的梅妃都深受宠爱、貌美倾城，关于她们的爱情故事有成百上千个。这些故事在统一性和复杂性上堪比西方小说的标准。故事里也有战争、危机和大团圆的结局，或直述或暗示。中国人说："我们一定要读唐朝的故事。虽然它们都不是惊天动地的大事，但却感人至深，催人泪下。"

6 这些故事中的爱情大多数并不以婚姻为结局，也不是讲的婚姻中的爱情。这并不奇怪。事实上，如

---

② racy ['reɪsɪ] *adj.* 生动的，活泼的　如：a racy novel 生动的小说

③ earthy ['ɜːθɪ] *adj.* 朴实的，粗俗的　如：an earthy sense of humor 粗俗的幽默感

④ lusty ['lʌstɪ] *adj.* 精力充沛的　如：lusty singing 洪亮的歌声

the marriage relationship. Indeed, it is significant that when marriage is the theme the story nearly always ends in tragedy. Two famous stories, *Pei Li Shi* and *Chiao Fang Chi*, deal entirely with extramarital love, and are written apparently to show the superiority of the courtesans, who could read and write and sing and were clever and beautiful besides, beyond the ordinary wife who was, as the Chinese say even today, "a yellow-faced woman", and usually illiterate.

7 So strong did this tendency become that officialdom grew alarmed at the popularity of such stories among the common people, and they were denounced as revolutionary and dangerous because it was thought they attacked that foundation of Chinese civilization, the family system. A reactionary tendency was not lacking, such as is to be seen in *Hui Chen Chi*, one of the earlier forms of a famous later work, the story of the young scholar who loved the beautiful Ying Ying and who renounced her, saying prudently as he went away, "All extraordinary women are dangerous. They destroy themselves and others. They have ruined even emperors. I am not an emperor and I had better give her up"—which he did, to the admiration of all wise men. And to him the modest Ying Ying replied, "If you possess me and leave me, it is your right. I do not reproach you." But five hundred years later the sentimentality of the Chinese popular heart comes forth and sets the thwarted romance right again. In this last version of the story the author makes Chang and Ying Ying husband and wife and says

果婚姻成为故事的主题，那么结局往往是悲剧。两个著名的故事《裴丽诗》和《教坊记》写的都是婚外情，显然都是为显示妓女之美。她们不但能读、会写、会唱，而且聪颖美丽，不像传统的中国妻子——通常目不识丁，今天的中国人还称之为"黄脸婆"。

7 这样的趋势愈演愈烈，朝廷开始对这类民间故事警惕起来。朝廷将其斥为革命和危险思想，因为它破坏了中华文明的基础——家庭制度。而反其势而行的思想也不是没有，后来成为一部作品的《会真记》就是一个例子。秀才张生爱上了美丽的崔莺莺，后来却又抛弃了她，他在离开时决绝地说："大凡天之所命尤物也，不妖其身，必妖与人……昔殷之辛，周之幽，据万乘之国，其势甚厚；然而一女子败之，溃其众，屠其身，至今为天下僇笑。予之德不足以胜妖孽，是用忍情。"时人多赞张生的做法。而谦卑的莺莺则答曰："始乱之，终弃之，固其宜矣，愚不敢恨。"但是五百年后，中国人多愁善感的心性又占据上风，使这个遭遇阻挠的爱情故事归于正位了。最后一版故事的作者使张生和崔莺莺最后结为夫妻，以满足中国人"有情人终成眷属"的愿望。在中国，随着时间的推移，用五百年等一个幸福的结局并不算久。

in closing, "This is in the hope that all the lovers of the world may be united in happy marriage." And as time goes in China, five hundred years is not long to wait for a happy ending.

8   This story, by the way, is one of China's most famous. It was repeated in the Sung dynasty in a poetic form by Chao Teh Liang, under the title *The Reluctant Butterfly*, and again in the Yuan dynasty by Tung Chai-yuen as a drama to be sung, entitled *Suh Hsi Hsiang*. In the Ming dynasty, with two versions intervening, it appears as Li Reh Hua's *Nan Hsi Hsiang Chi*, written in the southern **metrical**⑤ form called "ts'e", and so to the last and most famous *Hsi Hsiang Chi*. Even children in China know the name of Chang Sen.

9   If I seem to emphasize the romances of the T'ang period, it is because romance between man and woman is the chief gift of T'ang to the novel, and not because there were no other stories. There were many novels of a humorous and satirical nature and one curious type of story which concerned itself with cockfighting, an important **pastime**⑥ of that age and particularly in favor at court. One of the best of these tales is *Tung Chen Lao Fu Chuan*, by Ch'en Hung, which tells how Chia Chang, a famous cockfighter, became so famous that he was loved by emperor and people alike.

10   But time and the stream pass on. The novel form really begins to be clear in the Sung

8   这个故事是中国最著名的故事之一。宋朝时赵令畤以诗歌形式将其重写，题名《商调蝶恋花》。元朝时，董解元又将其写成戏剧《西厢记诸宫调》。明朝时，李日华将两个版本融合改写成《南西厢记》，以南词形式写成。而《西厢记》是最后一版，也是最著名的版本。就连中国的小孩都知道"张生"这个名字。

9   如果说我强调唐代的爱情故事，那是因为男女间的爱情是唐代赠予小说的一份礼物，而不是说没有其他故事了。还有许多幽默、讽刺小说，以及一种与斗鸡有关的故事，在宫廷尤其流行。陈鸿写的《东城老父传》就是这里面最好的故事之一，讲了一个有名的斗鸡者贾昌如何名噪一时，赢得皇帝和同道中人喜爱的故事。

10   时间如流水。到了宋代和元代，小说的形式开始日渐清晰，发展

⑤ metrical ['metrɪk(ə)l] *adj.* 韵律的

⑥ pastime ['pɑːstaɪm] *n.* 消遣，娱乐   如：Sailing is her favorite pastime. 航海是她最喜欢的娱乐方式。

29

Dynasty, and in the Yuan Dynasty it flowers into that height which was never again surpassed and only equalled, indeed, by the single novel *Hung Lou Meng*, or *The Dream of the Red Chamber*, in the Ts'ing Dynasty. It is as though for centuries the novel had been developing unnoticed and from deep roots among the people, spreading into trunk and branch and twig and leaf to burst into this flowering in the Yuan Dynasty, when the young Mongols brought into the old country they had conquered their vigorous, hungry, untutored minds and demanded to be fed. Such minds could not be fed with the husks of the old classical literature, and they turned therefore the more eagerly to the drama and the novel, and in this new life, in the sunshine of imperial favor, though still not with literary favor, there came two of China's three great novels, *Shui Hu Chuan* and *San Kuo*—*Hung Lou Meng* being the third.

11 I wish I could convey to you what these three novels mean and have meant to the Chinese people. But I can think of nothing comparable to them in Western literature. We have not in the history of our novel so clear a moment to which we can point and say, "There the novel is at its height." These three are the *vindication*⑦ of that literature of the common people, the Chinese novel. They stand as completed monuments of that popular literature, if not of letters. They, too, were ignored by men of letters and banned by censors and damned in succeeding dynasties as dangerous, revolutionary, decadent. But they lived

到了无可超越的高度，后代的小说也只有清朝的《红楼梦》可与之媲美。似乎几个世纪以来小说都根植于民间，悄然发展，开枝散叶，到了元朝终于开出了一片春天。年轻的蒙古民族征服了这片中原大地，他们精力旺盛，如饥似渴，缺乏教养的头脑急需补充营养。这样的头脑不可能用中国古老的文学经典来补充，于是他们迫不及待地转向了戏剧和小说。在这种新生活里，有了朝廷的支持，尽管小说仍然不被文人们看好，但还是出现了中国最伟大的三部小说：《水浒传》、《三国演义》和后来的《红楼梦》。

11 我希望我能尽可能向你们传达这三部小说过去和现在对中国人的意义。但遗憾的是我找不到任何西方小说可以与之相提并论。我们的小说史上找不到这样明确的一段时期可以说"小说发展到了顶峰"。这三部中国小说是普通民众文学的见证。它们是大众文学完整的纪念碑——即使不能说是所有文字的纪念碑。文人忽略它们，监察机关禁止它们，后继朝代视其危险、反叛、颓废。但是它们还是存活下来了，因为人们阅读、讲述着它们，将其编成歌谣和戏剧来演

⑦ vindication [ˌvɪndɪˈkeɪʃən] *n.* 辩护，见证

30

on, because people read them and told them as stories and sang them as songs and ballads and acted them as dramas, until at last *grudgingly* [8] even the scholars were compelled to notice them and to begin to say they were not novels at all but allegories, and if they were allegories perhaps then they could be looked upon as literature after all, though the people paid no heed to such theories and never read the long treatises which scholars wrote to prove them. <u>They rejoiced in the novels they had made as novels and for no purpose except for joy in story and in story through which they could express themselves.</u>

12 And indeed the people had made them. *Shui Hu Chuan*, though the modern versions carry the name of Shi Nai'an as author, was written by no one man. Out of a handful of tales centering in the Sung Dynasty about a band of robbers there grew this great, structured novel. Its beginnings were in history. The original *lair* [9] which the robbers held still exists in Shantung, or did until very recent times. Those times of the thirteenth century of our Western era were, in China, sadly distorted. The dynasty under the emperor Huei Chung was falling into decadence and disorder. The rich grew richer and the poor poorer and when none other came forth to set this right, these *righteous* [10] robbers came forth.

13 I cannot here tell you fully of the long growth of this novel, nor of its changes at many

绎。最后连文人们都被迫去关注它们，开始说它们并不是小说，而是寓言。如果把它们说成寓言故事，那就可以视其为文学了。尽管人们从来不关注这些文学理论，也从不阅读文人们写的长篇大论证明其文学性的论文。人民大众只是以他们创作的小说为乐，在他们自己的故事中表达自己，除此之外，别无其他目的。

12 事实上，是人民大众创造了这些故事。尽管现代版本的《水浒传》冠以施耐庵的名字，但其实这本书的作者不详。关于宋朝的一帮反叛者的故事有一大批，而《水浒传》这部伟大小说的框架完全由这些故事发展而来。它的起源在历史上也有记载。这些绿林好汉的据点仍在，或者说近年来还一直存在于山东省。按照西方的纪元，中国的 13 世纪是一个悲惨的时代：宋徽宗的王朝日益衰落混乱。富者愈富，穷者愈穷，没有人去纠正这一切，于是这些充满正义感的强盗应运而生。

13 我并不能完全讲出这部小说的成长史，也不知道它经过多少人之

---

[8] grudgingly ['grʌdʒɪŋlɪ] *adv.* 勉强地，不情愿地

[9] lair [leə] *n.* 据点，藏身处

[10] righteous ['raɪtʃəs] *adj.* 正义的   如：a righteous judgment 公正的判决

hands. Shih Nai An, it is said, found it in rude form in an old book shop and took it home and rewrote it. After him the story was still told and re-told. Five or six versions of it today have importance, one with a hundred chapters entitled *Chung Yi Shui Hu*, one of a hundred and twenty-seven chapters, and one of a hundred chapters. The original version attributed to Shih Nai An, had a hundred and twenty chapters, but the one most used today has only seventy. This is the version arranged in the Ming Dynasty by the famous Ching Shen T'an, who said that it was idle to forbid his son to read the book and therefore presented the lad with a copy revised by himself, knowing that no boy could ever refrain from reading it. There is also a version written under official command, when officials found that nothing could keep the people from reading *Shui Hu*. This official version is entitled *Tung K'ou Chi*, or, *Laying Waste the Robbers*, and it tells of the final defeat of the robbers by the state army and their destruction. But the common people of China are nothing if not independent. They have never adopted the official version, and their own form of the novel still stands. It is a struggle they know all too well, the struggle of everyday people against a corrupt officialdom.

14　I might add that *Shui Hu Chuan* is in partial translation in French under the title *Les Chevaliers Chinois*, and the seventy-chapter version is in complete English translation by myself under the title *All Men Are Brothers*. The original title, *Shui Hu Chuan*, in English is

手，做了多少改编。据说，施耐庵在一家旧书店发现了这个故事的粗劣版本，就将其带回家重写。在他之后，这个故事还经历过很多次改编。今天大概有五六个版本是相对比较重要的，其中一个是 100 回的《忠义水浒》，另一个是 127 回的，还有另一种也是 100 回的。施耐庵的原版是 120 回，但是今天流行最广的一版只有 70 回。这个版本是由明朝著名的金圣叹改编的，他说禁止儿子读这本书是徒劳的，于是自己就重新做了修订，因为他知道不可能有哪个孩子能忍住不去读它。当官方发现已经没有办法阻止人们阅读《水浒》之后，他们也只好组织修订了自己的新版本。官定版本题名为《荡寇志》，其中官兵最后打败并摧毁了强盗。但是中国的普通民众还有独立之精神。他们从未接受官方版本，而这个故事的民间版本则长盛不衰。这是一个大家再熟悉不过的故事，讲述了平民如何反抗贪污腐败的官府。

14　除此之外，《水浒传》被部分翻译成法语，题名《中国骑士》，我自己也将 70 回的版本完全译成了英文，题名为《四海之内皆兄弟》。它的原名《水浒传》在英语里是没有任何意义的，只能反映出当时这群好

meaningless, denoting merely the watery margins of the famous marshy lake which was the robbers' lair. To Chinese the words invoke instant century-old memory, but not to us.

15 This novel has survived everything and in this new day in China has taken on an added significance. The Chinese Communists have printed their own edition of it with a preface by a famous Communist and have issued it anew as the first Communist literature of China. The proof of the novel's greatness is in this timelessness. It is as true today as it was dynasties ago. The people of China still march across its pages, priests and courtesans, merchants and scholars, women good and bad, old and young, and even naughty little boys. The only figure lacking is that of the modern scholar trained in the West, holding his Ph.D. diploma in his hand. But be sure that if he had been alive in China when the final hand laid down the brush upon the pages of that book, he, too, would have been there in all the **pathos** [①] and humor of his new learning, so often useless and inadequate and laid like a patch too small upon an old robe.

16 The Chinese say "The young should not read *Shui Hu* and the old should not read *San Kuo*." This is because the young might be charmed into being robbers and the old might be led into deeds too vigorous for their years. For if *Shui Hu Chuan* is the great social document of Chinese life, *San Kuo* is the document of wars and statesmanship, and in its turn *Hung Lou Meng*

汉聚集在一片水边湿地。对中国人来说，这几个字能瞬间激发出几百年的回忆，但对我们并非如此。

15 这部小说历经磨难，流传至今，在今天的中国已经有了新的意义。中国共产党印发了他们自己的新版本，由一名著名的共产主义者为之作序，而且将其列为中国首部共产主义文学作品。这部小说的伟大就在于它的不朽。这是从古至今的事实。中国人至今还在阅读这部小说，无论是和尚或妓女，商人或学者，或善或恶的妇女，也不论老幼，甚至淘气的男孩都在读这本书。唯一没有读过的人可能要属那些接受西方教育、拿着博士学位的现代学者，但可以肯定的是只要他们生活在中国，最终将手放在那本书页上时，也会为自己所学的新知识哭笑不得，因为那些在这本书面前是如此无用而不足，就像一件古老的长袍上面的一小片补丁。

16 中国人说"少不看《水浒》，老不看《三国》"，因为年轻人很容易铤而走险被吸引去做强盗，而老年人会做出超越他们年龄的过火事情。如果说《水浒传》是中国社会生活的伟大史诗，《三国》是国家间征战的记录的话，那么《红楼梦》就是家庭生活和人类爱情的见证。

---

① pathos ['peɪθɒs] *n.* 悲悯，悲痛

is the document of family life and human love.

17 The history of the *San Kuo* or *Three Kingdoms* shows the same architectural structure and the same doubtful authorship as *Shui Hu*. The story begins with three friends swearing eternal brotherhood in the Han Dynasty and ends ninety-seven years later in the succeeding period of the Six Dynasties. It is a novel rewritten in its final form by a man named Lo Kuan Chung, thought to be a pupil of Shih Nai An, and one who perhaps even shared with Shih Nai An in the writing, too, of *Shui Hu Chuan*. But this is a Chinese Bacon-and-Shakespeare controversy which has no end.

18 Lo Kuan Chung was born in the late Yuan Dynasty and lived on into the Ming. He wrote many dramas, but he is more famous for his novels, of which *San Kuo* is easily the best. The version of this novel now most commonly used in China is the one revised in the time of K'ang Hsi by Mao Chen Kan, who revised as well as criticised the book. He changed, added and omitted material, as for example when he added the story of Suan Fu Ren, the wife of one of the chief characters. He altered even the style. If *Shui Hu Chuan* has importance today as a novel of the people in their struggle for liberty, *San Kuo* has importance because it gives in such detail the science and art of war as the Chinese conceive it, so differently, too, from our own. The guerillas, who are today China's most effective fighting units against Japan, are peasants who know *San Kuo* by heart, if not from their own reading, at least from hours spent in the idleness

17 由《三国》的形成史来看，不仅其总体结构跟《水浒传》相像，它还像《水浒》一样没有确定的作者。这个故事开始于汉朝末年，三个朋友宣誓结义，结束于 97 年后的六朝时代。《三国》的最终版可能是罗贯中改编而成的。而罗贯中可能是施耐庵的学生，而且可能同施耐庵一道参与了《水浒》的改写。但这是中国式的培根与莎士比亚的争论，不可能有结果。

18 罗贯中出生于元朝末年，一直活到明朝。他曾写过许多戏剧，但不如他的小说出名，而小说中最出色的要数《三国》了。现在用得最多的《三国》版本是清朝康熙年间毛宗岗修改并作评的。他改变、增删了许多素材，例如，他在其中补充了孙夫人的故事——孙夫人为其中一个主要人物的妻子。他甚至改变了写作风格。如果说《水浒传》在今天还有意义是因为它是一部人民为自由而战的小说，那《三国》的重要地位则是因为它对科学和战争艺术的详尽描述，尽管中国人的这种看法与我们西方如此不同。作为今天中国打击日本侵略者最有效的力量，游击队员们就是一群熟知三国故事的农民，如果不是自己亲读，也一定在无所事事的冬日或在一个个夏夜里听讲故事的人说了无数遍三国勇士们的战斗故事。这些游

of winter days or long summer evenings when they sat listening to the storytellers describe how the warriors of the Three Kingdoms fought their battles. It is these ancient tactics of war which the guerillas trust today. What a warrior must be and how he must attack and retreat, how retreat when the enemy advances, how advance when the enemy retreats—all this had its source in this novel, so well known to every common man and boy of China.

19 *Hung Lou Meng*, or *The Dream of the Red Chamber*, the latest and most modern of these three greatest of Chinese novels, was written originally as an autobiographical novel by Ts'ao Hsüeh Ching, an official highly in favor during the Manchu regime and indeed considered by the Manchus as one of themselves. There were then eight military groups among the Manchus, and Ts'ao Hsüeh Ching belonged to them all. He never finished his novel, and the last forty chapters were added by another man, probably named Kao O. The thesis that Ts'ao Hsüeh Ching was telling the story of his own life has been in modern times elaborated by Hu Shih, and in earlier times by Yuan Mei. Be this as it may, the original title of the book was *Shih T'ou Chi*, and it came out of Peking about 1765 of the Western era, and in five or six years, an incredibly short time in China, it was famous everywhere. Printing was still expensive when it appeared, and the book became known by the method that is called in China, "You-lend-me-a-book-and-I-lend-you-a-book".

20 The story is simple in its theme but

击队信奉的就是这一套古老的战争策略。一个真正的勇士该是什么样，应该如何适时攻击和撤退，以及如何做到敌进我退，敌退我进——所有这些都可以在这本每个中国男人都熟知的小说中找到源头。

19《红楼梦》是这三部伟大小说的最后一部，也是最现代的一部，是曹雪芹的自传体小说。曹雪芹深得满清王朝的青睐，也被满族视为自己人。当时有八大军事集团，称为"八旗"，曹雪芹就是其中的成员。他自己并未完成《红楼梦》的著述，后40回由高鹗补充完成。近代的胡适和稍早一点的袁枚都认为曹雪芹是在讲自己的故事。这也许是对的。这本书原名叫做《石头记》，大约于1765年在北京出现，之后仅五六年的时间，它就红遍了大江南北。当时印刷书籍还相当昂贵，而这本书是大家通过中国所谓的"你借我，我借你"的方式流行起来的。

20 这本书主题虽简单，但它的

complex in implication, in character study and in its portrayal of human emotions. It is almost a pathological study, this story of a great house, once wealthy and high in imperial favor, so that indeed one of its members was an imperial concubine. But the great days are over when the book begins. The family is already declining. Its wealth is being *dissipated* [12] and the last and only son, Chia Pao Yü, is being corrupted by the *decadent* [13] influences within his own home, although the fact that he was a youth of exceptional quality at birth is established by the symbolism of a piece of jade found in his mouth. The preface begins, "Heaven was once broken and when it was mended, a bit was left unused, and this became the famous jade of Chia Pao Yü." Thus does the interest in the supernatural persist in the Chinese people; it persists even today as a part of Chinese life.

21 This novel seized hold of the people primarily because it portrayed the problems of their own family system, the absolute power of women in the home, the too great power of the matriarchy, the grandmother, the mother, and even the bondmaids, so often young and beautiful and fatally dependent, who became too frequently the playthings of the sons of the house and ruined them and were ruined by them. Women reigned supreme in the Chinese house, and because they were wholly confined in its walls and often

寓意、人物研究和人物情感的刻画都很复杂深刻。它几乎成了对心理病态的研究。故事讲了一个庞大、富有而高贵的家族，深得皇帝宠爱，家庭成员里有一位还是皇上的妃子。但是小说一开始这种繁荣就不再了。这个家族已经开始衰落。家族财富被大量挥霍，家里最后一个也是唯一的一个儿子贾宝玉也被家里颓废的气氛宠溺着，尽管他天赋异禀——因为生下来嘴里就含着一块玉。前言开始就写道："却说那女娲炼石补天之时……单单剩下一块未用，这就成了贾宝玉那块著名的玉了。"中国人有着对超自然现象的兴趣，直到今天这种兴趣还是中国人生活的一部分。

21 这部小说之所以能如此吸引人，主要是因为它讲述的是家庭制度的一些问题：妇女在家中的绝对地位，母权制有着强大的势力，祖母、母亲，甚至女仆都有很大的力量，她们年轻貌美，却不能左右自己的命运，经常沦为家中男子的玩物，最终毁了那些男人，自己也被毁掉。中国家庭里，妇女有着绝对的统治地位，因为她们终日被限制在高墙院内，而且通常不识字，她们的统治常常使每

---

⑫ dissipate [ˈdɪsɪpeɪt] *vt.* 浪费，挥霍　　如：dissipate one's energy 浪费精力

⑬ decadent [ˈdekədənt] *adj.* 颓废的　　如：a decadent lifestyle/society 腐化的生活方式 / 腐朽的社会

illiterate, they ruled to the hurt of all. They kept men children, and protected them from hardship and effort when they should not have been so protected. Such a one was Chia Pao Yü, and we follow him to his tragic end in *Hung Lou Meng*.

22 I cannot tell you to what lengths of allegory scholars went to explain away this novel when they found that again even the emperor was reading it and that its influence was so great everywhere among the people. I do not doubt that they were probably reading it themselves in secret. A great many popular jokes in China have to do with scholars reading novels privately and publicly pretending never to have heard of them. At any rate, scholars wrote treatises to prove that *Hung Lou Meng* was not a novel but a political allegory depicting the decline of China under the foreign rule of the Manchus, the word Red in the title signifying Manchu, and Ling Tai Yü, the young girl who dies, although she was the one destined to marry Pao Yü, signifying China, and Pao Ts'ai, her successful rival, who secures the jade in her place, standing for the foreigner, and so forth. The very name "Chia" signified, they said, "falseness". But this was a farfetched explanation of what was written as a novel and stands as a novel and as such a powerful delineation, in the characteristic Chinese mixture of realism and romance, of a proud and powerful family in decline. Crowded with men and women of the several generations accustomed to living under one roof in China, it stands alone as an intimate description of that life.

个人都倍感痛苦。她们把男人当小孩一样保护，不让男人受苦受累，但男人本身却并不需要这种保护。贾宝玉就是这样一个被保护的男人，在《红楼梦》中也是以悲剧收尾。

22 当文人学者发现这本书在民间影响如此之大，甚至连皇帝都开始读的时候，他们又开始想尽办法将其解释为寓言故事。我丝毫不怀疑，他们自己也在暗地里读过这本书。中国有许多笑话讲文人们自己私下里读小说，但在公开场合却说连听都没听说过。不管怎样，文人们写了许多论文证明《红楼梦》不是小说，而是政治性寓言故事，描述了满族统治下衰败的中国。他们认为题目中的"红"字就代表满族；林黛玉象征着中国，尽管她本该与贾宝玉结为连理，但结果却病死于贾府；而薛宝钗——黛玉的情敌，成功把玉收归己有，她象征着外族，等等。而姓氏"贾"则象征着"假"。但是这种解释对于这部小说来说很牵强。这是一部集浪漫主义与现实主义于一身的小说，它有力地描述了一个强大贵族家庭的衰落。书中中国的几代男男女女同住在一个屋檐下，所以它本身就是对那种生活的贴切描绘。

23　In so emphasizing these three novels, I have merely done what the Chinese themselves do. When you say "novel", the average Chinese replies, "*Shui Hu, San Kuo, Hung Lou Meng.*" Yet this is not to say that there are not hundreds of other novels, for there are. I must mention *Hsi Yü Chi*, or *Record of Travels in the West*, almost as popular as these three. I might mention *Feng Shen Chuan*, the story of a deified warrior, the author unknown but said to be a writer in the time of Ming. I must mention *Ru Ling Wai Shi*, a satire upon the evils of the Tsing dynasty, particularly of the scholars, full of a double-edged though not malicious dialogue, rich with incident, pathetic and humorous. The fun here is made of the scholars who can do nothing practical, who are lost in the world of useful everyday things, who are so bound by convention that nothing original can come from them. The book, though long, has no central character. Each figure is linked to the next by the thread of incident, person and incident passing on together until, as Lu Hsün, the famous modern Chinese writer, has said, "they are like scraps of brilliant silk and satin sewed together."

24　And there is *Yea Shou Pei Yin*, or *An Old Hermit Talks in the Sun*, written by a famous man disappointed in official **preferment** ⑭, Shia Kiang-yin, and there is that strangest of books, *Ching Hua Yuen*, a fantasy of women, whose ruler was an empress, whose scholars were all women. It is designed to show that the wisdom of women is equal to that of men, although I

23　我如此强调这三部小说，其实只是做了中国人会做的事情。只要你说到"小说"，一般中国人都会回答，《水浒传》、《三国》和《红楼梦》。但这并不是说中国就没有其他小说了，事实上确实还有成百上千的别的小说。我必须要提一下《西游记》，它几乎和这三部一样受欢迎。还有《封神演义》，它是一个神化了的武士的故事，作者不详，但据说是明朝人。还有《儒林外史》，这是清朝的一本讽刺小说，讽刺邪恶，尤其是当时的文人的邪恶。书中充满了并非恶意的双关语，情节丰富，感人而幽默。小说嘲讽那些空学无术、对日常事务一无所通的文人学者，他们拘泥于传统，不敢也不能做出任何创新。这本书虽长，却没有一个中心人物。每个人物都通过事件线索与另一个人物连接，人物和事件一起发展，就像中国著名现代作家鲁迅所说："他们就像编织在一起的精美的绫罗绸缎。"

24　除此之外还有《野叟曝言》，它是由一个官场失意的名人夏敬渠写的。还有那本奇怪的《镜花缘》，写了一个幻想的女人国，其中皇帝和知识分子都是女性。这本书是为了说明女人同男人一样有智慧，尽管我不得不承认书的最后女人和男人之间爆发了一场战争，男人取得了胜利，女皇

⑭ preferment [prɪˈfɜːmənt] *n.* 晋升

must acknowledge that the book ends with a war between men and women in which the men are triumphant and the empress is supplanted by an emperor.

25 But I can mention only a small fraction of the hundreds of novels which delight the common people of China. And if those people knew of what I was speaking to you today, they would after all say "tell of the great three, and let us stand or fall by *Shui Hu Chuan* and *San Kuo* and *Hung Lou Meng*." In these three novels are the lives which the Chinese people lead and have long led, here are the songs they sing and the things at which they laugh and the things which they love to do. Into these novels they have put the generations of their being and to refresh that being they return to these novels again and again, and out of them they have made new songs and plays and other novels. Some of them have come to be almost as famous as the great originals, as for example *Ching P'ing Mei*, that classic of romantic physical love, taken from a single incident in *Shui Hu Chuan*.

26 But the important thing for me today is not the listing of novels. The aspect which I wish to stress is that all this profound and indeed sublime development of the imagination of a great democratic people was never in its own time and country called literature. The very name for story was "hsiao shuo", denoting something slight and valueless, and even a novel was only a "ts'ang p'ien hsiao shuo", or a longer something which was still slight and useless. No, the people

的位置也被一个男性皇帝取代。

25 我只能给你们讲述中国人心仪的几百本小说中的一小部分。如果知道我今天要讲这些，他们肯定会说："告诉他们最伟大的三部吧，不论好歹也要讲讲《水浒传》、《三国》和《红楼梦》。"这三部小说讲的是中国人的生活，是他们长久以来所过的生活，里面有他们的欢歌笑语，也有他们平日的生活喜好。他们把几代人的发展都注入这些小说，又一遍遍地回顾这些小说来汲取营养，从中创作出新的诗歌、戏剧和小说。其中有些已经像原著一样有名，例如那个写情欲肉爱的《金瓶梅》就取材于《水浒传》中的一个故事。

26 但是我今天要做的重要的事并不是列举小说。我要强调的是人民大众的想象力发展到如此深刻卓越的程度，而这些小说在他们自己的国家和时代里却不被称为文学。这些故事的特有名称"小说"在当时是无足轻重，不具任何价值的，甚至"长篇小说"也只是较长的一些卑微无用之物。不，除了文人的文学，中国人民还创造了他们自己的文学。今天存留

of China forged their own literature apart from letters. And today this is what lives, to be part of what is to come, and all the formal literature, which was called art, is dead. The plots of these novels are often incomplete, the love interest is often not brought to solution, heroines are often not beautiful and heroes often are not brave. Nor has the story always an end; sometimes it merely stops, in the way life does, in the middle of it when death is not expected.

27　In this tradition of the novel have I been born and reared as a writer. My ambition, therefore, has not been trained toward the beauty of letters or the grace of art. It is, I believe, a sound teaching and, as I have said, illuminating for the novels of the West.

28　For here is the essence of the attitude of Chinese novelists—perhaps the result of the contempt in which they were held by those who considered themselves the priests of art. I put it thus in my own words, for none of them has done so.

29　The instinct which creates the arts is not the same as that which produces art. The creative instinct is, in its final analysis and in its simplest terms, an enormous extra vitality, a super-energy, born inexplicably in an individual, a vitality great beyond all the needs of his own living—an energy which no single life can consume. This energy consumes itself then in creating more life, in the form of music, painting, writing, or whatever is its most natural medium of expression. Nor can the individual keep himself from this process,

下来的正是这些，而在今后那些正式的文学，所谓的艺术，却即将消亡。这些小说的情节大都不完整，爱情纠缠往往都没有解决方法，女主角往往不够美丽，而男主角又大都不够勇敢。而且故事也并非都有一个结局，有时会突然中止，就像生活本身一样，死亡不期而至。

27　我就是在这样的小说传统中出生并被培养起来的。因此，我从小就没有接受过追求华丽辞藻和艺术之美的教育。我相信这是一种很好的教育，就像我说的，这对西方小说会是一次无声的启示。

28　这就是中国小说家的态度之精华——也许这是那些自称大师的人对他们的轻蔑，但我自己说的话里并没有一丝轻蔑的意思。

29　创造艺术的本能和制造艺术的天性是不同的。创造的本能，从根本上分析，用简单的话说就是，一种巨大的外力，是超能力，是一个人莫名其妙生来就有的能力，这种能力远远超出一个人的基本生活需要——是单独一个人绝对消耗不尽的能力。于是这种力量通过创造更多的生命来消耗自己，音乐、画作、文字或者随便什么都能作为表达媒介。个人本身也不能阻止这个过程，因为只有将其释

because only by its full function is he relieved of the burden of this extra and peculiar energy—an energy at once physical and mental, so that all his senses are more alert and more profound than another man's, and all his brain more sensitive and quickened to that which his senses reveal to him in such abundance that actuality overflows into imagination. It is a process proceeding from within. It is the heightened activity of every cell of his being, which sweeps not only himself, but all human life about him, or in him, in his dreams, into the circle of its activity.

30 From the product of this activity, art is deducted—but not by him. The process which creates is not the process which deduces the shapes of art. The defining of art, therefore, is a secondary and not a primary process. And when one born for the primary process of creation, as the novelist is, concerns himself with the secondary process, his activity becomes meaningless. When he begins to make shapes and styles and techniques and new schools, then he is like a ship stranded upon a reef whose propeller, whirl wildly as it will, cannot drive the ship onward. Not until the ship is in its element again can it regain its course.

31 And for the novelist the only element is human life as he finds it in himself or outside himself. The sole test of his work is whether or not his energy is producing more of that life. Are his creatures alive? That is the only question. And who can tell him? Who but those living human beings, the people? Those people are not

放出来，他自己才能卸下这多余的负担和独特的能量，这种能量既是肉体上的，也是精神上的。拥有这种力量的人，他所有的感觉都会比他人更敏锐，更深刻，他的大脑也会对感觉传达的信息更敏感，反应更快，这种能量发散过剩，以至于最后都发展成了想象力。它是一个由内而外的过程。它需要调动全身细胞，这种力量不止会辐射他自己，还会囊括所有与他相关的人，他心里的、梦里的，以及所生活的圈子里的人。

30 这种活动的成品诠释了艺术——但做诠释的人并不是作者本身。创造的过程并非塑造艺术形象的过程。因此，定义艺术就成了次要的，而非主要过程。如果一个为主要的创造活动而生的人，就像小说家，把他自己与次要活动联系起来，那他的活动就失去了意义。当一个小说家开始塑造小说的形象、风格和流派，注意写作技巧的时候，他就会像一艘搁浅在礁石上的船只，只管打转，却怎么也不能前行。直到船重新进入到自己的环境，它才能继续前行。

31 对小说家来说，唯一的环境就是他自己身处其中的或在其身外的人类生活。检验他成果的唯一标准就是看他的能量是否创造出了更多生活的东西。创造的人物是否生动？这是唯一的问题。谁能回答这个问题呢？只能是活着的人民大众吧？这些群众

absorbed in what art is or how it is made. No, they are absorbed only in themselves, in their own hungers and despairs and joys and above all, perhaps, in their own dreams. These are the ones who can really judge the work of the novelist, for they judge by that single test of reality. And the standard of the test is not to be made by the device of art, but by the simple comparison of the reality of what they read, to their own reality.

32 I have been taught, therefore, that though the novelist may see art as cool and perfect shapes, he may only admire them as he admires marble statues standing aloof in a quiet and remote gallery; for his place is not with them. His place is in the street. He is happiest there. The street is noisy and the men and women are not perfect in the technique of their expression as the statues are. They are ugly and imperfect, incomplete even as human beings, and where they come from and where they go cannot be known. But they are people and therefore infinitely to be preferred to those who stand upon the pedestals of art.

33 And like the Chinese novelist, I have been taught to want to write for these people. If they are reading their magazines by the million, then I want my stories there rather than in magazines read only by a few. For story belongs to the people. They are sounder judges of it than anyone else, for their senses are unspoiled and their emotions are free. No, a novelist must not think of pure literature as his goal. He must not even know this field too well, because people, who

对艺术不感兴趣，对怎么产生艺术也不感兴趣，他们感兴趣的只是他们自己，他们的温饱、绝望、欢乐，还有最重要的——他们的梦想。他们是真正可以评价小说家成果的一批人，他们评价的唯一标准就是现实。检验的标准并不是艺术策略，而是人们读到的故事和他们自己的现实之间简单的对比。

32 因此，我所受的教育告诉我，虽然小说家可以把艺术看成冷酷完美的形式，但他只是像欣赏矗立在僻静处画廊里的大理石雕像一样来欣赏艺术，他自己的位置却并不在那里。他的位置在大街上，那是最令他感到快乐的地方。街道热闹而喧哗，那里的男女们也不会像雕像一样有着完美的表达技巧。他们没有美丽的容貌，也并不完美，甚至不完整，他们只是普通的人类，你不知道他们来自哪里要到哪里去。但是他们是实实在在的人，肯定要比落在基座上的雕像更讨人喜欢。

33 就像其他中国小说家一样，我所受的教育使我想为这些人写作。如果他们中有一百万人读杂志，那我想让我的小说在他们的杂志上发表，而不想发表在只有很少人阅读的杂志上。因为故事属于人民。人民才是小说最好的评判者，因为他们的情感是自由的，他们的感官没有被宠坏。不，一个小说家绝不能把纯粹的文学当成自己的目标。他甚至绝不能太了

are his material, are not there. He is a storyteller in a village tent, and by his stories he *entices* [15] people into his tent. He need not raise his voice when a scholar passes. But he must beat all his drums when a band of poor pilgrims pass on their way up the mountain in search of gods. To them he must cry, "I, too, tell of gods!" And to farmers he must talk of their land, and to old men he must speak of peace, and to old women he must tell of their children, and to young men and women he must speak of each other. He must be satisfied if the common people hear him gladly. At least, so I have been taught in China.

解文学，因为作为他素材的人民大众并不在那儿。他是村庄帐篷里讲故事的人，他通过自己的故事将人民吸引到自己的帐篷里。当一个文人经过时，他没有必要提高自己的声音。但是若是一群上山朝圣的穷人路过时，他一定要使劲把鼓敲响，向他们高呼："我也在讲神的故事！"对农民，他一定要讲土地；对老人，他一定要讲和平安详；对老妇人，他一定要讲她们的孩子；而对年轻的男女，他一定要讲彼此的故事。如果普通人乐意听他的故事，那他自己也一定很满意。至少，我在中国所学就是这样的。

 演讲关键词 Practical Expressions

1. folklore 民间传说
2. family system 家族制度
3. realism 现实主义
4. transmigration and resurrection from the dead 轮回转世
5. *The Dream of the Red Chamber*《红楼梦》

1. They rejoiced in the novels they had made as novels and for no purpose except for joy in story and in story through which they could express themselves.

   人民大众只是以他们创作的小说为乐，在他们自己的故事中表达自己，除此之外，别无其他目的。

---

[15] entice [ɪn'taɪs] *vt.* 引诱　如：The animal refused to be enticed from its hole. 怎么引诱，那只动物也不肯出洞。

2. When he begins to make shapes and styles and techniques and new schools, then he is like a ship stranded upon a reef whose propeller, whirl wildly as it will, cannot drive the ship onward.

当一个小说家开始塑造小说的形象、风格和流派，注意写作技巧的时候，他就会像一艘搁浅在礁石上的船只，只管打转，却怎么也不能前行。

诺贝尔奖背后的那些趣事

诺贝尔奖的摇篮

　　若论起培养诺贝尔奖得主最多的大学排行榜，毫无疑问，剑桥大学会摘得桂冠。剑桥大学至今已拥有 80 多位诺贝尔奖得主，而牛顿、培根所在的三一学院则培养出了 30 多位诺贝尔奖得主。古老的三一学院入口处有亨利八世的雕像，大门右侧的草坪中间长着一棵苹果树。据说这就是当年苹果落下砸中牛顿的那棵树。后来无数人来到剑桥，都要慕名来到这棵树下顿足。遗憾的是，牛顿去世的时间比诺贝尔奖的创立还要早 100 多年，所以他是无缘诺贝尔奖了。

Speech 4
Writing Makes Man Endure
写作使人类不朽

—Speech by William Faulkner for the Nobel Prize in Literature in 1949

——意识流文学在美国的代表人物威廉·福克纳 1949 年诺贝尔文学奖获奖演讲

 名家速览 About the Author

诺贝尔奖大师	威廉·福克纳
奖 项 归 属	诺贝尔文学奖
获 奖 理 由	因为他对当代美国小说做出了强有力的，艺术上无与伦比的贡献。
获 奖 作 品	《我弥留之际》

　　威廉·福克纳（William Faulkner, 1897 年 9 月 25 日 —
1962 年 7 月 6 日），是美国文学史上最具影响力的作家之一，
是美国意识流文学的代表人物。福克纳出身于没落的庄园主家
庭，其祖父是小有名气的政治家、作家、实业家，对福克纳一
生产生了重大影响。福克纳性格不羁，热爱阅读，没有接受过
多少正规教育，但从小受文学熏陶，显示出与众不同的天赋。
他曾强烈渴望参军，但加入部队后却没有参加过战斗。福克纳
是一位多产的作家，一生共写了 19 部长篇小说和 120 多篇短
篇小说。他的大部分小说的故事背景都是约克纳帕塔法县，讲
述了这个县不同社会阶层的若干个家族几代人的故事，时间跨
度从 1800 年起直到第二次世界大战以后。其作品风格多变，常常不按照时空顺序来组织情
节，使故事呈现出意义上的无限可能。他最有代表性的作品是《喧哗与骚动》、《八月之光》。
在本篇演讲中福克纳谈到了诺贝尔文学奖的意义，以及诗人、作家的使命。

演讲现场
Speech Script

精美译文
Suggested Translation

1 I feel that this award was not made to me as a man, but to my work—a life's work in the **agony** ① and sweat of the human spirit, not for glory and **least of all** ② for profit, but to create out of the materials of the human spirit something which did not exist before. So this award is only mine in trust. It will not be difficult to find a **dedication** ③ for the money part of it **commensurate** ④ with the purpose and significance of its origin. But I would like to do the same with the acclaim too, by using this moment as a **pinnacle** ⑤ from which I might be listened to by the young men and women already dedicated to the same anguish and **travail** ⑥, among whom is already that one who will some day stand here where I am standing.

2 Our tragedy today is a general and universal physical fear so long sustained by now that we can even bear it. There are no longer problems of the spirit. There is only the question: When will I be **blown up** ⑦? Because of this, the

1 这个奖并不是颁给我个人的，而是授予我所从事的工作——这是关于人类精神的一份含辛茹苦的工作，无关荣耀，更非为了利益，只是从人类精神中寻求素材，创造出前所未有的东西。因此，这个奖项只是暂时托我保管而已。要做一篇同奖金相符又能兼顾奖项最初的目的和意义的献词并不难。但我还是想借此万众欢呼的时刻，站在这举世瞩目的高度，向那些投身于这项艰苦劳动的男女同仁们致敬，终将有一天他们中有些人也要站在这同一个地方。

2 如今我们的悲剧在于一种普遍存在的生理上的恐惧，这种恐惧由来已久，以至于我们已经开始承受，并渐渐麻木了。精神的困扰已经不复存在。存在的只有一种困惑：我什么

---

① agony ['ægənɪ] *n.* 苦恼，极大的痛苦　如：be in agony 苦恼不堪

② least of all　最不，尤其　如：No one could ever tell what he was thinking about, Scarlett least of all. 谁也不明白他在想些什么，而斯嘉丽是最不明白的。

③ dedication [ˌdedɪ'keɪʃən] *n.* 献词，题词

④ commensurate [kə'menʃərɪt] *adj.* 相称的，相当的　如：a salary commensurate with performance 薪水与工作表现相称

⑤ pinnacle ['pɪnəkl] *n.* 顶点，顶峰　如：the pinnacle of one's career 事业的顶峰

⑥ travail ['træveɪl] *n.* 艰辛，辛勤劳动

⑦ blow (sb.) up　吹捧，追捧

young man or woman writing today has forgotten the problems of the human heart in conflict with itself which alone can make good writing because only that is worth writing about, worth the agony and the sweat.

3　He must learn them again. He must teach himself that the basest of all things is to be afraid; and, teaching himself that, forget it forever, leaving no room in his workshop for anything but the old verities and truths of the heart, the old universal truths lacking which any story is *ephemeral* [8] and doomed—love and honor and pity and pride and compassion and sacrifice. Until he does so, he labors under a curse. He writes not of love but of lust, of defeats in which nobody loses anything of value, of victories without hope and, worst of all, without pity or compassion. His griefs *grieve* [9] on no universal bones, leaving no scars. He writes not of the heart but of the glands.

4　Until he relearns these things, he will write as though he stood among and watched the end of man. I decline to accept the end of man. It is easy enough to say that man is immortal simply because he will endure: that when the last dingdong of doom has *clanged* [10] and faded from the last worthless rock hanging tideless in the last red and dying evening, that even then there

时候才能成名，受人追捧？怀着这样的心态，今天的年轻人已经忘却了人类内心的困扰和冲突，而只有这些才能创造出好作品，也只有这些才值得写作，值得付出血汗。

3　因此，必须重新认识这些问题，必须告诉自己最可鄙的事就是恐惧。告诉自己，要永远忘却恐惧。在工作坊里只留下人类内心古老的真理，因为缺少这些，任何故事都只能昙花一现，注定夭折——这些真理就是爱、荣誉、同情、自豪、怜悯和牺牲精神。如果不这样做，写作就像受了诅咒一样，不会成功。那么写出的爱情将不是爱，而仅仅是情欲；写出的失败将是所有人都不会损失任何价值的虚伪的失败；写出的胜利没有希望，甚至没有同情或怜悯。这样的悲哀没有深度，不会留下任何伤痕。这不是用心写作，而是靠器官劳动。

4　在重新认识这些之前，写作就犹如站着观望人类末日的到来。我不接受世界末日的说法。因为人类能够延续就说明我们能不朽，这样说很容易。或者说即使末日的最后一声叮咚也已消失在那晚霞灿烂却无潮起潮落的礁石旁，即使到了那时仍然会有一种不知疲倦的声音在轻微交谈。这

---

⑧　ephemeral [ɪ'femərəl] *adj.* 短暂的，短命的　如：ephemeral joys 短暂的欢乐；ephemeral flowers 朝开暮谢的花

⑨　grieve [gri:v] *vi.* 伤心

⑩　clang [klæŋ] *vi.* 叮当地响

will still be one more sound: that of his *puny* ⑪ inexhaustible voice, still talking.

5 I refuse to accept this. I believe that man will not merely endure: he will prevail. He is immortal, not because he alone among creatures has an inexhaustible voice, but because he has a soul, a spirit capable of compassion and sacrifice and endurance. The poet's, the writer's, duty is to write about these things. It is his privilege to help man endure by lifting his heart, by reminding him of the courage and honor and hope and pride and compassion and pity and sacrifice which have been the glory of his past. The poet's voice need not merely be the record of man, it can be one of the *props* ⑫, the pillars to help him endure and prevail.

样说也很容易。

5 但我拒绝接受这样的说法。我相信人类不只能够延续，而且能战胜一切并永存。人类之所以能不朽，不是因为在万物中只有他能永不疲倦地发出自己的声音，而是因为他有灵魂，有怜悯和牺牲的能力及精神。诗人和作家的任务就是书写这些，他们的特权就是去鼓舞人心，提醒世人他们曾拥有辉煌的过去——勇气、荣誉、希望、自豪、怜悯、同情和牺牲精神。诗人的声音不只是记录人类，它还支撑着人类取得胜利，以达到永恒。

演讲关键词 Practical Expressions

1. agony and sweat 含辛茹苦
2. lift one's heart 鼓舞人心
3. so long by now 由来已久
4. be blown up 受人追捧

1. Because of this, the young man or woman writing today has forgotten the problems of the human heart in conflict with itself which alone can make good writing because only

---

⑪ puny ['pju:nɪ] *adj.* 小的，弱的，微不足道的 如：They laughed at my puny efforts. 他们嘲笑我微不足道的努力。

⑫ prop [prɒp] *n.* 支撑物，架

that is worth writing about, worth the agony and the sweat.

怀着这样的心态，今天的年轻人已经忘却了人类内心的困扰和冲突，而只有这些才能创造出好作品，也只有这些才值得写作，值得付出血汗。

2. He is immortal, not because he alone among creatures has an inexhaustible voice, but because he has a soul, a spirit capable of compassion and sacrifice and endurance.

人类之所以能不朽，不是因为在万物中只有他能永不疲倦地发出自己的声音，而是因为他有灵魂，有怜悯和牺牲的能力及精神。

 诺贝尔奖背后的那些趣事

蓝厅不蓝

瑞典不仅国旗中有蓝色，国内的一些重要建筑的主色调也都是蓝色。诺贝尔奖的颁奖大厅是一座蓝色的音乐厅，除此之外，诺贝尔奖的盛大晚宴也是在市政厅的"蓝厅"举行。但这个"蓝厅"其实并不蓝，其主要建材是红砖。在当年建造的时候，设计师无意中发现，红色的砖墙在阳光照耀下显得格外温暖而又辉煌，这种温暖的感觉对于这个位于寒冷地区的国家来说是没有理由拒绝的，于是设计师就不再往墙面上贴蓝色马赛克了。

Speech 5
Two Worlds
两个世界

—Speech by V. S. Naipaul for the Nobel Prize in Literature in 2001
——英语作家中的佼佼者维·苏·奈保尔 2001 年诺贝尔文学奖获奖演讲

 名家速览 About the Author

诺贝尔奖大师	维·苏·奈保尔
奖 项 归 属	诺贝尔文学奖
获 奖 理 由	其著作将极具洞察力的叙述与不为世俗左右的探索融为一体，是驱策我们从扭曲的历史中探寻真实的动力。
主 要 作 品	《神秘的按摩师》、《米格尔大街》、《河湾》等

  维·苏·奈保尔 1932 年生于中美洲的特立尼达和多巴哥共和国的一个印度婆罗门家庭。他 1948 年毕业于特立尼达和多巴哥共和国的首都西班牙港的一所学校，之后获奖学金赴英国牛津大学留学。毕业后奈保尔做了自由撰稿人，也曾为 BBC 做"西印度之声"广播员，1955 年在英国结婚并定居。20 世纪 60 年代他曾在世界各地广泛游历，游记写作成为他后半生写作的主要内容。

  奈保尔一家是移民到中美洲的印度婆罗门家庭，虽然在印度婆罗门已经是较高的种姓，但在特立尼达岛上，这些印度移民的生活却并不如意。他们远离家乡，先后在西班牙和英国的殖民下过着封闭的生活，他们虽然刚开始保留着自己的生活习惯和文化宗教，但这些都随着时间的推移渐渐淡去。到了奈保尔这一代，他们几乎成了没有根的人。来自印度、西班牙、英国和当地土著的多元文化混合，让他们迷失了自己。后来奈保尔到英国留学也曾因为印裔身份和人种问题遭受歧视。这种身份的焦虑给他造成了极大的负担，但同时也成了他写作的原动力和灵感的源泉，给了他观察事物的独特视角。本篇演讲中，奈保尔讲述了他自己对写作的看法，包括他自己的写作动机和写作历程。他解释了许多他自己的背景来历，以及这些对他写作的影响，使我们得以窥见一个写作大师关于写作的真实想法。

演讲现场
Speech Script

精美译文
Suggested Translation

1 This is unusual for me. I have given readings and not lectures. I have told people who ask for lectures that I have no lecture to give. And that is true. It might seem strange that a man who has dealt in words and emotions and ideas for nearly fifty years shouldn't have a few to spare, so to speak. But everything of value about me is in my books. Whatever extra there is in me at any given moment isn't fully formed. I am hardly aware of it; it awaits the next book. It will—with luck—come to me during the actual writing, and it will take me by surprise. That element of surprise is what I look for when I am writing. It is my way of judging what I am doing—which is never an easy thing to do.

2 Proust has written with great penetration of the difference between the writer as writer and the writer as a social being. You will find his thoughts in some of his essays in *Against Sainte-Beuve*, a book reconstituted from his early papers.

3 The nineteenth-century French critic Sainte-Beuve believed that to understand a writer it was necessary to know as much as possible about the exterior man, the details of his life. It is a **_beguiling_** ① method, using the man to illuminate the work. It might seem **_unassailable_** ②. But Proust is able very convincingly to pick it apart. "This

1 这次演讲对我来说是极不寻常的。我写过很多东西供人阅读，但却没有做过演讲。我告诉那些请我演讲的人们，我不会演讲。这是真的。一个同文字、情感和思想打了将近50年交道的人不该有所保留，可以说这很奇怪。但是我一切有价值的东西都在我的书里面。在其他任何场合所需的品质我都还没有形成。我刚刚意识到，这些在下一本书里等着我。幸运的话，在我实际写作的时候这些都会涌现出来，会给我意外的惊喜。我写作时一直在寻找的就是这样的惊喜。这是我评判自己所做的事情的方式——而这做起来并不容易。

2 普鲁斯特曾以颇具洞察力的文章分析过作为写作者的作家和作为社会人的作家之间的区别。他的思想在《反对圣伯夫》这本早期文集的一些散文里有所表露。

3 19世纪法国文学评论家圣伯夫认为要理解一位作家的作品，就有必要尽可能多地了解这位作家的外在，即他的生活细节。这个方法很具欺骗性——通过人来映射作品。看起来似乎无懈可击，但普鲁斯特却不无说服力地将其推翻。普鲁斯特写道：

---

① beguiling [bɪˈgaɪlɪŋ] *adj.* 欺骗的，诱骗的　如：beguiling advertisements 富有诱惑力的广告
② unassailable [ˌʌnəˈseɪləbl] *adj.* 无懈可击的，不容置疑的　如：The party now has an unassailable lead. 这个党的领先地位坚不可摧。

method of Sainte-Beuve," Proust writes, "ignores what a very slight degree of self-acquaintance teaches us: that a book is the product of a different self from the self we manifest in our habits, in our social life, in our vices. If we would try to understand that particular self, it is by searching our own bosoms, and trying to reconstruct it there, that we may arrive at it."

4 Those words of Proust should be with us whenever we are reading the biography of a writer—or the biography of anyone who depends on what can be called inspiration. All the details of the life and the *quirks* ③ and the friendships can be laid out for us, but the mystery of the writing will remain. No amount of documentation, however fascinating, can take us there. The biography of a writer—or even the autobiography—will always have this incompleteness.

5 Proust is a master of happy amplification, and I would like to go back to *Against Sainte-Beuve* just for a little. "In fact," Proust writes, "it is the secretions of one's innermost self, written in solitude and for oneself alone that one gives to the public. What one bestows on private life—in conversation... or in those drawing-room essays that are scarcely more than conversation in print—is the product of a quite superficial self, not of the innermost self which one can only recover by putting aside the world and the self that frequents the world."

6 When he wrote that, Proust had not yet

"圣伯夫的这个方法忽略了哪怕一点点的自我认知就可以告诉我们的道理：书中所表现的自我与我们在日常习惯、社会生活和恶习中表现的自我并非同一个。我们需要剖析内心，试图在内部重构自我才可能窥见内部真正的自我。"

4 无论何时读一本作家或者任何依靠灵感写作的人物传记时，我们都应该想想普鲁斯特的这些话。生活中所有的细节、弯路和友情都可以很明白地展现在我们面前，只有写作的奥秘仍然无解。没有任何文件，不管有多吸引人，能带我们解开写作之谜。作家的传记，甚至自传，永远都是不完整的。

5 普鲁斯特是一个放大快乐的大师，我想回过头来再看看《反对圣伯夫》这本书。"事实上，"普鲁斯特写道，"人内心最深处的自我在孤独的状态下为自己写出的东西其实是作家给大众看的东西。一个人展现出的私人生活——谈话或者一些和印刷的谈话无异的客厅文章——只是一个非常表面的自己，而不是那个将世界和经常混迹于世界的自我置之度外的最内部的自我。"

6 普鲁斯特写这些的时候还没

---

③ quirk [kwɜːk] *n.* 急转　如：a quirk of fate 命运难料

found the subject that was to lead him to the happiness of his great literary labour. And you can tell from what I have quoted that he was a man trusting to his intuition and waiting for luck. I have quoted these words before in other places. The reason is that they defined how I have gone about my business. I have trusted to intuition. I did it at the beginning. I do it even now. I have no idea how things might turn out, where in my writing I might go next. I have trusted to my intuition to find the subjects, and I have written intuitively. I have an idea when I start, I have a shape; but I will fully understand what I have written only after some years.

7 I said earlier that <u>everything of value about me is in my books. I will go further now. I will say I am the sum of my books.</u> Each book, intuitively sensed and, in the case of fiction, intuitively worked out, stands on what has gone before, and grows out of it. I feel that at any stage of my literary career it could have been said that the last book contained all the others.

8 It's been like this because of my background. My background is at once *exceedingly* ④ simple and exceedingly confused. I was born in Trinidad. It is a small island in the mouth of the great Orinoco river of Venezuela. So Trinidad is not strictly of South America, and not strictly of the Caribbean. It was developed as a New World plantation colony, and when I was born in 1932 it had a population of about 400,000.

发现那个能带给他文学创作的快乐的东西。从我引用的话里你也可以发现，他相信直觉，等待着时来运转。在其他地方我也引用过这段话，因为它们定义了我的工作。我一开始也曾相信直觉，甚至现在还相信。我写作时往往不知道事情会怎样发展，以及什么时候该进行下一步。我就依靠直觉来做这些决定，靠直觉写作。我开始写作的时候会有自己的想法，有基本的形态概念；但是常常要到若干年后我才能完全理解自己写的东西。

7 之前我说过，我自己有价值的东西都在我的书里。现在我想进一步说，我就是我那些书的总和。每一本靠直觉写就的书，以及凭直觉创作的小说都建立在过去之上，从过去发展而来。我觉得在我事业的任何阶段都可以说，最后一本书囊括了之前所有的书。

8 之所以会这样，与我的背景有很大关系。我的背景极其简单，却又非常令人迷惑不解。我出生在特立尼达拉岛。这是一个位于委内瑞拉奥里诺科河河口处的小岛。所以，特立尼达拉严格上说既不属于南美洲，也不属于加勒比地区。这个地方作为新世界的殖民地，开辟了许多种植园，1932 年我出生时人口有 40 万，其中

---

④ exceedingly [ɪkˈsiːdɪŋli] *adv.* 非常，极度地   如：The girl is exceedingly beautiful. 这女孩貌美无比。

Of this, about 150,000 were Indians, Hindus and Muslims, nearly all of peasant origin, and nearly all from the Gangetic plain.

9　This was my very small community. The bulk of this migration from India occurred after 1880. The deal was like this. People *indentured* ⑤ themselves for five years to serve on the estates. At the end of this time they were given a small piece of land, perhaps five acres, or a passage back to India. In 1917, because of *agitation* ⑥ by Gandhi and others, the indenture system was abolished. And perhaps because of this, or for some other reason, the pledge of land or *repatriation* ⑦ was dishonoured for many of the later arrivals. These people were absolutely *destitute* ⑧. They slept in the streets of Port of Spain, the capital. When I was a child I saw them. I suppose I didn't know they were destitute—I suppose that idea came much later—and they made no impression on me. This was part of the cruelty of the plantation colony.

10　I was born in a small country town called Chaguanas, two or three miles inland from the Gulf of Paria. Chaguanas was a strange name, in spelling and pronunciation, and many of the Indian people—they were in the majority in the area—preferred to call it by the Indian caste name of Chauhan.

有 15 万是印第安人、印度教徒和穆斯林，几乎所有人都是农民出身，都来自恒河平原。

9　这就是我所在的小社区。大多数印度移民都在 1880 年以后来到这里。开始的交易是这样的。人们签署在这片土地上服务五年的契约，五年后能得到一小片土地，约有 5 英亩，或者可以拿到返回印度的路费。1917 年，由于甘地等人的煽动，契约制度取消了。可能因为这个或其他一些原因，有关土地和遣返回国的承诺在后来许多移民身上都没有履行。这些人真的是无比穷困。他们平时就睡在首都西班牙港的大街上。我小时候见过他们，但我想那时候我并不知道他们很穷——可能是后来才知道的——他们也没有留给我太深的印象。这是种植园殖民地的残酷表现之一。

10　我出生在一个叫查古纳斯的小镇上，距离帕里亚湾约两到三英里。查古纳斯这个名字无论在拼写还是发音上都有点奇怪，许多印度人——印度人占了这里居民的大多数——更喜欢根据印度的种姓制度叫它乔汉。

⑤ indenture [ɪnˈdentʃə] *vt.* 订契约

⑥ agitation [ˌædʒɪˈteɪʃən] *n.* 煽动　如：conduct propaganda and agitation 进行宣传鼓动

⑦ repatriation [ˌriːpætrɪˈeɪʃən] *n.* 遣送回国，归国

⑧ destitute [ˈdestɪtjuːt] *adj.* 穷困的，匮乏的　如：be destitute of morality 无道德的；be destitute of good feeling 无同情心

11 I was thirty-four when I found out about the name of my birthplace. I was living in London, had been living in England for sixteen years. I was writing my ninth book. This was a history of Trinidad, a human history, trying to re-create people and their stories. I used to go to the British Museum to read the Spanish documents about the region. These documents—recovered from the Spanish archives—were copied out for the British government in the 1890s at the time of a nasty boundary dispute with Venezuela. The documents begin in 1530 and end with the disappearance of the Spanish Empire.

12 I was reading about the foolish search for El Dorado, and the *murderous* [9] interloping of the English hero, Sir Walter Raleigh. In 1595 he raided Trinidad, killed all the Spaniards he could, and went up the Orinoco looking for El Dorado. He found nothing, but when he went back to England he said he had. He had a piece of gold and some sand to show. He said he had hacked the gold out of a cliff on the bank of the Orinoco. The Royal Mint said that the sand he asked them to assay was worthless, and other people said that he had bought the gold beforehand from North Africa. He then published a book to prove his point, and for four centuries people have believed that Raleigh had found something. The magic of Raleigh's book, which is really quite difficult to read, lay in its very long title: The Discovery of the Large, Rich, and Beautiful Empire of Guiana, with a relation of the great and golden city of

11 我34岁时发现自己出生地名字的资料。当时我住在伦敦，而且在英国居住已经16年了。当时我正在写自己的第九本书。这是一段关于特立尼达拉岛的历史，一段试图重塑当地人和故事的人类历史。我那时常常去大英博物馆阅读这个地区的资料。这些资料——从西班牙文的档案恢复而来——是19世纪90年代在与委内瑞拉的一场领土争端中复制过来的。资料中的记载开始于1530年，止于西班牙王朝的覆灭。

12 我读到了寻找传说中的宝山的故事。1595年，英国的大英雄瓦尔特·罗里爵士闯入此地，杀光了所有西班牙人，到奥里诺科河找寻宝山。他什么也没找到，但是回到英国后却说自己找到了，并拿出一些金子和沙土作证。他说他从奥里诺科河岸边的悬崖上砍下了这些金子。他拿着这些沙子让皇家造币厂化验，但造币厂说这些一点价值都没有，而其他人则说他是事先从北非买好了这些金子。之后他出了一本书来举证自己的观点，于是连续四个世纪，人们都相信罗里真的找到了一些东西。罗里这本一点也不好看的书自有它的魔力，那就是书的题目：广袤富饶美丽的圭亚那王国的发现之旅，有关那个巨大的金子之城马诺阿（西班牙人称之为"宝山"）以及伊美黎、阿若麦亚、

---

⑨ murderous ['mɜːdərəs] *adj.* 杀人致死的，残忍的　　如：a murderous plot 谋杀计划

Manoa (which the Spaniards call El Dorado) and the provinces of Emeria, Aromaia, Amapaia, and other countries, with their rivers adjoining. How real it sounds! And he had hardly been on the main Orinoco.

13 And then, as sometimes happens with confidence men, Raleigh was caught by his own fantasies. Twenty-one years later, old and ill, he was let out of his London prison to go to Guiana and find the gold mines he said he had found. In this *fraudulent*[10] venture his son died. The father, for the sake of his reputation, for the sake of his lies, had sent his son to his death. And then Raleigh, full of grief, with nothing left to live for, went back to London to be executed.

14 The story should have ended there. But Spanish memories were long—no doubt because their imperial correspondence was so slow: it might take up to two years for a letter from Trinidad to be read in Spain. Eight years afterwards the Spaniards of Trinidad and Guiana were still settling their scores with the Gulf Indians. One day in the British Museum I read a letter from the King of Spain to the governor of Trinidad. It was dated 12 October 1625.

15 "I asked you," the King wrote, "to give me some information about a certain nation of Indians called Chaguanes, who you say number above one thousand, and are of such bad disposition that it was they who led the English when they captured the town. Their crime hasn't been punished because forces were not

阿玛帕亚，还有其他一些国家，这些地区以河相连。听起来多么真实啊！但实际上他几乎连奥里诺科河的主干都没去过。

13 后来，就像大多数骗子的遭遇一样，罗里被自己编织的谎言坑害了。21 年后，又老又病的他被驱逐出伦敦监狱，发配到圭亚那地区，去找寻他自己当年发现的金矿。在这场谎言造就的探险中，他的儿子丧了命。这位父亲为了自己的名誉和谎言，断送了自己儿子的性命。悲痛难忍的罗里已经没有了活下去的动力，他只好返回伦敦接受处决。

14 故事到此本该结束了。但是西班牙人的记忆总是很长，也难怪，因为西班牙帝国的通信那么慢：从特立尼达拉岛发出的信要两年后才能到西班牙。八年后，特立尼达拉岛和圭亚那的西班牙人还在和海湾地区的印度人算账。有一天，我在大英博物馆读到了一封西班牙国王给特立尼达拉岛都督的信。日期写的是 1625 年 10 月 12 日。

15 国王写道："关于印度人的一个叫查古纳斯的地区，你要给我汇报一些信息，之前你说这个地区有超过一千人，他们不安分守己，在英国进攻该镇的时候帮英国人带路。他们的行为没有得到惩罚，因为兵力不够，而且印度人觉得没有人能左右他

---

⑩ fraudulent [ˈfrɔːdjulənt] *adj.* 欺骗性的　　如：fraudulent business practices 欺骗的交易行为

available for this purpose and because the Indians acknowledge no master save their own will. You have decided to give them a punishment. Follow the rules I have given you; and let me know how you get on."

16 What the governor did I don't know. I could find no further reference to the Chaguanes in the documents in the Museum. Perhaps there were other documents about the Chaguanes in the mountain of paper in the Spanish archives in Seville which the British government scholars missed or didn't think important enough to copy out. What is true is that the little tribe of over a thousand—who would have been living on both sides of the Gulf of Paria—disappeared so completely that no one in the town of Chaguanas or Chauhan knew anything about them. And the thought came to me in the Museum that I was the first person since 1625 to whom that letter of the king of Spain had a real meaning. And that letter had been dug out of the archives only in 1896 or 1897. A disappearance, and then the silence of centuries.

17 We lived on the Chaguanes' land. Every day in term time—I was just beginning to go to school—I walked from my grandmother's house—past the two or three main-road stores, the Chinese parlour, the Jubilee Theatre, and the high-smelling little Portuguese factory that made cheap blue soap and cheap yellow soap in long bars that were put out to dry and harden in the mornings—every day I walked past these eternal-seeming things—to the Chaguanas Government

16 我不知道都督是如何做的。博物馆找不到更多查古纳斯的资料了。可能在西班牙塞维利亚的堆积成山的档案里还有关于查古纳斯的文件，但英国学者没注意到，或者认为那些并不值得复制。事实是一千年前居住在帕里亚湾两岸的这个小部落消失得无影无踪，查古纳斯镇上没有一个人知道它的信息。在大英博物馆的时候我在想，自1625年以来我是第一个了解到国王那封信的意义的人。那封信大概是在1896或1897年从档案里挖出来的。后来就不见了，接着便是几个世纪的悄无声息。

17 我们住在查古纳斯岛上。那时我刚开始上学，每天都从祖母的房子出发，经过两三个街边商店，有中国饭店，犹太人开的剧院，散发着浓味的葡萄牙工厂，它生产黄色或蓝色的便宜长条肥皂，每天早上这些肥皂都要铺在外面风干硬化。我每天就这样途经这些似乎亘古不变的东西，去查古纳斯的公办学校里上课。学校外面是甘蔗地和房产地，一直通到帕里

School. Beyond the school was sugar-cane, estate land, going up to the Gulf of Paria. The people who had been dispossessed would have had their own kind of agriculture, their own calendar, their own codes, their own sacred sites. They would have understood the Orinoco-fed currents in the Gulf of Paria. Now all their skills and everything else about them had been *obliterated* [11].

18　The world is always in movement. People have everywhere at some time been dispossessed. I suppose I was shocked by this discovery in 1967 about my birthplace because I had never had any idea about it. But that was the way most of us lived in the agricultural colony, blindly. There was no plot by the authorities to keep us in our darkness. I think it was more simply that the knowledge wasn't there. The kind of knowledge about the Chaguanes would not have been considered important, and it would not have been easy to recover. They were a small tribe, and they were *aboriginal* [12]. Such people—on the mainland, in what was called B.G., British Guiana—were known to us, and were a kind of joke. People who were loud and ill-behaved were known, to all groups in Trinidad, I think, as warrahoons. I used to think it was a made-up word, made up to suggest wildness. It was only when I began to travel in Venezuela, in my forties, that I understood that a word like that was the name of a rather large aboriginal tribe there.

亚湾。过去的穷人们会有他们自己的农业，自己的历法和规则，以及圣地。他们可能懂得奥里诺科河的水流在帕里亚湾形成的洋流。但现在那些技术，以及所有与他们有关的东西都消失了。

18　世界总是在变化。世界各地的人都曾成为无产者。当1967年知道这个关于自己家乡的消息时我是很震惊的，因为我之前一点都不知道。但这就是我们大多数生活在农业殖民地人的命运，总是很盲目。官方也并没有计划使我们一直处于黑暗中。我想可能只是他们并不知道这些消息吧。有关查古纳斯的消息对他们来说并不重要，而且复兴这样一个地方也并不容易。毕竟这是一个小地方，居民又都是土著居民。我们都知道居住在大陆上的是英籍圭亚那人，而且说起来简直有点好笑。他们动静很大，举止不雅，这些特立尼达拉岛的人都把他们叫做warrahoons。以前我以为这是一个合成词，表示"野蛮"的意思。直到后来，我40多岁开始游历委内瑞拉时才知道那个词是当地一个很大的土著部落的名字。

---

⑪ obliterate [əˈblɪtəreɪt] *vt.* 抹去，消失　如：Everything that happened that night was obliterated from his memory. 那天晚上发生的一切都从他的记忆中消失了。

⑫ aboriginal [ˌæbəˈrɪdʒənəl] *adj.* 土著的　如：the aboriginal people of Canada 加拿大土著居民

19 There was a vague story when I was a child—and to me now it is an unbearably affecting story—that at certain times aboriginal people came across in canoes from the mainland, walked through the forest in the south of the island, and at a certain spot picked some kind of fruit or made some kind of offering, and then went back across the Gulf of Paria to the sodden estuary of the Orinoco. The rite must have been of enormous importance to have survived the upheavals of four hundred years, and the extinction of the aborigines in Trinidad. Or perhaps—though Trinidad and Venezuela have a common flora—they had come only to pick a particular kind of fruit. I don't know. I can't remember anyone inquiring. And now the memory is all lost; and that sacred site, if it existed, has become common ground.

20 What was past was past. I suppose that was the general attitude. And we Indians, immigrants from India, had that attitude to the island. We lived for the most part ritualised lives, and were not yet capable of self-assessment, which is where learning begins. Half of us on this land of the Chaguanes were pretending—perhaps not pretending, perhaps only feeling, never formulating it as an idea—that we had brought a kind of India with us, which we could, as it were, unroll like a carpet on the flat land.

21 My grandmother's house in Chaguanas was in two parts. The front part, of bricks and plaster, was painted white. It was like a kind of Indian house, with a grand balustraded terrace on the upper floor, and a prayer-room on the floor

19 我小时候还有一个模糊的故事，对现在的我来说是相当感人的。有段时间土著居民会从大陆乘船过来，穿过岛南的密林，在某个特定的地方摘一些水果或其他东西，然后再穿过帕里亚湾回到奥里诺科河河口。这个习俗肯定意义十分重大才能经受住那四百年的沧桑巨变和特立尼达拉岛上原住民的灭绝。或者可能虽然特立尼达拉和委内瑞拉有着共同的植物区系，但他们过来只是捡拾一种特殊的水果呢。我不知道。我不记得有谁问过这类问题。现在记忆都遗失了，那个神圣之地即使存在，也要变成普普通通的一块地了。

20 过去的都过去了。我想这才是通常的态度。我们这些印第安人，从印度来的移民，对这个岛屿也是这种态度。我们过了那么多年仪式化了的生活，到头来却不能自我定位，这才是教训的开始。岛上一半的人假装——也可能不是假装，只是感觉——从来没有这样的想法：我们带着一种印度身份，我们本可以在那片岛上像铺地毯一样将其展现出来的。

21 岛上我祖母的房子分为两部分。前面一部分是粉刷成白色的水泥砖墙。这是一种印度房子，上层有一个很大的带栏杆的阳台，再上面是一个祷告室。房子装饰很奢华，柱子上

above that. It was ambitious in its decorative detail, with lotus capitals on pillars, and sculptures of Hindu deities, all done by people working only from a memory of things in India. In Trinidad it was an architectural oddity. At the back of this house, and joined to it by an upper bridge room, was a timber building in the French Caribbean style. The entrance gate was at the side, between the two houses. It was a tall gate of corrugated iron on a wooden frame. It made for a fierce kind of privacy.

22 So as a child I had this sense of two worlds, the world outside that tall corrugated-iron gate, and the world at home—or, at any rate, the world of my grandmother's house. It was a *remnant* [13] of our caste sense, the thing that excluded and shut out. In Trinidad, where as new arrivals we were a disadvantaged community, that excluding idea was a kind of protection; it enabled us—for the time being, and only for the time being—to live in our own way and according to our own rules, to live in our own fading India. It made for an extraordinary self-centredness. We looked inwards; we lived out our days; the world outside existed in a kind of darkness; we inquired about nothing.

23 There was a Muslim shop next door. The little loggia of my grandmother's shop ended against his blank wall. The man's name was Mian. That was all that we knew of him and his family. I suppose we must have seen him, but I have no mental picture of him now. We knew nothing of

砌有莲花和印度教神明的图案，这些都是靠着在印度的记忆完成的。在特立尼达拉岛，这是一栋很怪异的房子。房子有一座法国加勒比风格的建筑通过桥房与之相连。大门在侧面，位于两座房子中间，是木框的铁门。这门象征着强烈的隐私感。

22 所以我还是孩子的时候身处两个世界，一个是高高的大铁门之外的世界，另一个是家里的世界，或者说是我祖母房子里的世界。在印度的种姓制度下，门外的世界是多余的。但在特立尼达拉岛，作为新来者我们这个团体处于不利地位，那种排斥态度对我们来说是一种保护。至少在当时，仅限于当时，这种保护使我们按照自己的方式生活，生活在我们即将消失的印度世界里。这使我们非常以自我为中心，我们总是向内看，过着自己的日子，外面的世界是一片黑暗，我们从不过问。

23 隔壁是一家穆斯林商店。我祖母店铺的小凉廊与他家的墙相对。那个男子叫米兰。这是我们知道的所有关于他和他家庭的信息。我想我们一定见过他，但现在我却想不起来他长什么样子了。我们对穆斯林一无所

---

⑬ remnant ['remnənt] *n.* 剩余　如：the remnants of a feast 筵席的残汤剩菜

Muslims. This idea of strangeness, of the thing to be kept outside, extended even to other Hindus. For example, we ate rice in the middle of the day, and wheat in the evenings. There were some extraordinary people who reversed this natural order and ate rice in the evenings. I thought of these people as strangers—you must imagine me at this time as under seven, because when I was seven all this life of my grandmother's house in Chaguanas came to an end for me. We moved to the capital, and then to the hills to the northwest.

24 But the habits of mind engendered by this shut-in and shutting-out life lingered for quite a while. If it were not for the short stories my father wrote I would have known almost nothing about the general life of our Indian community. Those stories gave me more than knowledge. They gave me a kind of solidity. They gave me something to stand on in the world. I cannot imagine what my mental picture would have been without those stories.

25 The world outside existed in a kind of darkness; and we inquired about nothing. I was just old enough to have some idea of the Indian epics, the Ramayana in particular. The children who came five years or so after me in our extended family didn't have this luck. No one taught us Hindi. Sometimes someone wrote out the alphabet for us to learn, and that was that; we were expected to do the rest ourselves. So, as English penetrated, we began to lose our language. My grandmother's house was full of religion; there were many ceremonies and

知。对其他印度教徒我们也有这种将其屏蔽的陌生感。例如，我们中午吃米饭，晚上吃小麦制品。但是有些特别的人反过来做，他们在晚上吃米饭。我就觉得这些人很奇怪。你想象我的这段生活时一定要把我当作七岁以下的小孩，因为七岁时我在查古纳斯岛上祖母家里的生活就结束了。我们搬到了首都，然后又到了西北部的山区。

24 但是这种两个世界的生活中形成的心理习惯在之后仍旧持续了很久。如果没有我父亲写的那些短篇小说，我不会了解印度的日常生活。这些故事不只扩充了我的知识，更给了我一种坚定的信念，使我能够立足于这个世界。我不敢想象，没有这些故事我的心态会变成什么样子。

25 外面的世界对我们来说是一片黑暗，我们对其一无所知。我的年纪刚好能理解一些印度史诗，尤其是罗摩传。后来家里比我小四五岁的人就没有这么好的运气了，因为没有人教我们北印度语。有时有人写出字母表教我们，但仅限于此，接下来的都要靠我们自己。所以，后来随着英语的入侵，我们开始失去我们自己的语言。我祖母家里有着浓郁的宗教氛围，经常有各种仪式和诵读，有时甚至可以持续好几天。但是没有人给我

readings, some of which went on for days. But no one explained or translated for us who could no longer follow the language. So our ancestral faith receded, became mysterious, not pertinent to our day-to-day life.

26 We made no inquiries about India or about the families people had left behind. When our ways of thinking had changed, and we wished to know, it was too late. I know nothing of the people on my father's side; I know only that some of them came from Nepal. Two years ago a kind Nepalese who liked my name sent me a copy of some pages from an 1872 gazetteer-like British work about India, Hindu Castes and Tribes as Represented in Benares; the pages listed—among a multitude of names—those groups of Nepalese in the holy city of Banaras who carried the name Naipal. That is all that I have.

27 Away from this world of my grandmother's house, where we ate rice in the middle of the day and wheat in the evenings, there was the great unknown—in this island of only 400,000 people. There were the African or African-derived people who were the majority. They were policemen; they were teachers. One of them was my very first teacher at the Chaguanas Government School; I remembered her with adoration for years. There was the capital, where very soon we would all have to go for education and jobs, and where we would settle permanently, among strangers. There were the white people, not all of them English; and the Portuguese and the Chinese, at one time also immigrants like us. And, more mysterious

们这些跟不上语言的人解释或翻译。于是我们的祖先信仰就逐渐衰退了，这些变得神秘起来，不再与我们的日常生活相干。

26 我们没有问过印度，没有问过那些被我们留下的家人。当我们的思维方式改变了的时候，我们才希望了解那些，但为时已晚了。我父亲这边的人我一点也不了解，只知道他们有些来自尼泊尔。两年前一个好心的喜欢我名字的尼泊尔人送给我一份复制来的1872年英国制作的类似于印度地名辞典一样的东西，记录了尼泊尔圣城贝拿勒斯地区有代表性的种姓和部落。这就是我拥有的全部关于祖先的东西。

27 在那个只有40万人的小岛上，我祖母房子里的世界之外，那些中午吃米饭晚上吃小麦的日子之外，是一个巨大的未知世界。那里大部分是非洲人以及非裔外籍人。他们有的是警察，有的是教师。其中一个是我在查古纳斯公立学校的启蒙老师，因为喜欢她，我好多年都没忘记她。除此之外还有首都，我们不久将在那里受教育、找工作，甚至永久定居在陌生的人群里。那里有白种人，但不全是英国人，还有葡萄牙人、中国人，有时也会有像我们一样的移民。比这些更显神秘的是我们称为"西班牙人"的一群人，他们是有着棕黄色皮

than these, were the people we called Spanish, mixed people of warm brown complexions who came from the Spanish time, before the island was detached from Venezuela and the Spanish Empire—a kind of history absolutely beyond my child's comprehension.

28　To give you this idea of my background, I have had to call on knowledge and ideas that came to me much later, principally from my writing. As a child I knew almost nothing, nothing beyond what I had picked up in my grandmother's house. All children, I suppose, come into the world like that, not knowing who they are. But for the French child, say, that knowledge is waiting. That knowledge will be all around them. It will come indirectly from the conversation of their elders. It will be in the newspapers and on the radio. And at school the work of generations of scholars, scaled down for school texts, will provide some idea of France and the French.

29　In Trinidad, bright boy though I was, I was surrounded by areas of darkness. School elucidated nothing for me. I was crammed with facts and formulas. Everything had to be learned by heart; everything was abstract for me. Again, I do not believe there was a plan or plot to make our courses like that. What we were getting was standard school learning. In another setting it would have made sense. And at least some of the failing would have lain in me. With my limited social background it was hard for me imaginatively to enter into other societies or societies that were far away. I loved the idea

肤的混血人，来自西班牙时代，当时这个岛屿还没有从委内瑞拉和西班牙王朝的统治下分离出来——这段历史已经远远超出了我的孩子的理解范围。

28　给你们讲的这些有关我背景的故事，我借助的是自己后来的知识库，尤其是我的写作。儿童时代的我什么都不了解，所知仅限于我祖母的家里。我想，所有的孩子来到这个世界上时都同我差不多，不知道他们自己的来历。但是对法国的孩子们来说，那些信息都在等着他们，就等在他们周围。同大人谈话时这些信息会间接地传达出来；从报纸上、广播里也都能获取。在学校，一代又一代编写教材的学者们都会加入关于法国和法国人的知识。

29　在特立尼达拉岛上，虽然我也是个阳光的男孩，但还是被一片黑暗包围着。学校没有对我们做任何解释。我整日填鸭式地接受大量事实和公式。所有东西都要靠心记，每样东西对我来说都很抽象。我也不相信我的课程是故意设计成那样的。我们接受的也是正规的学校教育。也许换个环境，这种课程就可行。至少不会有那么多失败。我社会背景有限，不可能想象着自己进入其他社会或者远离这个社会。我喜欢书中的思想，但却不喜欢那些书。我学得最好的是那些

of books, but I found it hard to read them. I got on best with things like Andersen and Aesop, timeless, placeless, not excluding. And when at last in the sixth form, the highest form in the college, I got to like some of our literature texts—Moliere, Cyrano de Bergerac—I suppose it was because they had the quality of the fairytale.

30 When I became a writer those areas of darkness around me as a child became my subjects. The land; the aborigines; the New World; the colony; the history; India; the Muslim world, to which I also felt myself related; Africa; and then England, where I was doing my writing. That was what I meant when I said that my books stand one on the other, and that I am the sum of my books. That was what I meant when I said that my background, the source and prompting of my work, was at once exceedingly simple and exceedingly complicated. You will have seen how simple it was in the country town of Chaguanas. And I think you will understand how complicated it was for me as a writer. Especially in the beginning, when the literary models I had—the models given me by what I can only call my false learning—dealt with entirely different societies. But perhaps you might feel that the material was so rich it would have been no trouble at all to get started and to go on. What I have said about the background, however, comes from the knowledge I acquired with my writing. And you must believe me when I tell you that the pattern in my work has only become clear in the last two months or so. Passages from old books were read to me,

没有时间和地点限制，不具排斥性的东西，如关于安徒生、伊索的。到了六年级，大学里最高的年级，我才开始喜欢上文学课——莫里哀、大鼻子情圣——可能是因为他们有童话故事的特点吧。

30 我成了作家以后，以前儿童时代周围的黑暗都变成了我作品的主题。陆地；原住民；新世界；殖民地；历史；印度；穆斯林世界，我觉得我与它也有关系；非洲，然后是英国，也就是我写作的地方。因此我才会说我的书都是互相依赖的，我自己就是这些书的总和。这也是我为什么会说我的背景就是我写作的灵感源泉，它既简单又极其复杂。你也看到了，在查古纳斯镇上的生活是多么简单，而想必你也能理解对于身为作家的我来说，这又是多么复杂。尤其是刚开始时，我的文学榜样——那些我在错误的学习中遇见的榜样——讨论的都是不同社会的问题。也许你会认为，这样的信息很丰富，要想开始并坚持下去并没有多大问题。然而，我所说的背景来自于我自己写作时出现的知识。你们一定要相信，我的写作模式直到近两个月才清晰起来。通过阅读古老的书籍，我找到了联系。直到两个月前，我面临的最大问题还是如何对人描述我的作品，如何向人解释我做了什么。

and I saw the connections. Until then the greatest trouble for me was to describe my writing to people, to say what I had done.

31 I said I was an intuitive writer. That was so, and that remains so now, when I am nearly at the end. I never had a plan. I followed no system. I worked intuitively. <u>My aim every time was do a book, to create something that would be easy and interesting to read. At every stage I could only work within my knowledge and sensibility and talent and world-view.</u> Those things developed book by book. And I had to do the books I did because there were no books about those subjects to give me what I wanted. I had to clear up my world, elucidate it, for myself.

32 I had to go to the documents in the British Museum and elsewhere, to get the true feel of the history of the colony. I had to travel to India because there was no one to tell me what the India my grandparents had come from was like. There was the writing of Nehru and Gandhi; and strangely it was Gandhi, with his South African experience, who gave me more, but not enough. There was Kipling; there were British-Indian writers like John Masters (going very strong in the 1950s, with an announced plan, later abandoned, I fear, for thirty-five connected novels about British India); there were romances by women writers. The few Indian writers who had come up at that time were middle-class people, town-dwellers; they didn't know the India we had come from.

33 And when that Indian need was satisfied, others became apparent: Africa, South America,

31 我说过我是一个靠直觉写作的作家。以前是这样，现在我都行将就木了，但还是这样。我从来没有计划，也不遵循什么规则制度。我总是靠直觉。我每次的目标都是写一本书，写一本简单易读又有趣的书。不管在哪个阶段，我都只能根据自己的知识、感受、天赋和世界观来写作。这些东西构成了我的书。我之所以写这些书，是因为已有的有关这些主题的书都不是我想要的。我得理清自己的世界，为自己解释自己。

32 我不得不去大英博物馆或其他地方来真实地感受殖民历史。我不得不到印度游历，因为没有人能告诉我祖父母的故乡是什么样子。尼赫鲁和甘地也写书，奇怪的是，有南非经历的甘地给了我更多启示，但还是不够。还有吉卜林，以及一些英籍印度作家像约翰·马斯特斯（20世纪50年代名噪一时，曾宣布过要写35本与英国统治下的印度有关的书，但恐怕后来放弃了），此外还有一些女性作家写的浪漫故事。那个时代兴起的印度作家几乎没有中产阶级或城镇居民，他们不了解我们离开时的印度。

33 有关印度的需要满足之后，其他需要也就变得很明显了：非洲、

the Muslim world. The aim has always been to fill out my world picture, and the purpose comes from my childhood: to make me more at ease with myself. Kind people have sometimes written asking me to go and write about Germany, say, or China. But there is much good writing already about those places; I am willing to depend there on the writing that exists. And those subjects are for other people. Those were not the areas of darkness I felt about me as a child. So, just as there is a development in my work, a development in narrative skill and knowledge and sensibility, so there is a kind of unity, a focus, though I might appear to be going in many directions.

34 When I began I had no idea of the way ahead. I wished only to do a book. I was trying to write in England, where I stayed on after my years at the university, and it seemed to me that my experience was very thin, was not truly of the stuff of books. I could find in no book anything that came near my background. The young French or English person who wished to write would have found any number of models to set him on his way. I had none. My father's stories about our Indian community belonged to the past. My world was quite different. It was more urban, more mixed. The simple physical details of the chaotic life of our extended family—sleeping rooms or sleeping spaces, eating times, the sheer number of people—seemed impossible to handle. There was too much to be explained, both about my home life and about the world outside. And at the same time there was also too much about us—like our

南美、穆斯林世界。我的目的总是要完善我对世界的印象，而且这目的来自于我的童年：为了使我自己更随意。有些好心人给我写信建议我去写德国或者中国。但是这些地方已经有很好的作品了，我想我愿意依靠那些已经存在的作品来了解它们。而且那些主题是留给别人的。那些也不是我儿时深觉黑暗的地方。所以，我的书有所发展，在叙事技巧、知识和感受描写上有所发展，虽然表面上看我还是有很多方向，但实际上是有一个统一和焦点的。

34 刚开始我不知道前路在哪里。我只是想写一本书。我试图在英国写书，自从大学毕业后我就住在那里，但是我的经历似乎太浅薄，不能满足写书的需要。我从任何书里都找不到与我的背景接近的东西。对于想写作的年轻法国人或英国人来说，他们想找多少榜样就可以找到多少。而我却找不到。我父亲写的短篇是关于过去的印度社会的。我的世界却大不相同，更城市化，也更复杂。仅仅是我们庞大家庭中简单的日常生活细节——卧室或睡觉的地方、吃饭时间、人口数量等——似乎都很难掌握。关于我家乡的生活和外面的世界有太多需要解释的东西了。同时，有关我的祖先和历史我也知道得太少。

own ancestry and history—that I didn't know.

35 At last one day there came to me the idea of starting with the Port of Spain street to which we had moved from Chaguanas. There was no big corrugated-iron gate shutting out the world there. The life of the street was open to me. It was an intense pleasure for me to observe it from the verandah. This street life was what I began to write about. I wished to write fast, to avoid too much self-questioning, and so I simplified. I suppressed the child-narrator's background. I ignored the racial and social complexities of the street. I explained nothing. I stayed at ground level, so to speak. I presented people only as they appeared on the street. I wrote a story a day. The first stories were very short. I was worried about the material lasting long enough. But then the writing did its magic. The material began to present itself to me from many sources. The stories became longer; they couldn't be written in a day. And then the inspiration, which at one stage had seemed very easy, rolling me along, came to an end. But a book had been written, and I had in my own mind become a writer.

36 The distance between the writer and his material grew with the two later books; the vision was wider. And then intuition led me to a large book about our family life. During this book my writing ambition grew. But when it was over I felt I had done all that I could do with my island material. No matter how much I meditated on it, no further fiction would come.

37 Accident, then, rescued me. I became a

35 最后终于有一天，我想到了西班牙港——那个我们为之搬离查古纳斯岛的地方——我要从那里的街道开始我的写作。那里没有将世界拒之门外的高大铁门。街上的生活完全展现在我面前。从阳台上观察街上的生活是我的一大乐趣。我开始写的也是那里的街道生活。我希望能写快一点，避免过多的自我质疑，所以我写得很简化。我压制了少年主人公的背景，忽略了街上的种族和社会复杂性。我没有做任何解释。也就是说，我非常接地气。我书里展现的人们就是他们在街上的样子。我一天写一个故事。最开始的一些都很短，我担心材料不够用。但是后来写作就有了魔性，素材也源源不断地涌来。故事开始变长，一天写不完了。灵感对我来说唾手可得，一直在推着我走，但是后来竟突然停止了。好在写成了一本书，我自己心里认为我已经是一个作家了。

36 写后来的两本书时，作者和素材之间的距离随之拉近，视野也更宽广了。直觉告诉我我该写一本有关我家庭生活的大书。我的雄心也在写这本书时开始变大。写完这本书后，我觉得关于这个岛的素材我已经写完了。不管我在此沉思多久，都不可能再写出一部小说了。

37 后来，我碰到了意外，成了

traveller. I travelled in the Caribbean region and understood much more about the colonial set-up of which I had been part. I went to India, my ancestral land, for a year; it was a journey that broke my life in two. The books that I wrote about these two journeys took me to new realms of emotion, gave me a world-view I had never had, extended me technically. I was able in the fiction that then came to me to take in England as well as the Caribbean—and how hard that was to do. I was able also to take in all the racial groups of the island, which I had never before been able to do.

38 This new fiction was about colonial shame and fantasy, a book, in fact, about how the powerless lie about themselves, and lie to themselves, since it is their only resource. The book was called *The Mimic Men*. And it was not about mimics. It was about colonial men mimicking the condition of manhood, men who had grown to distrust everything about themselves. Some pages of this book were read to me the other day—I hadn't looked at it for more than thirty years—and it occurred to me that I had been writing about colonial *schizophrenia*⑭. But I hadn't thought of it like that. I had never used abstract words to describe any writing purpose of mine. If I had, I would never have been able to do the book. The book was done intuitively, and only out of close observation.

39 I have done this little survey of the early part of my career to try to show the stages by which, in just ten years, my birthplace had altered

一名旅者。我在加勒比地区游历，关于自己曾身在其中的殖民地，我了解了更多。我去了印度，我祖先的所在地，在那里待了一年；那次旅行将我的世界分成了两半。关于这两次旅行的书使我在感情上经历了新的改变，大大提升了自我，给了我一个全新的世界观。在后来的小说里，我开始能够领会我在英国和加勒比海的经历了——这对我来说是多么困难啊。同时我也能够了解岛上所有种族的人了，过去我从未做到过。

38 这本新小说讲的是殖民地人民的耻辱和幻想，事实上，讲了没有力量的他们如何向别人隐瞒自己，欺骗自己，因为这是他们唯一的资源。这本书叫做《模仿者》。但它与模仿无关，它讲的是殖民地人民模拟人类世界的生活环境，他们成长过程中从不相信任何有关自己的事。前几天有人给我读了这本书的一部分内容——我自己有30多年没看这本书了——我这才想起来我还写过有关殖民地人精神分裂的书，但是我写的时候并没有这样的想法。我从不用抽象的词汇去描述我的写作目的。如果真那样做了，那我肯定写不出来了。书是靠直觉写就的，它来源于近距离观察。

39 我对自己早期的事业做了一个小调查，在那十年间我有关出生地的写作改变、发展了不少：从对街头

⑭ schizophrenia [ˌskɪzəˈfriːnɪə] *n.* 精神分裂症

or developed in my writing: from the comedy of street life to a study of a kind of widespread schizophrenia. What was simple had become complicated.

40 Both fiction and the travel-book form have given me my way of looking; and you will understand why for me all literary forms are equally valuable. It came to me, for instance, when I set out to write my third book about India—twenty-six years after the first—that what was most important about a travel book were the people the writer travelled among. The people had to define themselves. A simple enough idea, but it required a new kind of book; it called for a new way of travelling. And it was the very method I used later when I went, for the second time, into the Muslim world.

41 I have always moved by intuition alone. I have no system, literary or political. I have no guiding political idea. I think that probably lies with my ancestry. The Indian writer R. K. Narayan, who died this year, had no political idea. My father, who wrote his stories in a very dark time, and for no reward, had no political idea. Perhaps it is because we have been far from authority for many centuries. It gives us a special point of view. I feel we are more inclined to see the humour and pity of things.

42 Nearly thirty years ago I went to Argentina. It was at the time of the guerrilla crisis. People were waiting for the old dictator Perón to come back from exile. The country was full of hate. Peronists were waiting to settle old scores. One

喜剧的描绘，发展到了对广泛存在的精神分裂症的探究。本来简单的事情变得复杂起来。

40 小说和旅行游记都影响了我看事物的方式，因此你应该能理解为什么不管什么文学形式对我来说都有同等的价值。例如，我开始写关于印度的第三本书时——距离第一本已经 26 年——我想到旅行游记类的书重要的其实是作者在旅程中经历过的那些人。人们需要定义自己。这是一个再简单不过的道理，但是却需要用一种新书去诠释，这又是旅行的一种新方式。这也是我第二次到访穆斯林世界时所用的方法。

41 我常常被直觉本身打动。我不遵循任何文学或政治的规则制度。我也没有政治上的指导思想。我想这可能源于我的祖先。今年逝世的印度作家 R·K·纳拉扬就没有政治倾向性。我的父亲在非常黑暗的岁月里写他的短篇故事，他也没有政治倾向性。可能是因为我们几百年来都离当局太远了吧。这给了我们一种独特的视角。我觉得我们更倾向于看到事物的诙谐和遗憾面。

42 大约 30 年前，我去了阿根廷。当时正是游击队危机盛行的时候。人们正在等待过去的独裁者裴隆流放归来。这个国家充满了仇恨。裴隆主义者等着要算旧账。有这样一个

such man said to me, "There is good torture and bad torture." Good torture was what you did to the enemies of the people. Bad torture was what the enemies of the people did to you. People on the other side were saying the same thing. There was no true debate about anything. There was only passion and the borrowed political jargon of Europe. I wrote, "Where jargon turns living issues into abstractions, and where jargon ends by competing with jargon, people don't have causes. They only have enemies."

43 And the passions of Argentina are still working themselves out, still defeating reason and consuming lives. No resolution is in sight.

44 I am near the end of my work now. I am glad to have done what I have done, glad creatively to have pushed myself as far as I could go. Because of the intuitive way in which I have written, and also because of the baffling nature of my material, every book has come as a blessing. Every book has amazed me; up to the moment of writing I never knew it was there. But the greatest miracle for me was getting started. I feel—and the anxiety is still vivid to me—that I might easily have failed before I began.

45 I will end as I began, with one of the marvellous little essays of Proust in *Against Sainte-Beuve*. "The beautiful things we shall write if we have talent," Proust says, "are inside us, indistinct, like the memory of a melody which delights us though we are unable to recapture its outline. Those who are obsessed by this blurred

人对我说："有好的苦难，也有坏的苦难。"好的苦难就是你对人民的敌人所做的事情，而坏的苦难则是人民的敌人对你所做的。另一派的人也是这么说。其实人们并没有争论任何实质性的问题，有的只是激情和从欧洲舶来的政治术语。我写道："在这里政治术语将生活变作抽象，政治术语之间互相竞争，打败彼此，人们没有事业，只有敌人。"

43 现在阿根廷还在用激情寻找出路，激情仍然在战胜理智，消耗生命。人们看不到解决办法。

44 我现在就快到我事业的终点了。我为自己做过的那些事而高兴，也很高兴在创作的路上将自己尽可能地推向远方。由于我依靠直觉的写作方式，也由于我那些令人费解的素材，我的每一本书都是一种恩赐。每一本书都使我自己惊奇，在开始写作之前我从来不知道它已经在那儿了。但是对我来说最大的奇迹就是开始写作。到现在我还时常感到焦虑——我感觉可能还没开始我就要轻易地失败了。

45 我还像开头那样，引用普鲁斯特在《反对圣伯夫》里的精彩言论来结尾："如果有天赋的话，我们要写的美好其实就在我们心中，模糊不清，就像关于一段旋律的记忆，虽然它曾让我们愉悦，但我们却想不起来它大概的轮廓。那些沉溺于这些模

memory of truths they have never known are the men who are gifted... Talent is like a sort of memory which will enable them finally to bring this indistinct music closer to them, to hear it clearly, to note it down..."

46 Talent, Proust says. I would say luck, and much labour. Thank you.

糊记忆而不自知的人才是有天赋的人……天资就像一种记忆，最终会将这段不分明的音乐拉近，使作家将其记录下来……"

46 普鲁斯特将写作归于天资，而我要说是运气，或者更多的是付出。谢谢

 演讲关键词 Practical Expressions

1. British Museum 大英博物馆
2. confidence men 骗子
3. plantation colony 种植殖民地
4. self-assessment 自我定位
5. unassailable 无懈可击
6. settle old scores 算旧账
7. Caribbean region 加勒比地区

精华佳句

1. Everything of value about me is in my books. I will go further now. I will say I am the sum of my books.
我自己有价值的东西都在我的书里。现在我想进一步说，我就是我那些书的总和。

2. My aim every time was do a book, to create something that would be easy and interesting to read. At every stage I could only work within my knowledge and sensibility and talent and world-view.
我每次的目标都是写一本书，写一本简单易读又有趣的书。不管在哪个阶段，我都只能根据自己的知识、感受、天赋和世界观来写作。

失约的诺贝尔奖

　　诺贝尔奖并非每届都如约而至，和奥运会一样，它也会受到外界很多不可抗因素的影响而取消颁发。从 1901 年算起，诺贝尔文学奖只颁发过 104 次。瑞典文学院和诺贝尔奖委员会为什么在这些年份没有宣读授奖词呢？除了外界不可抗因素之外，答案竟然出人意料——没有发"红包"就是没有符合评审机构口味的作品。根据诺贝尔奖基金会章程，若当年的参评作品中没有符合获奖标准的作品，那这一年的奖将自动保留至第二年，以激励后生晚辈为人类文学事业而奋斗。这样一来，肯定有人会问："如果到第二年仍然无法颁奖，那么奖金会继续积累保留到下一年吗？"那倒不是了。如果第二年仍然没有人得这笔奖金的话，这笔巨款将被归入基金会的专用基金。

Speech 6
Storytellers
讲故事的人

—Speech by Mo Yan for the Nobel Prize in Literature in 2012

——第一个获得诺贝尔文学奖的中国籍作家莫言 2012 年诺贝尔文学奖获奖演讲

名家速览 About the Author

诺贝尔奖大师	莫言
奖 项 归 属	诺贝尔文学奖
获 奖 理 由	用魔幻现实主义的写作手法，将民间故事、历史事件与当代背景融为一体。
主 要 作 品	《蛙》、《生死疲劳》、《丰乳肥臀》、《檀香刑》
所 获 奖 项	茅盾文学奖、红楼梦奖、诺贝尔文学奖

　　莫言，原名管谟业，1955 年 2 月 17 日出生于山东高密，是第一个获得诺贝尔文学奖的中国籍作家。莫言度过了物质贫乏的艰难童年，当时正值中国近代史上的"三年困难时期"。虽然物质上匮乏，但莫言并没有放弃精神营养。他小学时便经常偷看"闲书"，包括《封神演义》、《三国演义》、《水浒传》、《儒林外史》、《青春之歌》、《破晓记》、《三家巷》、《钢铁是怎样炼成的》等。除了看书，他也经常去听说书人讲故事，回来之后再把故事复述给家里人听。"文革"期间，他守着一本《新华字典》和《中国通史简编》度过了那段精神压抑的岁月。之后他入伍参军，在部队担任图书管理员，后来又考入解放军艺术学院文学系。自 20 世纪 80 年代以来，莫言以一系列乡土作品崛起，充满着"怀乡"以及"怨乡"的复杂情感，因此被归类为"寻根文学"作家。在这篇演讲中，莫言将自己称为"讲故事的人"，他讲述了自己在家乡的经历，以及那段经历对自己的创作之路的影响。他把这次演讲也当作讲故事，给大家呈现了一个个自己的和别人的真实故事，以及他自己创作的故事，这些故事使我们了解了一位作家创作的初衷和动力，以及他写作的方法和思路。

精美译文
Suggested Translation

1 Distinguished members of the Swedish Academy, Ladies and Gentlemen:

2 Through the mediums of television and the Internet, I imagine that everyone here has at least a nodding acquaintance with far-off Northeast Gaomi Township. You may have seen my ninety-year-old father, as well as my brothers, my sister, my wife and my daughter, even my granddaughter, now a year and four months old. But the person who is most on my mind at this moment, my mother, is someone you will never see. Many people have shared in the honor of winning this prize, everyone but her.

3 My mother was born in 1922 and died in 1994. We buried her in a peach orchard east of the village. Last year we were forced to move her grave farther away from the village in order to make room for a proposed rail line. When we dug up the grave, we saw that the coffin had rotted away and that her body had merged with the damp earth around it. So we dug up some of that soil, a symbolic act, and took it to the new gravesite. That was when I grasped the knowledge that my mother had become part of the earth, and that when I spoke to mother earth, I was really speaking to my mother.

4 I was my mother's youngest child. My earliest memory was of taking our only vacuum bottle to the public canteen for drinking water. Weakened by hunger, I dropped the bottle and

演讲现场
Speech Script

1 尊敬的瑞典学院各位院士，女士们、先生们：

2 通过电视或者网络，我想在座的各位，对遥远的高密东北乡，已经有了或多或少的了解。你们也许看到了我的九十岁的老父亲，看到了我的哥哥姐姐、我的妻子女儿和我的一岁零四个月的外孙女。但有一个我此刻最想念的人，我的母亲，你们永远无法看到了。我获奖后，很多人分享了我的光荣，但我的母亲却无法分享了。

3 我母亲生于 1922 年，卒于 1994 年。她的骨灰，埋葬在村庄东边的桃园里。去年，一条铁路要从那儿穿过，我们不得不将她的坟墓迁移到距离村子更远的地方。掘开坟墓后，我们看到，棺木已经腐朽，母亲的骨殖，已经与泥土混为一体。我们只好象征性地挖起一些泥土，移到新的墓穴里。也就是从那一时刻起，我感到，我的母亲是大地的一部分，我站在大地上的诉说，就是对母亲的诉说。

4 我是我母亲最小的孩子。我记忆中最早的一件事，是提着家里唯一的一把热水瓶去公共食堂打开水。因为饥饿无力，失手将热水瓶打碎，

broke it. Scared witless, I hid all that day in a haystack. Toward evening, I heard my mother calling my childhood name, so I crawled out of my hiding place, prepared to receive a beating or a scolding. But Mother didn't hit me, didn't even scold me. She just rubbed my head and **heaved** ① a sigh.

5 My most painful memory involved going out in the collective's field with Mother to **glean** ② ears of wheat. The gleaners scattered when they spotted the watchman. But Mother, who had bound feet, could not run; she was caught and slapped so hard by the watchman, a hulk of a man, that she fell to the ground. The watchman confiscated the wheat we'd gleaned and walked off whistling. As she sat on the ground, her lip bleeding, Mother wore a look of hopelessness I'll never forget.

6 Years later, when I encountered the watchman, now a gray-haired old man, in the marketplace, Mother had to stop me from going up to avenge her. "Son," she said evenly, "the man who hit me and this man are not the same person."

7 My clearest memory is of a Moon Festival day, at noontime, one of those rare occasions when we ate jiaozi at home, one bowl **apiece** ③. An aging beggar came to our door while we were at the table, and when I tried to send him away with half a bowlful of dried sweet potatoes, he

我吓得要命，钻进草垛，一天没敢出来。傍晚的时候，我听到母亲呼唤我的乳名。我从草垛里钻出来，以为会受到打骂，但母亲没有打我也没有骂我，只是抚摸着我的头，口中发出长长的叹息。

5 我记忆中最痛苦的一件事，就是跟随着母亲去集体的地里捡麦穗，看守麦田的人来了，捡麦穗的人纷纷逃跑，我母亲是小脚，跑不快，被捉住，那个身材高大的看守人搧了她一个耳光。她摇晃着身体跌倒在地。看守人没收了我们捡到的麦穗，吹着口哨扬长而去。我母亲嘴角流血，坐在地上，脸上那种绝望的神情让我终生难忘。

6 多年之后，当那个看守麦田的人成为一个白发苍苍的老人，在集市上与我相逢，我冲上去想找他报仇，母亲拉住了我，平静地对我说："儿子，那个打我的人，与这个老人，并不是一个人。"

7 我记得最深刻的一件事是一个中秋节的中午，我们家难得地包了一顿饺子，每人只有一碗。正当我们吃饺子时，一个乞讨的老人，来到了我们家门口。我端起半碗红薯干打发他，他却愤愤不平地说："我

---

① heave [hi:v] *vt.* 叹息，缓慢地发出声音　如：We all heaved a sigh of relief. 我们都如释重负地舒了一口气。

② glean [gli:n] *vt.* 拾落穗，收集

③ apiece [ə'pi:s] *adv.* 每人，每个

reacted angrily. "I'm an old man," he said, "You people are eating jiaozi, but want to feed me sweet potatoes. How heartless can you be?" I reacted just as angrily, "We're lucky if we eat jiaozi a couple of times a year, one small bowlful apiece, barely enough to get a taste! You should be thankful we're giving you sweet potatoes, and if you don't want them, you can get the hell out of here!" After *reprimanding* ④ me, Mother dumped her half bowlful of jiaozi into the old man's bowl.

8 My most *remorseful* ⑤ memory involves helping Mother sell cabbages at market, and me overcharging an old villager one jiao— intentionally or not, I can't recall—before heading off to school. When I came home that afternoon, I saw that Mother was crying, something she rarely did. Instead of scolding me, she merely said softly, "Son, you embarrassed your mother today."

9 Mother contracted a serious lung disease when I was still in my teens. Hunger, disease, and too much work made things extremely hard on our family. The road ahead looked especially bleak, and I had a bad feeling about the future, worried that Mother might take her own life. Every day, the first thing I did when I walked in the door after a day of hard labor was call out for Mother. Hearing her voice was like giving my heart a new lease on life. But not hearing her threw me

是一个老人，你们吃饺子，却让我吃红薯干，你们的心是怎么长的？"我气急败坏地说："我们一年也吃不了几次饺子，一人一小碗，连半饱都吃不了！给你红薯干就很好了，你要就要，不要就滚！"母亲训斥了我，然后端起她那半碗饺子，倒进老人碗里。

8 我最后悔的一件事，就是跟着母亲去卖白菜，有意无意地多算了一位买白菜的老人一毛钱。算完钱我就去了学校。当我放学回家时，看到很少流泪的母亲泪流满面。母亲并没有骂我，只是轻轻地说："儿子，你让娘丢了脸。"

9 我十几岁时，母亲患了严重的肺病，饥饿、病痛、劳累，使我们这个家庭陷入困境，看不到光明和希望。我产生了一种强烈的不祥之感，以为母亲随时都会自寻短见。每当我劳动归来，一进大门，就高喊母亲，听到她的回应，心中才感到一块石头落了地，如果一时听不到她的回应，我就心惊胆战，跑到厢房和磨坊里寻找。有一次，找遍了所有的房间也没

---

④ reprimand ['reprɪmɑːnd] *vt.* 谴责，斥责　如：He was reprimanded for playing truant. 他因逃学而受严斥。

⑤ remorseful [rɪ'mɔːsful] *adj.* 懊悔的，悔恨的　如：He felt remorseful for not believing her. 他后悔没有相信她。

into a panic. I'd go looking for her in the side building and in the mill. One day, after searching everywhere and not finding her, I sat down in the yard and cried like a baby. That is how she found me when she walked into the yard carrying a bundle of firewood on her back. She was very unhappy with me, but I could not tell her what I was afraid of. She knew anyway. "Son," she said, "don't worry, there may be no joy in my life, but I won't leave you till the God of the Underworld calls me."

10 I was born ugly. Villagers often laughed in my face, and school bullies sometimes beat me up because of it. I'd run home crying, where my mother would say, "You're not ugly, son. You've got a nose and two eyes, and there's nothing wrong with your arms and legs, so how could you be ugly? If you have a good heart and always do the right thing, what is considered ugly becomes beautiful." Later on, when I moved to the city, there were educated people who laughed at me behind my back, some even to my face; but when I recalled what Mother had said, I just calmly offered my apologies.

11 My illiterate mother held people who could read in high regard. We were so poor we often did not know where our next meal was coming from, yet she never denied my request to buy a book or something to write with. By nature hard-working, she had no use for lazy children, yet I could skip my chores as long as I had my nose in a book.

12 A storyteller once came to the marketplace,

有看到母亲的身影。我便坐在院子里大哭。这时，母亲背着一捆柴草从外边走进来。她对我的哭很不满，但我又不能对她说出我的担忧。母亲看透我的心思，她说："孩子，你放心，尽管我活着没有一点乐趣，但只要阎王爷不叫我，我是不会去的。"

10 我生来相貌丑陋，村子里很多人当面嘲笑我，学校里有几个性格霸蛮的同学甚至为此打我。我回家痛哭，母亲对我说："儿子，你不丑。你不缺鼻子不缺眼，四肢健全，丑在哪里？而且，只要你心存善良，多做好事，即便是丑，也能变美。"后来我进入城市，有一些很有文化的人依然在背后甚至当面嘲笑我的相貌，我想到了母亲的话，便心平气和地向他们道歉。

11 我母亲不识字，但对识字的人十分敬重。我们家生活困难，经常吃了上顿没下顿，但只要我对她提出买书买文具的要求，她总是会满足我。她是个勤劳的人，讨厌懒惰的孩子，但只要是我因为看书耽误了干活，她从来没批评过我。

12 有一段时间，集市上来了一

and I *sneaked* ⑥ off to listen to him. She was unhappy with me for forgetting my chores. But that night, while she was stitching padded clothes for us under the weak light of a *kerosene* ⑦ lamp, I couldn't keep from retelling stories I'd heard that day. She listened impatiently at first, since in her eyes professional storytellers were smooth-talking men in a dubious profession. Nothing good ever came out of their mouths. But slowly she was dragged into my retold stories, and from that day on, she never gave me chores on market day, unspoken permission to go to the marketplace and listen to new stories. As repayment for Mother's kindness and a way to demonstrate my memory, I'd retell the stories for her in vivid detail.

13 It did not take long to find retelling someone else's stories unsatisfying, so I began *embellishing* ⑧ my narration. I'd say things I knew would please Mother, even changed the ending once in a while. And she wasn't the only member of my audience, which later included my older sisters, my aunts, even my maternal grandmother. Sometimes, after my mother had listened to one of my stories, she'd ask in a care-laden voice, almost as if to herself: "What will you be like when you grow up, son? Might you wind up prattling for a living one day?"

14 I knew why she was worried. Talkative kids are not well thought of in our village, for they can bring trouble to themselves and to their

个说书人。我偷偷地跑去听书，忘记了她分配给我的活儿。为此，母亲批评了我。晚上，当她就着一盏小油灯为家人赶制棉衣时，我忍不住地将白天从说书人那里听来的故事复述给她听，起初她有些不耐烦，因为在她心目中，说书人都是油嘴滑舌、不务正业的人，从他们嘴里，冒不出什么好话来。但我复述的故事，渐渐地吸引了她。以后每逢集日，她便不再给我排活儿，默许我去集上听书。为了报答母亲的恩情，也为了向她炫耀我的记忆力，我会把白天听到的故事，绘声绘色地讲给她听。

13 很快地，我就不满足复述说书人讲的故事了，我在复述的过程中，不断地添油加醋。我会投我母亲所好，编造一些情节，有时候甚至改变故事的结局。我的听众，也不仅仅是我的母亲，连我的姐姐、我的婶婶、我的奶奶都成为了我的听众。我母亲在听完我的故事后，有时会忧心忡忡地，像是对我说，又像是自言自语："儿啊，你长大后会成为一个什么人呢？难道要靠耍贫嘴吃饭吗？"

14 我理解母亲的担忧，因为在村子里，一个贫嘴的孩子，是招人厌烦的，有时候还会给自己和家庭带来

---

⑥ sneak [sni:k] *vi.* 溜走，鬼鬼祟祟　如：I sneaked up the stairs. 我蹑手蹑脚地上了楼。

⑦ kerosene ['kerəsi:n] *n.* 煤油，灯油

⑧ embellish [ɪm'belɪʃ] *vt.* 修饰，润色

families. There is a bit of a young me in the talkative boy who falls afoul of villagers in my story *Bulls*. Mother habitually cautioned me not to talk so much, wanting me to be a ***taciturn*** ⑨, smooth, and steady youngster. Instead I was possessed of a dangerous combination—remarkable speaking skills and the powerful desire that went with them. My ability to tell stories brought her joy, but that created a dilemma for her.

15 A popular saying goes, "It is easier to change the course of a river than a person's nature." Despite my parents' tireless guidance, my natural desire to talk never went away, and that is what makes my name—Mo Yan, or "don't speak"—an ironic expression of self-mockery.

16 After dropping out of elementary school, I was too small for heavy labor, so I became a cattle-and-sheep-herder on a nearby grassy riverbank. The sight of my former schoolmates playing in the schoolyard when I drove my animals past the gate always saddened me and made me aware of how tough it is for anyone— even a child—to leave the group.

17 I turned the animals loose on the riverbank to graze beneath a sky as blue as the ocean and grass-carpeted land as far as the eye could see—not another person in sight, no human sounds, nothing but bird calls above me. I was all by myself and terribly lonely; my heart felt empty. Sometimes I lay in the grass and watched clouds float lazily by, which gave rise to all sorts of fanciful images. That part of the country

麻烦。我在小说《牛》里所写的那个因为话多被村里人厌恶的孩子，就有我童年时的影子。我母亲经常提醒我少说话，她希望我能做一个沉默寡言、安稳大方的孩子。但在我身上，却显露出极强的说话能力和极大的说话欲望，这无疑是极大的危险，但我的说故事的能力，又带给了她愉悦，这使她陷入深深的矛盾之中。

15 俗话说"江山易改，本性难移"，尽管有我父母亲的谆谆教导，但我并没改掉我喜欢说话的天性，这使得我的名字"莫言"，很像对自己的讽刺。

16 我小学未毕业即辍学，因为年幼体弱，干不了重活，只好到荒草滩上去放牧牛羊。当我牵着牛羊从学校门前路过，看到昔日的同学们在校园里打打闹闹，我心中充满悲凉，深深地体会到一个人——哪怕是一个孩子——离开群体后的痛苦。

17 到了荒滩上，我把牛羊放开，让它们自己吃草。蓝天如海，草地一望无际，周围看不到一个人影，没有人的声音，只有鸟儿在天上鸣叫。我感到很孤独，很寂寞，心里空空荡荡。有时候，我躺在草地上，望着天上懒洋洋地飘动着的白云，脑海里便浮现出许多莫名其妙的幻象。我们那地方流传着许多狐狸变成美女的

⑨ taciturn [ˈtæsɪtɜːn] *adj.* 沉默寡言的，不爱说话的　　如：a taciturn child 一个沉默寡言的孩子

is known for its tales of foxes in the form of beautiful young women, and I would fantasize a fox-turned-beautiful girl coming to tend animals with me. She never did come. Once, however, a fiery red fox bounded out of the brush in front of me, scaring my legs right out from under me. I was still sitting there trembling long after the fox had vanished.

18　Sometimes I'd crouch down beside the cows and gaze into their deep blue eyes, eyes that captured my reflection. At times I'd have a dialogue with birds in the sky, mimicking their cries, while at other times I'd *divulge*⑩ my hopes and desires to a tree. But the birds ignored me, and so did the trees. Years later, after I'd become a novelist, I wrote some of those fantasies into my novels and stories. People frequently bombard me with compliments on my vivid imagination, and lovers of literature often ask me to divulge my secret to developing a rich imagination. My only response is a wan smile. Our Taoist master Laozi said it best: "Fortune depends on misfortune. Misfortune is hidden in fortune."

19　I left school as a child, often went hungry, was constantly lonely, and had no books to read. But for those reasons, like the writer of a previous generation, Shen Congwen, I had an early start on reading the great book of life. My experience of going to the marketplace to listen to a storyteller was but one page of that book. After leaving school, I was thrown uncomfortably into the world of adults, where I embarked on the long journey

故事。我幻想着能有一个狐狸变成美女与我来做伴放牛，但她始终没有出现。但有一次，一只火红色的狐狸从我面前的草丛中跳出来时，我却被吓得一屁股蹲在地上。狐狸跑没了踪影，我还在那里颤抖。

18　有时候我会蹲在牛的身旁，看着湛蓝的牛眼和牛眼中的我的倒影。有时候我会模仿着鸟儿的叫声试图与天上的鸟儿对话，有时候我会对一棵树诉说心声。但鸟儿不理我，树也不理我。许多年后，当我成为一个小说家，当年的许多幻想，都被我写进了小说。很多人夸我想象力丰富，有一些文学爱好者，希望我能告诉他们培养想象力的秘诀，对此，我只能报以苦笑。就像中国的先贤老子所说的那样："福兮祸所伏，祸兮福所倚。"

19　我童年辍学，饱受饥饿、孤独、无书可读之苦，但我因此也像我们的前辈作家沈从文那样，及早地开始阅读社会人生这本大书。前面所提到的到集市上去听说书人说书，仅仅是这本大书中的一页。辍学之后，我混迹于成人之中，开始了"用耳朵阅读"的漫长生涯。两百多年前，我的故乡曾出了一个讲故事的伟大天

⑩　divulge [daɪˈvʌldʒ] *vt.* 泄露　　如：divulge the source of one's information 泄露情报来源

of learning through listening. Two hundred years ago, one of the great storytellers of all time—Pu Songling—lived near where I grew up, and where many people, me included, carried on the tradition he had perfected. Wherever I happened to be—working the fields with the collective, in production team cowsheds or stables, on my grandparents' heated kang, even on oxcarts bouncing and swaying down the road—my ears filled with tales of the supernatural, historical romances, and strange and captivating stories, all tied to the natural environment and clan histories, and all of which created a powerful reality in my mind. Even in my wildest dreams, I could not have envisioned a day when all this would be the stuff of my own fiction, for I was just a boy who loved stories, who was *infatuated* [11] with the tales people around me were telling. Back then I was, without a doubt, a theist, believing that all living creatures were endowed with souls. I'd stop and pay my respects to a towering old tree; if I saw a bird, I was sure it could become human any time it wanted; and I suspected every stranger I met of being a transformed beast. At night, terrible fears accompanied me on my way home after my work points were tallied, so I'd sing at the top of my lungs as I ran to build up a bit of courage. My voice, which was changing at the time, produced scratchy, squeaky songs that grated on the ears of any villager who heard me.

20 I spent my first twenty-one years in that

才——蒲松龄，我们村里的许多人，包括我，都是他的传人。我在集体劳动的田间地头，在生产队的牛棚马厩，在我爷爷奶奶的热炕头上，甚至在摇摇晃晃地行进着的牛车上，聆听了许许多多神鬼故事、历史传奇、逸闻趣事，这些故事都与当地的自然环境、家族历史紧密联系在一起，使我产生了强烈的现实感。我做梦也想不到有朝一日这些东西会成为我的写作素材，我当时只是一个迷恋故事的孩子，醉心地聆听着人们的讲述。那时我是一个绝对的有神论者，我相信万物都有灵性。我见到一棵大树会肃然起敬；我看到一只鸟会感到它随时会变化成人；我遇到一个陌生人，也会怀疑他是一个动物变化而成的。每当夜晚我从生产队的记工房回家时，无边的恐惧便包围了我，为了壮胆，我一边奔跑一边大声歌唱。那时我正处在变声期，嗓音嘶哑，声调难听，我的歌唱，是对我的乡亲们的一种折磨。

20 我在故乡生活了二十一年，

---

[11] infatuated [ɪnˈfætjʊeɪtɪd] *adj.* 着迷的   如：She was completely infatuated with him. 她完全迷恋上了他。

village, never traveling farther from home than to Qingdao, by train, where I nearly got lost amid the giant stacks of wood in a lumber mill. When my mother asked me what I'd seen in Qingdao, I reported sadly that all I'd seen were stacks of lumber. But that trip to Qingdao planted in me a powerful desire to leave my village and see the world.

21 In February 1976 I was recruited into the army and walked out of the Northeast Gaomi Township village I both loved and hated, entering a critical phase of my life, carrying in my backpack the four-volume *Brief History of China* my mother had bought by selling her wedding jewelry. Thus began the most important period of my life. I must admit that were it not for the thirty-odd years of tremendous development and progress in Chinese society, and the subsequent national reform and opening of her doors to the outside, I would not be a writer today. In the midst of mind-numbing military life, I welcomed the ideological emancipation and literary fervor of the 1980s, and evolved from a boy who listened to stories and passed them on by word of mouth into someone who experimented with writing them down. It was a rocky road at first, a time when I had not yet discovered how rich a source of literary material my two decades of village life could be. I thought that literature was all about good people doing good things, stories of heroic deeds and model citizens, so that the few pieces of mine that were published had little literary value.

22 In the fall of 1984 I was accepted into the

期间离家最远的是乘火车去了一次青岛，还差点迷失在木材厂的巨大木材之间，以至于我母亲问我去青岛看到了什么风景时，我沮丧地告诉她：什么都没看到，只看到了一堆堆的木头。但也就是这次青岛之行，使我产生了想离开故乡到外边去看世界的强烈愿望。

21 1976年2月，我应征入伍，背着我母亲卖掉结婚时的首饰帮我购买的四本《中国通史简编》，走出了高密东北乡这个既让我爱又让我恨的地方，开始了我人生的重要时期。我必须承认，如果没有三十多年来中国社会的巨大发展与进步，如果没有改革开放，也不会有我这样一个作家。在军营的枯燥生活中，我迎来了八十年代的思想解放和文学热潮，我从一个用耳朵聆听故事，用嘴巴讲述故事的孩子，变成了一个开始尝试用笔来讲述故事的人。起初的道路并不平坦，我那时并没有意识到我二十多年的农村生活经验是文学的富矿，那时我以为文学就是写好人好事，就是写英雄模范，所以，尽管也发表了几篇作品，但大部分文学价值都不高。

22 1984年秋，我考入解放军艺

Literature Department of the PLA Art Academy, where, under the guidance of my revered mentor, the renowned writer Xu Huaizhong, I wrote a series of stories and novellas, including: *Autumn Floods*, *Dry River*, *The Transparent Carrot*, and *Red Sorghum*. Northeast Gaomi Township made its first appearance in *Autumn Floods*, and from that moment on, like a wandering peasant who finds his own piece of land, this literary **vagabond**⑫ found a place he could call his own. I must say that in the course of creating my literary domain, Northeast Gaomi Township, I was greatly inspired by the American novelist William Faulkner and the Columbian Gabriel García Márquez. I had not read either of them extensively, but was encouraged by the bold, unrestrained way they created new territory in writing, and learned from them that a writer must have a place that belongs to him alone. Humility and compromise are ideal in one's daily life, but in literary creation, supreme self-confidence and the need to follow one's own instincts are essential. For two years I followed in the footsteps of these two masters before realizing that I had to escape their influence. This is how I characterized that decision in an essay: They were a pair of blazing furnaces; I was a block of ice. If I got too close to them, I would dissolve into a cloud of steam. In my understanding, one writer influences another when they enjoy a profound spiritual kinship, what is often referred to as "hearts beating in unison". That explains why, though I had read little of their work, a few pages

术学院文学系。在我的恩师著名作家徐怀中的启发指导下，我写出了《秋水》、《枯河》、《透明的红萝卜》、《红高粱》等一批中短篇小说。在《秋水》这篇小说里，第一次出现了"高密东北乡"这个字眼，从此，就如同一个四处游荡的农民有了一片土地，我这样一个文学的流浪汉，终于有了一个可以安身立命的场所。我必须承认，在创建我的文学领地"高密东北乡"的过程中，美国的威廉·福克纳和哥伦比亚的加西亚·马尔克斯给了我重要启发。我对他们的阅读并不认真，但他们开天辟地的豪迈精神激励了我，使我明白了一个作家必须要有一块属于自己的领地。一个人在日常生活中应该谦卑退让，但在文学创作中，必须颐指气使，独断专行。我追随在这两位大师身后两年，即意识到，必须尽快地逃离他们。我在一篇文章中写道：他们是两座灼热的火炉，而我是冰块，如果离他们太近，会被他们蒸发掉。根据我的体会，一个作家之所以会受到某一位作家的影响，其根本是因为影响者和被影响者灵魂深处的相似之处，正所谓"心有灵犀一点通"。所以，尽管我没有很好地去读他们的书，但只读过几页，我就明白了他们干了什么，也明白了他们是怎样干的，随即我也就明白了我该干什么和我该怎样干。

---

⑫ vagabond ['væɡəbɒnd] *n.* 流浪汉

were sufficient for me to comprehend what they were doing and how they were doing it, which led to my understanding of what I should do and how I should do it.

23 What I should do was simplicity itself: Write my own stories in my own way. My way was that of the marketplace storyteller, with which I was so familiar, the way my grandfather and my grandmother and other village old-timers told stories. In all candor, I never gave a thought to audience when I was telling my stories; perhaps my audience was made up of people like my mother, and perhaps it was only me. The early stories were narrations of my personal experience: the boy who received a whipping in *Dry River*, for instance, or the boy who never spoke in *The Transparent Carrot*. I had actually done something bad enough to receive a whipping from my father, and I had actually worked the bellows for a blacksmith on a bridge site. Naturally, personal experience cannot be turned into fiction exactly as it happened, no matter how unique that might be. Fiction has to be fictional, has to be imaginative. To many of my friends, *The Transparent Carrot* is my very best story; I have no opinion one way or the other. What I can say is, *The Transparent Carrot* is more symbolic and more profoundly meaningful than any other story I've written. That dark-skinned boy with the superhuman ability to suffer and a superhuman degree of sensitivity represents the soul of my entire fictional output. Not one of all the fictional characters I've created since then is as close to my soul as he is. Or put a different way, among all the characters a writer

23 我该干的事情其实很简单，那就是用自己的方式，讲自己的故事。我的方式，就是我所熟知的集市说书人的方式，就是我的爷爷奶奶、村里的老人们讲故事的方式。坦率地说，讲述的时候，我没有想到谁会是我的听众，也许我的听众就是那些如我母亲一样的人，也许我的听众就是我自己。我自己的故事，起初就是我的亲身经历，譬如《枯河》中那个遭受痛打的孩子，譬如《透明的红萝卜》中那个自始至终一言不发的孩子。我的确曾因为干过一件错事而受到过父亲的痛打，我也的确曾在桥梁工地上为铁匠师傅拉过风箱。当然，个人的经历无论多么奇特也不可能原封不动地写进小说，小说必须虚构，必须想象。很多朋友说《透明的红萝卜》是我最好的小说，对此我不反驳，也不认同，但我认为《透明的红萝卜》是我的作品中最有象征性、最意味深长的一部。那个浑身漆黑、具有超人的忍受痛苦的能力和超人的感受能力的孩子，是我全部小说的灵魂，尽管在后来的小说里，我写了很多的人物，但没有一个人物，比他更贴近我的灵魂。或者可以说，一个作家所塑造的若干人物中，总有一个领头的，这个沉默的孩子就是一个领头的，他一言不发，但却有力地领导着

creates, there is always one that stands above all the others. For me, that laconic boy is the one. Though he says nothing, he leads the way for all the others, in all their variety, performing freely on the Northeast Gaomi Township stage.

24 A person can experience only so much, and once you have exhausted your own stories, you must tell the stories of others. And so, out of the depths of my memories, like conscripted soldiers, rose stories of family members, of fellow villagers, and of long-dead ancestors I learned of from the mouths of old-timers. They waited expectantly for me to tell their stories. My grandfather and grandmother, my father and mother, my brothers and sisters, my aunts and uncles, my wife and my daughter have all appeared in my stories. Even unrelated residents of Northeast Gaomi Township have made cameo appearances. Of course they have undergone literary modification to transform them into larger-than-life fictional characters. An aunt of mine is the central character of my latest novel, *Frogs*. The announcement of the Nobel Prize sent journalists swarming to her home with interview requests. At first, she was patiently accommodating, but she soon had to escape their attentions by fleeing to her son's home in the provincial capital. I don't deny that she was my model in writing *Frogs*, but the differences between her and the fictional aunt are extensive. The fictional aunt is arrogant and ***domineering*** [13], in places virtually thuggish,

形形色色的人物，在高密东北乡这个舞台上，尽情地表演。

24 自己的故事总是有限的，讲完了自己的故事，就必须讲他人的故事。于是，我的亲人们的故事，我的乡亲们的故事，以及我从老人们口中听到过的祖先们的故事，就像听到集合令的士兵一样，从我的记忆深处涌出来。他们用期盼的目光看着我，等待着我去写他们。我的爷爷、奶奶、父亲、母亲、哥哥、姐姐、姑姑、叔叔、妻子、女儿，都在我的作品里出现过，还有很多的我们高密东北乡的乡亲，也都在我的小说里露过面。当然，我对他们，都进行了文学化的处理，使他们超越了他们自身，成为文学中的人物。我最新的小说《蛙》中，就出现了我姑姑的形象。因为我获得诺贝尔奖，许多记者到她家采访，起初她还很耐心地回答提问，但很快便不胜其烦，跑到县城里她儿子家躲起来了。姑姑确实是我写《蛙》时的模特，但小说中的姑姑，与现实生活中的姑姑有着天壤之别。小说中的姑姑专横跋扈，有时简直像个女匪，现实中的姑姑和善开朗，是一个标准的贤妻良母。现实中的姑姑晚年生活幸福美满，小说中的姑姑到了晚

---

⑬ domineering [ˌdɒmɪˈnɪərɪŋ] *adj.* 跋扈的，盛气凌人的 如：a cold and domineering father 冷漠而专横的父亲

while my real aunt is kind and gentle, the classic caring wife and loving mother. My real aunt's golden years have been happy and fulfilling; her fictional counterpart suffers insomnia in her late years as a result of spiritual torment, and walks the nights like a specter, wearing a dark robe. I am grateful to my real aunt for not being angry with me for how I changed her in the novel. I also greatly respect her wisdom in comprehending the complex relationship between fictional characters and real people.

25 After my mother died, in the midst of almost crippling grief, I decided to write a novel for her. *Big Breasts and Wide Hips* is that novel. Once my plan took shape, I was burning with such emotion that I completed a draft of half a million words in only eighty-three days. In *Big Breasts and Wide Hips* I shamelessly used material associated with my mother's actual experience, but the fictional mother's emotional state is either a total fabrication or a composite of many of Northeast Gaomi Township's mothers. Though I wrote "To the spirit of my mother" on the dedication page, the novel was really written for all mothers everywhere, evidence, perhaps, of my overweening ambition, in much the same way as I hope to make tiny Northeast Gaomi Township a microcosm of China, even of the whole world.

26 The process of creation is unique to every writer. Each of my novels differs from the others in terms of plot and guiding inspiration. Some, such as *The Transparent Carrot*, were born in dreams, while others, like *The Garlic Ballads*

年却因为心灵的巨大痛苦患上了失眠症，身披黑袍，像个幽灵一样在暗夜中游荡。我感谢姑姑的宽容，她没有因为我在小说中把她写成那样而生气；我也十分敬佩我姑姑的明智，她正确地理解了小说中人物与现实中人物的复杂关系。

25 母亲去世后，我悲痛万分，决定写一部书献给她。这就是那本《丰乳肥臀》。因为胸有成竹，因为情感充盈，仅用了83天，我便写出了这部长达50万字的小说的初稿。在《丰乳肥臀》这本书里，我肆无忌惮地使用了与我母亲的亲身经历有关的素材，但书中的母亲情感方面的经历，则是虚构或取材于高密东北乡诸多母亲的经历。在这本书的卷前语上，我写下了"献给母亲在天之灵"的话，但这本书，实际上是献给天下母亲的，这是我狂妄的野心，就像我希望把小小的"高密东北乡"写成中国乃至世界的缩影一样。

26 作家的创作过程各有特色，我每本书的构思与灵感触发也都不尽相同。有的小说起源于梦境，譬如《透明的红萝卜》，有的小说则发端于现实生活中发生的事件——譬如《天

have their origin in actual events. Whether the source of a work is a dream or real life, only if it is integrated with individual experience can it be imbued with individuality, be populated with typical characters molded by lively detail, employ richly evocative language, and boast a well-crafted structure. Here I must point out that in *The Garlic Ballads* I introduced a real-life storyteller and singer in one of the novel's most important roles. I wish I hadn't used his real name, though his words and actions were made up. This is a recurring phenomenon with me. I'll start out using characters' real names in order to achieve a sense of intimacy, and after the work is finished, it will seem too late to change those names. This has led to people who see their names in my novels going to my father to vent their displeasure. He always apologizes in my place, but then urges them not to take such things so seriously. He'll say: "The first sentence in *Red Sorghum*, 'My father, a bandit's offspring', didn't upset me, so why should you be unhappy?"

27 My greatest challenges come with writing novels that deal with social realities, such as *The Garlic Ballads*, not because I'm afraid of being openly critical of the darker aspects of society, but because heated emotions and anger allow politics to suppress literature and transform a novel into reportage of a social event. As a member of society, a novelist is entitled to his own stance and viewpoint; but when he is writing he must take a humanistic stance, and write accordingly. Only then can literature not just originate in events, but

堂蒜薹之歌》。但无论是起源于梦境还是发端于现实，最后都必须和个人的经验相结合，才有可能变成一部具有鲜明个性的，用无数生动细节塑造出了典型人物的、语言丰富多彩、结构匠心独运的文学作品。有必要特别提及的是，在《天堂蒜薹之歌》中，我让一个真正的说书人登场，并在书中扮演了十分重要的角色。我十分抱歉地使用了这个说书人的真实姓名，当然，他在书中的所有行为都是虚构的。在我的写作中，出现过多次这样的现象，写作之初，我使用他们的真实姓名，希望能借此获得一种亲近感，但作品完成之后，我想为他们改换姓名时却感到已经不可能了，因此也发生过与我小说中人物同名者找到我父亲发泄不满的事情，我父亲替我向他们道歉，但同时又开导他们不要当真。我父亲说："他在《红高粱》中，第一句就说'我父亲这个土匪种'，我都不在意你们还在意什么？"

27 我在写作《天堂蒜薹之歌》这类逼近社会现实的小说时，面对着的最大问题，其实不是我敢不敢对社会上的黑暗现象进行批评，而是这燃烧的激情和愤怒会让政治压倒文学，使这部小说变成一个社会事件的纪实报告。小说家是社会中人，他自然有自己的立场和观点，但小说家在写作时，必须站在人的立场上，把所有的人都当做人来写。只有这样，文学才能发端事件但超越事件，关心政治但

transcend them, not just show concern for politics but be greater than politics.

28 Possibly because I've lived so much of my life in difficult circumstances, I think I have a more profound understanding of life. I know what real courage is, and I understand true compassion. I know that nebulous terrain exists in the hearts and minds of every person, terrain that cannot be adequately characterized in simple terms of right and wrong or good and bad, and this vast territory is where a writer gives free rein to his talent. So long as the work correctly and vividly describes this nebulous, massively contradictory terrain, it will inevitably transcend politics and be endowed with literary excellence.

29 Prattling on and on about my own work must be annoying, but my life and works are inextricably linked, so if I don't talk about my work, I don't know what else to say. I hope you are in a forgiving mood.

30 I was a modern-day storyteller who hid in the background of his early work; but with the novel *Sandalwood Death* I jumped out of the shadows. My early work can be characterized as a series of soliloquies, with no reader in mind; starting with this novel, however, I visualized myself standing in a public square spiritedly telling my story to a crowd of listeners. This tradition is a worldwide phenomenon in fiction, but is especially so in China. At one time, I was a diligent student of Western modernist fiction, and I experimented with all sorts of narrative styles. But in the end I came back to my traditions. To be

大于政治。

28 可能是因为我经历过长期的艰难生活，因而我对人性有较为深刻的了解。我知道真正的勇敢是什么，也明白真正的悲悯是什么。我知道，每个人心中都有一片难用是非善恶准确定性的朦胧地带，而这片地带，正是文学家施展才华的广阔天地。只要是准确地、生动地描写了这个充满矛盾的朦胧地带的作品，也就必然地超越了政治并具备了优秀文学的品质。

29 喋喋不休地讲述自己的作品是令人厌烦的，但我的人生是与我的作品紧密相连的，不讲作品，我感到无从下嘴，所以还得请各位原谅。

30 在我的早期作品中，我作为一个现代的说书人，是隐藏在文本背后的，但从《檀香刑》这部小说开始，我终于从后台跳到了前台。如果说我早期的作品是自言自语，目无读者，从这本书开始，我感觉到自己是站在一个广场上，面对着许多听众，绘声绘色地讲述。这是世界小说的传统，更是中国小说的传统。我也曾积极地向西方的现代派小说学习，也曾经玩弄过形形色色的叙事花样，但我最终回归了传统。当然，这种回归，不是一成不变的回归，《檀香刑》和

sure, this return was not without its modifications. *Sandalwood Death* and the novels that followed are inheritors of the Chinese classical novel tradition but enhanced by Western literary techniques. What is known as innovative fiction is, for the most part, a result of this mixture, which is not limited to domestic traditions with foreign techniques, but can include mixing fiction with art from other realms. *Sandalwood Death*, for instance, mixes fiction with local opera, while some of my early work was partly nurtured by fine art, music, even acrobatics.

31 Finally, I ask your indulgence to talk about my novel *Life and Death Are Wearing Me Out*. The Chinese title comes from Buddhist scripture, and I've been told that my translators have had fits trying to render it into their languages. I am not especially well versed in Buddhist scripture and have but a superficial understanding of the religion. I chose this title because I believe that the basic tenets of the Buddhist faith represent universal knowledge, and that mankind's many disputes are utterly without meaning in the Buddhist realm. In that lofty view of the universe, the world of man is to be pitied. My novel is not a religious tract; in it I wrote of man's fate and human emotions, of man's limitations and human generosity, and of people's search for happiness and the lengths to which they will go, the sacrifices they will make, to uphold their beliefs. Lan Lian, a character who takes a stand against contemporary trends, is, in my view, a true hero. A peasant in a neighboring village

之后的小说，是继承了中国古典小说传统又借鉴了西方小说技术的混合文本。小说领域的所谓创新，基本上都是这种混合的产物。不仅仅是本国文学传统与外国小说技巧的混合，也是小说与其他的艺术门类的混合，就像《檀香刑》是与民间戏曲的混合，就像我早期的一些小说从美术、音乐、甚至杂技中汲取了营养一样。

31 最后，请允许我再讲一下我的《生死疲劳》。这个书名来自佛教经典，据我所知，为翻译这个书名，各国的翻译家都很头痛。我对佛教经典并没有深入研究，对佛教的理解自然十分肤浅，之所以以此为题，是因为我觉得佛教的许多基本思想，是真正的宇宙意识，人世中许多纷争，在佛家的眼里，是毫无意义的。这样一种至高眼界下的人世，显得十分可悲。当然，我没有把这本书写成布道词，我写的还是人的命运与人的情感，人的局限与人的宽容，以及人为追求幸福、坚持自己的信念所做出的牺牲与努力。小说中那位以一己之身与时代潮流对抗的蓝脸，在我心目中是一位真正的英雄。这个人物的原型，是我们邻村的一位农民，我童年时，经常看到他推着一辆吱吱作响的木轮车，从我家门前的道路上通过。给他拉车的，是一头瘸腿的毛驴，为

was the model for this character. As a youngster I often saw him pass by our door pushing a creaky, wooden-wheeled cart, with a lame donkey up front led by his bound-foot wife. Given the collective nature of society back then, this strange labor group presented a bizarre sight that kept them out of step with the times. In the eyes of us children, they were clowns marching against historical trends, provoking in us such indignation that we threw stones at them as they passed us on the street. Years later, after I had begun writing, that peasant and the tableau he presented floated into my mind, and I knew that one day I would write a novel about him, that sooner or later I would tell his story to the world. But it wasn't until the year 2005, when I viewed the Buddhist mural "The Six Stages of Samsara" on a temple wall that I knew exactly how to go about telling his story.

32 The announcement of my Nobel Prize has led to controversy. At first I thought I was the target of the disputes, but over time I've come to realize that the real target was a person who had nothing to do with me. Like someone watching a play in a theater, I observed the performances around me. I saw the winner of the prize both garlanded with flowers and besieged by stone-throwers and mudslingers. I was afraid he would succumb to the assault, but he emerged from the garlands of flowers and the stones, a smile on his face; he wiped away mud and grime, stood calmly off to the side, and said to the crowd: For a writer, the best way to speak is by writing. You

他牵驴的，是他小脚的妻子。这个奇怪的劳动组合，在当时的集体化社会里，显得那么古怪和不合时宜，在我们这些孩子的眼里，也把他们看成是逆历史潮流而动的小丑，以至于当他们从街上经过时，我们会充满义愤地朝他们投掷石块。事过多年，当我拿起笔来写作时，这个人物，这个画面，便浮现在我的脑海中。我知道，我总有一天会为他写一本书，我迟早要把他的故事讲给天下人听，但一直到了2005年，当我在一座庙宇里看到"六道轮回"的壁画时，才明白了讲述这个故事的正确方法。

32 我获得诺贝尔文学奖后，引发了一些争议。起初，我还以为大家争议的对象是我，渐渐地，我感到这个被争议的对象，是一个与我毫不相关的人。我如同一个看戏人，看着众人的表演。我看到那个得奖人身上落满了花朵，也被掷上了石块、泼上了污水。我生怕他被打垮，但他微笑着从花朵和石块中钻出来，擦干净身上的脏水，坦然地站在一边，对着众人说：对一个作家来说，最好的说话方式是写作。我该说的话都写进了我的作品里。用嘴说出的话随风而散，用笔写出的话永不磨灭。我希望你们能

will find everything I need to say in my works. Speech is carried off by the wind; the written word can never be obliterated. I would like you to find the patience to read my books. I cannot force you to do that, and even if you do, I do not expect your opinion of me to change. No writer has yet appeared, anywhere in the world, who is liked by all his readers; that is especially true during times like these. Even though I would prefer to say nothing, since it is something I must do on this occasion, let me just say this: I am a storyteller, so I am going to tell you some stories.

33 When I was a third-grade student in the 1960s, my school organized a field trip to an exhibit of suffering, where, under the direction of our teacher, we cried bitter tears. I let my tears stay on my cheeks for the benefit of our teacher, and watched as some of my classmates spat in their hands and rubbed it on their faces as pretend tears. I saw one student among all those wailing children—some real, some phony—whose face was dry and who remained silent without covering his face with his hands. He just looked at us, eyes wide open in an expression of surprise or confusion. After the visit I reported him to the teacher, and he was given a disciplinary warning. Years later, when I expressed my remorse over informing on the boy, the teacher said that at least ten students had done what I did. The boy himself had died a decade or more earlier, and my conscience was deeply troubled when I thought of him. But I learned something important from this incident, and that is: <u>When everyone around you</u>

耐心地读一下我的书，当然，我没有资格强迫你们读我的书。即便你们读了我的书，我也不期望你们能改变对我的看法，世界上还没有一个作家，能让所有的读者都喜欢他。在当今这样的时代里，更是如此。尽管我什么都不想说，但在今天这样的场合我必须说话，那我就简单地再说几句。我是一个讲故事的人，我还是要给你们讲故事。

33 上世纪六十年代，我上小学三年级的时候，学校里组织我们去观看一个苦难展览，我们在老师的引领下放声大哭。为了能让老师看到我的表现，我舍不得擦去脸上的泪水。我看到有几位同学悄悄地将唾沫抹到脸上冒充泪水。我还看到在一片真哭假哭的同学之间，有一位同学，脸上没有一滴泪，嘴巴里没有一点声音，也没有用手掩面。他睁着大眼看着我们，眼睛里流露出惊讶或者说是困惑的神情。事后，我向老师报告了这位同学的行为。为此，学校给了这位同学一个警告处分。多年之后，当我因自己的告密向老师忏悔时，老师说，那天来找他说这件事的，有十几个同学。这位同学十几年前就已去世，每当想起他，我就深感歉疚。这件事让我悟到一个道理，那就是：<u>当众人都哭时，应该允许有的人不哭。当哭成为一种表演时，更应该允许有的人</u>

is crying, you deserve to be allowed not to cry, and when the tears are all for show, your right not to cry is greater still.

34　Here is another story: More than thirty years ago, when I was in the army, I was in my office reading one evening when an elderly officer opened the door and came in. He glanced down at the seat in front of me and muttered, "Hm, where is everyone?" I stood up and said in a loud voice, "Are you saying I'm no one?" The old fellow's ears turned red from embarrassment, and he walked out. For a long time after that I was proud about what I considered a gutsy performance. Years later, that pride turned to intense qualms of conscience.

35　Bear with me, please, for one last story, one my grandfather told me many years ago: A group of eight out-of-town bricklayers took refuge from a storm in a rundown temple. Thunder rumbled outside, sending fireballs their way. They even heard what sounded like dragon shrieks. The men were terrified, their faces ashen. "Among the eight of us," one of them said, "is someone who must have offended the heavens with a terrible deed. The guilty person ought to volunteer to step outside to accept his punishment and spare the innocent from suffering." Naturally, there were no volunteers. So one of the others came up with a proposal, "Since no one is willing to go outside, let's all fling our straw hats toward the door. Whoever's hat flies out through the temple door is the guilty party, and we'll ask him to go out and accept his punishment." So they flung their

不哭。

34　我再讲一个故事：三十多年前，我还在部队工作。有一天晚上，我在办公室看书，有一位老长官推门进来，看了一眼我对面的位置，自言自语道："噢，没有人？"我随即站起来，高声说："难道我不是人吗？"那位老长官被我顶得面红耳赤，尴尬而退。为此事，我洋洋得意了许久，以为自己是个英勇的斗士，但事过多年后，我却为此深感内疚。

35　请允许我讲最后一个故事，这是许多年前我爷爷讲给我听的：有八个外出打工的泥瓦匠，为避一场暴风雨，躲进了一座破庙。外边的雷声一阵紧似一阵，一个个的火球，在庙门外滚来滚去，空中似乎还有吱吱的龙叫声。众人都胆战心惊，面如土色。有一个人说："我们八个人中，必定有一个人干过伤天害理的事情，谁干过坏事，就自己走出庙接受惩罚吧，免得让好人受到牵连。"自然没有人愿意出去。又有人提议道："既然大家都不想出去，那我们就将自己的草帽往外抛吧，谁的草帽被刮出了庙门，就说明谁干了坏事，那就请他出去接受惩罚。"于是大家就将自己的草帽往庙门外抛，七个人的草帽被刮回了庙内，只有一个人的草帽

hats toward the door. Seven hats were blown back inside; one went out the door. They pressured the eighth man to go out and accept his punishment, and when he balked, they picked him up and flung him out the door. I'll bet you all know how the story ends: They had no sooner flung him out the door than the temple collapsed around them.

36 I am a storyteller. Telling stories earned me the Nobel Prize in Literature. Many interesting things have happened to me in the wake of winning the prize, and they have convinced me that truth and justice are alive and well. So I will continue telling my stories in the days to come.

37 Thank you all.

(Translated by Howard Goldblatt)

被卷了出去。大家就催这个人出去受罚，他自然不愿出去，众人便将他抬起来扔出了庙门。故事的结局我估计大家都猜到了——那个人刚刚被扔出庙门，那座破庙就轰然坍塌了。

36 我是一个讲故事的人。因为讲故事我获得了诺贝尔文学奖。我获奖后发生了很多精彩的故事，这些故事，让我坚信真理和正义是存在的。在今后的岁月里，我将继续讲我的故事。

37 谢谢大家！

 演讲关键词 Practical Expressions

1. nodding acquaintance 或多或少地了解
2. bound feet 缠足
3. the God of the Underworld 阎王爷
4. walk off whistling 吹着口哨扬长而去
5. take one's own life 自寻短见
6. be born ugly 生来相貌丑陋

精华佳句

1. A writer must have a place that belongs to him alone. Humility and compromise are ideal in one's daily life, but in literary creation, supreme self-confidence and the need to follow one's own instincts are essential.

一个作家必须要有一块属于自己的领地。一个人在日常生活中应该谦卑退让，但在文学创作中必须颐指气使，独断专行。

2. When everyone around you is crying, you deserve to be allowed not to cry, and when the tears are all for show, your right not to cry is greater still.

当众人都哭时，应该允许有的人不哭。当哭成为一种表演时，更应该允许有的人不哭。

诺贝尔奖背后的那些趣事

吃西瓜"吃出"诺贝尔奖

1928 年，英国细菌学家亚历山大·弗莱明发现了能杀死细菌的青霉素，但他未能将其提纯用于临床。他的研究成果也一直未得到重视。

10 年后，德国化学家恩斯特·钱恩开始对青霉素做提纯实验。1940 年冬，钱恩提炼出了一点点青霉素，但离临床应用还差得很远。

1941 年，澳大利亚病理学家瓦尔特·弗洛里开始接力青霉素提纯的工作。在他的不懈努力及军方协助下，青霉素的产量从每立方厘米 2 单位提高到了 40 单位。虽然这离生产青霉素还差得很远，但弗洛里还是非常高兴。一天，弗洛里下班后散步的时候见路边水果店里摆满了西瓜，想着最近的成果就想买个西瓜犒劳一下自己，他走进了水果店。

他从一大堆上好的西瓜里挑了几个，付了钱，刚要走，忽然瞥见柜台上放着一个被挤破了的西瓜。溃烂的瓜皮面长了一层绿色的霉斑。弗洛里盯着这个烂瓜看了好久，又皱着眉头想了一会，忽然对老板说："我要这一个。"

"先生，那个坏瓜我们正打算扔掉呢，会吃坏肚子的。"老板提醒道。

"我就要这一个。"说着，弗洛里已放下怀里的西瓜，捧着那个烂瓜走出了水果店。

"先生，您把那几个好瓜也抱走吧，这个烂瓜算我送你的。"老板跟在后面喊。

"可我抱不了那么多的瓜啊，再说，要是把这个打烂了怎么办？"

老板满怀歉意要退钱给他，但弗洛里已走远了。望着弗洛里远去的背影，老板迷惑极了。

捧着这个烂西瓜回到实验室后，弗洛里立即从瓜上取下一点绿霉，开始培养菌种。不久，令人振奋的实验结果出来了，从烂西瓜里得到的青霉素，竟从每立方厘米 40 单位一下子猛增到了 200 单位。

1943 年 10 月，弗洛里和美国军方签订了首批青霉素生产合同。青霉素在第二次世界大战末期横空出世，迅速扭转了盟国的战局。战后，青霉素又拯救了数千万人的生命。因这项伟大发明，弗洛里和弗莱明、钱恩分享了 1945 年的诺贝尔生物及医学奖。

Chapter **2**

独立的人格：以卓越思想启迪人生的诺贝尔奖大师演讲

Speech 1

On Not Winning the Nobel Prize (1)
远离诺贝尔奖的人们（1）

—Speech by Doris Lessing for the Nobel Prize in Literature in 2007
——英国文坛祖母多丽丝·莱辛 2007 年诺贝尔文学奖获奖演讲

 名家速览 **About the Author**

诺贝尔奖大师	多丽丝·莱辛
奖 项 归 属	诺贝尔文学奖
获 奖 理 由	她以怀疑主义、激情和想象力审视一个分裂的文明，她登上了这方面女性体验的史诗巅峰。
相关采访链接	http://www.nobelprize.org/mediaplayer/index.php?id=978

多丽丝·莱辛，英国女作家，代表作有《野草在歌唱》、《金色笔记》等，2007 年获诺贝尔文学奖。莱辛出生于今伊朗西部克曼沙的一个英国殖民官员家庭，她父亲是当时帝国银行的职员。1925 年在靠玉米种植致富的潮流鼓动下，她随父母迁居非洲的英属殖民地罗得西亚（即今"津巴布韦"）南部。

由于早年作品带有浓厚的社会与政治批判色彩，对非洲殖民地黑人的悲惨际遇尤其同情，挞伐种族隔离制度不遗余力，导致罗德西亚与南非政府将她列为不受欢迎人物。直到白人政权倒台以后，莱辛才于 1995 年得以重访南非。她 2007 年获诺贝尔文学奖时已经 88 岁，是诺贝尔文学奖开设以来年龄最大的获奖者，也是第 11 位获得该奖项的女作家。本文所选取的是多丽丝·莱辛 2007 年获得诺贝尔文学奖时的获奖演讲，演讲中莱辛谈及非洲的阅读及教育现状，呼吁人们关注物资乏却对知识无比渴望的第三世界。

演讲现场
Speech Script

精美译文
Suggested Translation

1 I am standing in a doorway looking through clouds of blowing dust to where I am told there is still uncut forest. Yesterday I drove through miles of *stumps* ①, and charred remains of fires where, in '56, there was the most wonderful forest I have ever seen, all now destroyed. People have to eat. They have to get fuel for fires.

2 This is northwest Zimbabwe in the early eighties, and I am visiting a friend who was a teacher in a school in London. He is here "to help Africa", as we put it. He is a gently idealistic soul and what he found in this school shocked him into a depression, from which it was hard to recover. This school is like every other built after Independence. It consists of four large brick rooms side by side, put straight into the dust, one two three four, with a half room at one end, which is the library. In these classrooms are blackboards, but my friend keeps the chalks in his pocket, as otherwise they would be stolen. There is no atlas or globe in the school, no textbooks, no exercise books, or biros. In the library there are no books of the kind the pupils would like to read, but only tomes from American universities, hard even to lift, rejects from white libraries, or novels with titles like *Weekend in Paris* and *Felicity Finds Love.*

3 There is a goat trying to find sustenance in

1 我站在门口，远远望去，目光穿过云雾般缭绕的尘土，据说远处还有未被砍伐的森林。昨天，我驱车数英里，一路都是砍伐留下的枯树桩以及焚烧过后的余烬。1956 年时，这里还有我曾见过的最美的森林，现在，全毁了。因为人们要吃饭，要有柴烧。

2 20 世纪 80 年代初在津巴布韦的西北部，我拜访了一位曾在伦敦一所学校教书的朋友。正如我们所说的那样，他来这里"支援非洲"。他本人彬彬有礼，满怀理想，但非洲这所学校的情景却让他大为吃惊，甚至陷入消沉，难以自拔。这所学校同其他津巴布韦独立后建立的学校没什么两样。四间大砖房并排而立，整齐地排列在层层尘土里，一、二、三、四，最后一间留了半个房间作图书馆。教室里有黑板，但我这位朋友却一直把粉笔装在自己口袋里，否则就要被偷。学校没有地图、地球仪，没有教科书、练习册，甚至没有圆珠笔。图书馆里没有小学生喜欢读的书，有的只是来自美国大学的，连拿起来都十分困难的大部头著作，一些被白人图书馆弃置的书，还有诸如《巴黎周末》、《费莉希蒂找到了爱情》之类的小说。

3 一只山羊正试图在枯草中寻

---

① stump [stʌmp] *n.* 树桩

some aged grass. The headmaster has **embezzled** ②
the school funds and is suspended, arousing the
question familiar to all of us but usually in more
august contexts: How is it these people behave
like this when they must know everyone is
watching them?

4　My friend doesn't have any money because
everyone, pupils and teachers, borrow from him
when he is paid and will probably never pay
him back. The pupils range from six to twenty-
six, because some who did not get schooling as
children are here to make it up. Some pupils walk
many miles every morning, rain or shine and
across rivers. They cannot do homework because
there is no electricity in the villages, and you can't
study easily by the light of a burning log. The
girls have to fetch water and cook before they set
off for school and when they get back.

5　As I sit with my friend in his room,
people drop in shyly, and everyone begs for
books. "Please send us books when you get back
to London," one man says, "They taught us to
read but we have no books," Everybody I met,
everyone, begged for books.

6　I was there some days. The dust blew. The
pumps had broken and the women were having
to fetch water from the river. Another idealistic
teacher from England was rather ill after seeing
what this "school" was like.

7　On the last day they slaughtered the goat.
They cut it into bits and cooked it in a great tin.

找食物。校长挪用了学校的资金，已
经被停职。由此引发了一个我们都很
熟悉，但一般在更庄严的情景下才会
产生的问题：在众目睽睽之下，这些
人怎么敢如此行事？

4　我朋友没有一分钱，因为每
个人，不管是学生还是老师，都在他
领工资时向他借钱，而这些钱可能永
远都还不回来。学生的年龄从 6 岁
到 26 岁不等，因为有些在儿童时代
没上过学的人现在也回来补习。有些
孩子每天早晨要走数英里路来上学，
跋山涉水，风雨无阻。他们没法写作
业，因为村子里没电，借着柴火的光
学习又很困难。而女孩子们上学前、
放学后都要打水做饭。

5　我和朋友坐在他房间里，顺
道而来的人们羞涩地走进来，每个人
都向我们讨要书本。"你回伦敦后请
给我们寄些书吧，"一个人说道，"他
们教我们读书，可是我们却无书可
读。"我见过的每个人，每个人都在
讨要书籍。

6　我在那里待了几天。风卷黄
土，沙尘飞扬。水泵坏掉了，妇女们
不得不从河里来回取水。另一个从英
国来的满怀抱负的老师看了这样的
"学校"之后大病了一场。

7　学期结束的那天，他们宰了
那只山羊。把羊肉切碎了，放在一个

---

② embezzle [ɪmˈbezl] *vt.* 盗用；挪用；贪污　　如：embezzle public funds 挪用公款

This was the much anticipated end-of-term feast: boiled goat and porridge. I drove away while it was still going on, back through the charred remains and stumps of the forest.

8 I do not think many of the pupils of this school will get prizes.

9 The next day I am to give a talk at a school in North London, a very good school, whose name we all know. It is a school for boys, with beautiful buildings and gardens.

10 These children here have a visit from some well known person every week, and it is in the nature of things that these may be fathers, relatives, even mothers of the pupils. A visit from a celebrity is not unusual for them.

11 As I talk to them, the school in the blowing dust of north-west Zimbabwe is in my mind, and I look at the mildly expectant English faces in front of me and try to tell them about what I have seen in the last week. Classrooms without books, without textbooks, or an *atlas* [3], or even a map pinned to a wall. A school where the teachers beg to be sent books to tell them how to teach, they being only eighteen or nineteen themselves. I tell these English boys how everybody begs for books: "Please send us books." I am sure that anyone who has ever given a speech will know that moment when the faces you are looking at are blank. Your listeners cannot hear what you are saying, there are no images in their minds to

大罐子里煮。这就是人们期望已久的期末盛宴：水煮羊肉和燕麦粥。"宴会"还在进行时，我驾车离开了，再次经过那片烧伐殆尽、满是树桩和余烬的森林。

8 我觉得这所学校大多数的孩子都不会获得什么奖项。

9 第二天，我应邀在伦敦北部的一所学校做演讲。一个非常好的学校，学校的名字我们都熟知。这是一所专门为男生开办的学校，学校里有上等建筑和漂亮花园。

10 这儿的孩子每周都会见到名人，这些名人可能是他们的父亲、亲戚或者母亲。这都是家常便饭。名人到访对他们来说并不是什么稀罕事。

11 在我演讲时，津巴布韦西北部那所尘土飞扬的学校还在我脑海里挥之不去，看着眼前一张张温和而有所期待的英国人的面孔，我试图向他们讲述我上周的见闻。教室里没有书、课本、地图册，甚至连一张钉在墙上的地图都没有。那里的老师乞求我给他们寄去书籍，告诉他们该如何教学，他们自己只有十八九岁的样子。我向这些英国的男孩子们讲述着，那里的每个人都在向我讨要书本："请给我们寄些书吧。"我相信每个做过演讲的人都能体会到那一刻的情形，你看到的只是一张张写满空白的脸。听众们不懂你在说些什么，他

③ atlas ['ætləs] *n.* 地图集；寰椎

match what you are telling them—in this case the story of a school standing in dust clouds, where water is short, and where the end of term treat is a just-killed goat cooked in a great pot.

12 Is it really so impossible for these *privileged* ④ students to imagine such bare poverty?

13 I do my best. They are polite.

14 I'm sure that some of them will one day win prizes.

15 Then, the talk is over. Afterwards I ask the teachers how the library is, and if the pupils read. In this privileged school, I hear what I always hear when I go to such schools and even universities.

16 "You know how it is," one of the teacher's says, "A lot of the boys have never read at all, and the library is only half used."

17 Yes, indeed we do know how it is. All of us.

18 We are in a fragmenting culture, where our certainties of even a few decades ago are questioned and where it is common for young men and women, who have had years of education, to know nothing of the world, to have read nothing, knowing only some speciality or other, for instance, computers.

19 What has happened to us is an amazing invention—computers and the internet and TV.

们无法把自己头脑中的任何图像和你讲的内容联系起来———所矗立在漫天尘土中的学校，那里水源匮乏，期末奖励只是宰一只山羊并在一口大锅里煮了吃。

12 对这些养尊处优的学生来说，想象这样赤贫的情景真的这么难吗？

13 我只能尽力讲。他们也只是礼貌地听。

14 我确信他们中有些人一定会得奖的。

15 演讲结束后，我向学校老师询问图书馆的情况，孩子们是否读书等。在这所贵族学校，我听到的回答与在其他同类学校甚至大学里听到的答案是一样的。

16 "你肯定也知道情况，"一位老师说，"很多学生压根就不读书，图书馆利用率不到一半。"

17 是的，事实上我们了解这情况。我们所有人都知道。

18 我们处在分裂的文化里。在这里，几十年前还确凿无疑的事情今天会遭到质疑；受过多年教育的青年人对这个世界还一无所知，他们从不读文学作品，只知道少数几个专业，例如，计算机。这些对他们来说都司空见惯。

19 我们人类拥有神奇的发明创造——计算机、互联网和电视机。这

---

④ privileged ['prɪvɪlɪdʒd] *adj.* 享有特权的；有特别恩典的　如：She comes from a privileged background. 她出身特权阶层。

It is a revolution. This is not the first revolution the human race has dealt with. The printing revolution, which did not take place in a matter of a few decades, but took much longer, transformed our minds and ways of thinking. A foolhardy lot, we accepted it all, as we always do, never asked, "What is going to happen to us now, with this invention of print?" In the same way, we never thought to ask, how will our lives, our way of thinking, be changed by this internet, which has seduced a whole generation with its inanities so that even quite reasonable people will confess that once they are hooked, it is hard to cut free, and they may find a whole day has passed in blogging, etc.

20 Very recently, anyone even mildly educated would respect learning, education, and our great store of literature. Of course, we all know that when this happy state was with us, people would pretend to read, would pretend respect for learning. But it is on record that working men and women longed for books, and this is evidenced by the founding of working men's libraries and institutes, the colleges of the 18th and 19th centuries.

21 Reading, books, used to be part of a general education.

22 Older people, talking to young ones, must understand just how much of an education reading was, because the young ones know so much less. And if children cannot read, it is because they have not read.

23 We all know this sad story.

是一场革命，而且并非人类经历的第一次变革。发生在远远超过几十年前的印刷术革命，改变了人类的意识和思维方式。我们稀里糊涂地接受了一切，像往常一样，从未问过"印刷术的出现会带给我们什么？"同样地，我们也从未想过要问一下，互联网会怎样影响我们的生活和思维方式。整整一代人已经沦陷在那个空虚的世界里，就连十分理智的人也承认一旦上钩就很难脱身，他们甚至一整天都泡在博客上。

20 不久之前，任何甚至没受过多少教育的人都会尊重知识教育和我们的文学宝库。当然，在上层生活圈里，人们会附庸风雅，假装阅读，假装对知识充满敬意。据18、19世纪的工人图书馆、大学等机构的记载，贫苦的劳工和妇女才渴望读书。

21 阅读，书籍，这在以前是通识教育的一部分。

22 老一辈人，如果同年轻人聊天的话，就会知道阅读应该在教育中扮演多么重要的角色；因为年轻一辈在这方面实在知之甚少。而孩子们如果不会读书，那是因为他们还没有读过。

23 我们都知道这样悲伤的故事。

24 But we do not know the end of it.

25 We think of the old adage, "Reading maketh a full man"—and forgetting about jokes to do with over-eating—reading makes a woman and a man full of information, of history, of all kinds of knowledge.

26 But we in the West are not the only people in the world. Not long ago a friend who had been in Zimbabwe told me about a village where people had not eaten for three days, but they were still talking about books and how to get them, about education.

27 I belong to an organisation which started out with the intention of getting books into the villages. There was a group of people who in another connection had travelled Zimbabwe at its grass roots. They told me that the villages, unlike what is reported, are full of intelligent people, teachers retired, teachers on leave, children on holidays, old people. I myself paid for a little survey to discover what people in Zimbabwe want to read, and found the results were the same as those of a Swedish survey I had not known about. People want to read the same kinds of books that we in Europe want to read—novels of all kinds, science fiction, poetry, detective stories, plays, and do-it-yourself books, like how to open a bank account. All of Shakespeare too.

28 A problem with finding books for villagers is that they don't know what is available, so a set book, like the *Mayor of Casterbridge*, becomes popular simply because it just happens

24 但我们并不知道故事的结局。

25 "读书使人充实。"让我们记住这句古老的箴言——并且忘掉那个饮食过量的笑话吧——读书扩大人们的信息量，使人博古通今。

26 但是我们西方人并不是世界上仅有的人类。不久之前一个曾经去过津巴布韦的朋友告诉我，那里一个村子的人们三天都没吃过饭了，他们却还在谈论书籍，谈论教育，以及怎么实现这些。

27 我参加了一个组织，这个组织发起的初衷就是给村里送去图书。而也有一群人通过别的渠道深入到津巴布韦的草根基层。他们告诉我那些村子并非报道的那样，实际上那里有许多智慧的人，有退休或休假的教师，有度假的孩子们，还有老人。我自己出资做了一个小调查，意在发现津巴布韦的人们想读什么书。结果同我起初未知的一个瑞典调查不谋而合：那里人们的阅读意向和欧洲人是一样的——各类小说、科幻作品、诗歌、侦探故事、戏剧、莎士比亚全集，以及各种指导自己动手的书籍，例如如何开一个银行账户。

28 为村民找书的一个麻烦在于，他们不知道能得到什么书。通常一本书在那里流行起来，如《卡斯塔乔市长》，仅仅是因为碰巧那儿有这

to be there. *Animal Farm*, for obvious reasons, is the most popular of all novels.

29 Our organisation was helped from the very start by Norway, and then by Sweden. Without this kind of support our supplies of books would have dried up. We got books from wherever we could. Remember, a good paperback from England costs a month's wages in Zimbabwe: that was before Mugabe's reign of terror. Now with inflation, it would cost several years' wages. But having taken a box of books out to a village—and remember there is a terrible shortage of petrol—I can tell you that the box was greeted with tears. The library may be a plank on bricks under a tree. And within a week there will be *literacy* ⑤ classes—people who can read teaching those who can't, citizenship classes—and in one remote village, since there were no novels written in the language Tonga, a couple of lads sat down to write novels in Tonga. There are six or so main languages in Zimbabwe and there are novels in all of them: violent, *incestuous* ⑥, full of crime and murder.

30 It is said that a people gets the government it deserves, but I do not think it is true of Zimbabwe. And we must remember that this respect and hunger for books comes, not from Mugabe's regime, but from the one before it, the whites. It is an astonishing phenomenon, this hunger for books, and it can be seen everywhere from Kenya down to the Cape of Good Hope.

本书而已。很显然，《动物庄园》就因此成为那里最受欢迎的小说了。

29 最初，我们的组织受到来自挪威的帮助，然后是瑞典的。没有这些支持，书的供应无法保障。我们尽最大的努力到处找书。要知道，买一本英国出版的好的平装书在津巴布韦要花费一个月工资，这还是在穆加贝的恐怖政权之前。现在，由于通货膨胀，这样一本书要花费几年的工资。因此，在汽油奇缺的情况下，当一箱书被带到一个村子时，人们往往会含泪相迎。而图书馆可能只是在一棵树下用砖头支起的一片木板。一周之内就会成立扫盲班——公民班，由那些识字的人教不识字的。在一个遥远的村庄，因为没有汤加语言写的小说，几个青年小伙子就开始坐下用汤加语写作。津巴布韦大约有六种主流语言，每种语言都有自己的小说：暴力的、乱伦的，充斥着犯罪和谋杀。

30 人们说，有什么样的人民，就有什么样的政府。但我觉得津巴布韦并非如此。要知道，这种对书籍的尊重和渴望不是穆加贝政权培养起来的，而是之前白人统治遗留下的。从肯尼亚南下到好望角，这种对书籍的饥渴随处可见，令人吃惊。

⑤ literacy ['lɪtərəsɪ] *n.* 读写能力；精通文学　如：basic literacy skills 基本的读写技巧

⑥ incestuous [ɪn'sestjʊəs] *adj.* 乱伦的；犯乱伦罪的

31 This links improbably with a fact: I was brought up in what was virtually a mud hut, thatched. This kind of house has been built always, everywhere there are reeds or grass, suitable mud, poles for walls. Saxon England for example. The one I was brought up in had four rooms, one beside another, and it was full of books. Not only did my parents take books from England to Africa, but my mother ordered books by post from England for her children. Books arrived in great brown paper parcels, and they were the joy of my young life. A mud hut, but full of books.

32 Even today I get letters from people living in a village that might not have electricity or running water, just like our family in our elongated mud hut. "I shall be a writer, too," they say, "because I've the same kind of house you lived in."

33 But here is the difficulty, no?

34 <u>Writing, writers, do not come out of houses without books.</u>

35 There is the gap. There is the difficulty.

36 I have been looking at the speeches by some of your recent prizewinners. Take the *magnificent*⑦ Pamuk. He said his father had 500 books. His talent did not come out of the air, he was connected with the great tradition.

37 Take V.S. Naipaul. He mentions that the Indian Vedas were close behind the memory of his family. His father encouraged him to write, and

31 事实上，我自己就是在茅草覆盖的小泥屋里长大的。这种撒克逊英格兰时代风格的房子到处都是，因为那里有芦苇和茅草，有适合造房子的泥巴和柱子。我住过的茅屋有四个房间，一个连着一个，藏书丰富。我父母从英国把书带到非洲，除此之外，我母亲还为孩子们邮购英国的图书。牛皮纸包裹的书籍一包一包地到来，成为我童年生活里的快乐。虽是陋室，却书香萦绕。

32 甚至今天我还收到村子里人们的来信，那里可能不通电、不通自来水，跟当年我们茅屋下的家庭差不多。但他们在信里说："我也要成为一个作家，因为我现在住的房子跟你当年住的一样。"

33 但是这很难实现，不是吗？

34 没有书的家庭怎么会有写作和作家？

35 这就是差距和艰难。

36 我一直在看近年来诺贝尔奖获得者的演讲。就拿了不起的帕慕克先生说吧。他说过他父亲有 500 册藏书，他的天赋不是凭空而来的，这与家里的优良传统分不开。

37 再看 V•S• 奈保尔。他也谈到印度的吠陀经深深地烙印在家人的记忆里。他父亲鼓励他写作，到了英

---

⑦ magnificent [mæg'nɪfɪsnt] *adj.* 值得赞扬的；壮丽的；华丽的　如：The Taj Mahal is a magnificent building. 泰姬陵是一座宏伟的建筑。

when he got to England he would visit the British Library. So he was close to the great tradition.

38 Let us take John Coetzee. He was not only close to the great tradition, he was the tradition: he taught literature in Cape Town. And how sorry I am that I was never in one of his classes, taught by that wonderfully brave, bold mind.

39 In order to write, in order to make literature, there must be a close connection with libraries, books, with the tradition.

40 I have a friend from Zimbabwe, a black writer. He taught himself to read from the labels on jam jars, the labels on preserved fruit cans. He was brought up in an area I have driven through, an area for rural blacks. The earth is grit and gravel, there are low sparse bushes. The huts are poor, nothing like the well cared-for huts of the better off. A school—but like one I have described. He found a discarded children's encyclopaedia on a rubbish heap and taught himself from that.

41 On Independence in 1980 there was a group of good writers in Zimbabwe, truly a nest of singing birds. They were bred in old Southern Rhodesia, under the whites—the mission schools, the better schools. Writers are not made in Zimbabwe. Not easily, not under Mugabe.

42 All the writers travelled a difficult road to literacy, let alone to becoming writers. I would say learning to read from the printed labels on

国他就会去大英图书馆。所以他的成就与伟大的传统也是分不开的。

38 还有约翰·库切，他不只是贴近这伟大传统，他自己就是经典：他在南非开普敦教授文学。遗憾的是，我从未听过他的课，那位伟大勇敢的天才讲的文学课。

39 要写作，要创造文学作品，就离不开图书馆，离不开书籍这伟大的传统。

40 我有一个黑人作家朋友，他来自津巴布韦。他是从保存下来的水果罐头的标签上自学的认字。他在一片黑人聚居的农村地区长大，我开车曾经过那里。满地的细沙碎石，还有稀疏的灌木丛。他们的小屋都很破败，跟那些富有人家的没法比。学校也就是像我描述过的那样。他在垃圾堆里找到一本被丢弃的儿童百科全书，就用那个开始自学。

41 1980 年民族独立时津巴布韦有一批优秀作家，也有百家争鸣的大好景象。他们是在旧时南罗得西亚的白人统治下长大的——接受教会学校的教育。津巴布韦并没有培养出这些作家，因为在穆加贝的统治下，这几乎不可能。

42 所有作家培养读写能力的过程都很艰辛，别更说成为作家了。我敢说从水果罐头标签和被丢弃的百科

jam jars and *discarded* [8] encyclopaedias was not uncommon. And we are talking about people hungering for standards of education beyond them, living in huts with many children—an overworked mother, a fight for food and clothing.

43 Yet despite these difficulties, writers came into being. And we should also remember that this was Zimbabwe, conquered less than a hundred years before. The grandparents of these people might have been storytellers working in the oral tradition. In one or two generations there was the transition from stories remembered and passed on, to print, to books. What an achievement.

44 Books, literally wrested from rubbish heaps and the detritus of the white man's world. But a sheaf of paper is one thing, a published book quite another. I have had several accounts sent to me of the publishing scene in Africa. Even in more privileged places like North Africa, with its different tradition, to talk of a publishing scene is a dream of possibilities.

45 Here I am talking about books never written, writers that could not make it because the publishers are not there. Voices unheard. It is not possible to estimate this great waste of talent, of potential. But even before that stage of a book's creation which demands a publisher, an advance, encouragement, there is something else lacking.

全书上学习读写也不是什么稀奇事。但是我们谈论的是怎样一个群体啊？劳累过度的母亲，带着一群孩子住在茅屋里，终日要为衣食挣扎奋斗。他们追求的教育标准远远超出了自己的生存现状。

43 但是尽管困难重重，还是有作家诞生在这片土地上。我们要知道这是在津巴布韦，将近一百年前被征服的土地。或许他们的祖父母就有口头讲故事的传统。几代相传之后，这些故事被印成了书。多么伟大的成就啊！

44 毫不夸张地说，即使是从白人世界的垃圾堆里讨来的书也是弥足珍贵的。因为一捆纸是一回事，一本出版的图书又是另一回事。我收到过几篇反映非洲出版业状况的报告。即使在稍微优越一点的北非，由于传统差异，谈论书籍出版也只是奢侈的美梦而已。

45 现在我要说说那些从未写出的书，那些无法做出一本书的作家，因为出版商不在那儿。他们的声音外界听不到。这种天赋和潜力的浪费不可估量。他们缺乏出书的平台，缺乏出版商、预付款和支持鼓励，即使有了这些，他们也还缺其他的东西。

---

⑧ discard [dɪsˈkɑːd] *vt.* 丢弃，抛弃　如：discard old beliefs 抛弃旧观念

独立的人格：以卓越思想启迪人生的诺贝尔奖大师演讲

 演讲关键词 Practical Expressions

1. idealistic soul 满怀理想
2. the nature of things 司空见惯
3. privileged school 贵族学校
4. store of literature 文学宝库
5. Reading makes a full man. 读书使人充实。
6. reign of terror 恐怖统治
7. brown paper 牛皮纸

精华佳句

1. We all know this sad story. But we do not know the end of it.

   我们都知道这样悲伤的故事。但我们并不知道故事的结局。

2. Writing, writers, do not come out of houses without books.

   没有书的家庭怎么有写作和作家？

 诺贝尔奖背后的那些趣事

睡梦中得奖

对有些人来说获诺贝尔奖也许是意料之中的事，因为他们已经期盼了太久；但有些得主即使接到了瑞典祝贺获奖的电话也不敢相信自己的耳朵。

2012 年的诺贝尔化学奖得主是美国科学家罗伯特·莱夫科维茨和布赖恩·库比尔卡。瑞典皇家科学院新闻发布会现场，主持人接通莱夫科维茨的电话，告诉他获奖的消息。不料，这位伟大的科学家正在家中戴着耳塞睡觉，太太将他叫醒，他还说："太激动了！得奖简直像做梦！"库比尔卡则表示，5 名诺贝尔奖评委的轮番祝贺之后，他才敢相信自己真的得奖了，因为"1 个人可能跟你开玩笑，但不会 5 个人同时这样做。"

Speech 2

On Not Winning the Nobel Prize (2)
远离诺贝尔奖的人们（2）

—Speech by Doris Lessing for the Nobel Prize in Literature in 2007
——英国文坛祖母多丽丝·莱辛 2007 年诺贝尔文学奖获奖演讲

名家速览 About the Author

诺贝尔奖大师	多丽丝·莱辛
奖项归属	诺贝尔文学奖
获奖理由	她以怀疑主义、激情和想象力审视一个分裂的文明，她登上了这方面女性体验的史诗巅峰。

多丽丝·莱辛早年在南非的生活经历对她后期的写作产生了非常大的影响。她的父母抱着致富的梦想迁居罗得西亚（也即今天的津巴布韦），但是在南非广袤土地上的农场生活不但不尽如人意，还很艰辛。莱辛从 16 岁开始就参加工作，先后做过电话接线员、保姆、速记员等。但她却是个从小爱幻想的孩子，她也并未浪费自己的这一天赋。她将自己的经历植入到作品中，因此她作品中的女主角常带有自传色彩，如《野草在歌唱》中的女主人公玛丽的很多遭遇都源于作者自己的生活。莱辛辛勤笔耕 50 多年，是一位不可多得的多产作家。她的作品风格也处于不断尝试和变化之中，从早期的批判现实主义，中期的心理分析和苏菲主义迷思，到晚期的"内太空"探索的科幻系列，风格独特多变，思想深邃独到，对人的生存处境有着深刻的思考和反映。

演讲现场
Speech Script

精美译文
Suggested Translation

1 Writers are often asked, How do you write? With a wordprocessor? An electric typewriter? A quill? Longhand? But the essential question is, "Have you found a space, that empty space, which should surround you when you write?" Into that space, which is like a form of listening, of attention, will come the words, the words your characters will speak, ideas—inspiration.

2 If a writer cannot find this space, then poems and stories may be *stillborn* ①. When writers talk to each other, what they discuss is always to do with this imaginative space, this other time. "Have you found it? Are you holding it fast?"

3 Let us now jump to an apparently very different scene. We are in London, one of the big cities. There is a new writer. We *cynically* ② enquire, Is she good-looking? If this is a man, charismatic? Handsome? We joke but it is not a joke.

4 This new find is *acclaimed* ③, possibly given a lot of money. The buzzing of *paparazzi* ④ begins in their poor ears. They are feted, lauded,

1 作家们经常被问：你是怎么写作的？用文字处理软件？打字机？羽毛笔？还是普通手写？但关键的问题是："你能否找到一个空间，一个供你写作、发挥的清净地方？"在那里，仿佛有人在聆听你、注视你，灵感自然而发，思绪飘舞，诉说你思想的文字倾泻而下。

2 如果一个作家找不到这样一个地方，可能他的诗歌或故事就像不幸的婴儿，生下来就是死的。当作家互相攀谈切磋时，他们讨论的往往还是这片想象的空间，"你找到了吗？你紧紧抓住了吗？"

3 现在我们看看另一幅完全不同的景象吧。伦敦，这样一个大城市，出现了一位文坛新秀。讽刺的是，我们会问：她漂亮吗？有魅力吗？帅气吗？我们开着玩笑，但这不是玩笑。

4 这样的文学新星赢得一片喝彩，可能还赚了一大把钱。摄影记者们开始在他们可怜的耳朵旁聒噪、骚

---

① stillborn ['stɪlbɔːn] *adj.* 未经实施就已失败的，行不通的　如：a stillborn plot to assassinate the President 刺杀总统的计划还未实施就已宣告失败

② cynically ['sɪnɪkəlɪ] *adv.* 爱嘲笑地；冷嘲地

③ acclaim [ə'kleɪm] *vt.* 称赞；为……喝彩，向……欢呼　如：He was acclaimed hero of the country. 大家都称赞他是国家英雄。

④ paparazzi [ˌpæpə'rætsɪ] *n.* 狗仔队（专门追逐名人，偷拍照片的摄影者或记者）

whisked ⑤ about the world. Us old ones, who have seen it all, are sorry for this **neophyte** ⑥, who has no idea of what is really happening.

5 He, she, is flattered, pleased. But ask in a year's time what he or she is thinking—I've heard them: "This is the worst thing that could have happened to me," they say.

6 Some much publicised new writers haven't written again, or haven't written what they wanted to, meant to. And we, the old ones, want to whisper into those innocent ears. "Have you still got your space? Your soul, your own and necessary place where your own voices may speak to you, you alone, where you may dream. Oh, hold onto it, don't let it go."

7 My mind is full of splendid memories of Africa which I can revive and look at whenever I want. How about those sunsets, gold and purple and orange, spreading across the sky at evening. How about butterflies and moths and bees on the **aromatic** ⑦ bushes of the Kalahari? Or, sitting on the pale grassy banks of the Zambesi, the water dark and glossy, with all the birds of Africa darting about. Yes, elephants, giraffes, lions and the rest, there were plenty of those, but how about the sky at night, still unpolluted, black and wonderful, full of **restless** ⑧ stars.

8 There are other memories too. A young

扰。他们接受款待、夸赞，世界为之喧嚣。我们这些老匠们看惯了这一切，为这个新宠儿深感遗憾，因为他对这些还一无所知。

5 他们受尽他人的百般诌媚和取悦。但是一年内你再问他们的想法，就会听到他们回答："这是我经历的最糟糕的事了。"

6 那么多被大肆宣传的文坛新秀都没有继续写作，或者没有写出他们本来想写的东西。而我们这些老人们，很想悄声对这些单纯的人说："你们的那片空间还在吗？你的灵魂，你自己独有的能让你梦想，让你自我对话的那片空间呢？抓住，别让它溜走了。"

7 我脑子里都是非洲的记忆，我可以随时回望和品味。落日余晖铺展在黄昏的天际，绚烂的金黄、浅紫和橘红；虫蛾蜂蝶飞舞在卡拉哈里的灌木丛间，芬芳阵阵，扑面而来；或是静坐于赞比河畔，河水闪烁着黯淡微光，非洲的各类鸟儿穿梭在身旁。是啊，还有大象、长颈鹿、狮子，以及很多很多……那时候还没有污染，夜晚的天空，漆黑而美妙，繁星满天。

8 记忆里当然还有其他事情。

---

⑤ whisk [(h)wɪsk] *vt.* 轰动，骚动

⑥ neophyte ['ni(:)əʊfaɪt] *n.* 新信徒；新入教者；初学者

⑦ aromatic [ˌærəʊ'mætɪk] *adj.* 芳香的，芬芳的；芳香族的

⑧ restless ['restlɪs] *adj.* 焦躁不安的；不安宁的

African man, eighteen perhaps, in tears, standing in what he hopes will be his "library". A visiting American seeing that his library had no books, had sent a crate of them. The young man had taken each one out, reverently, and wrapped them in plastic. "But," we say, "these books were sent to be read, surely?" "No," he replies, "they will get dirty, and where will I get any more?"

9 This young man wants us to send him books from England to use as teaching guides. "I only did four years in senior school," he says, "but they never taught me to teach."

10 I have seen a teacher in a school where there were no textbooks, not even a chalk for the blackboard. He taught his class of six to eighteen year olds by moving stones in the dust, chanting "Two times two is..." and so on. I have seen a girl, perhaps not more than twenty, also lacking textbooks, exercise books, biros, seen her teach the A B C by scratching the letters in the dirt with a stick, while the sun beat down and the dust swirled.

11 We are witnessing here that great hunger for education in Africa, anywhere in the Third World, or whatever we call parts of the world where parents long to get an education for their children which will take them out of poverty.

12 I would like you to imagine yourselves somewhere in Southern Africa, standing in an Indian store, in a poor area, in a time of bad drought. There is a line of people, mostly women, with every kind of container for water. This store gets a bowser of precious water every afternoon

一个非洲年轻人，18岁的样子，满含热泪站在他期望中的"图书馆"前面。一位到访的美国人看到他的图书馆没有书，就送了一箱给他。这个年轻人一本一本虔诚地将书取出，用塑料布包上。我们就说："这些书肯定要让大家读吧？""不，"他回答，"会弄脏的，要是弄脏了我去哪儿再弄啊？"

9 这个年轻人想让我们从英国给他寄些关于教学的书。他说："我只在大龄儿童学校教了四年，但他们从来不跟我说怎么教。"

10 我还在一所学校见过一位老师，那里没有课本，连一支粉笔都没有。他的学生小的6岁，大的有18岁，平时就用石头在尘土里比画着教学，做着"2×2=？"的算术。还有一位可能不到20岁的女教师，教学也没有课本、练习本和圆珠笔。她用小木棍在尘埃里写写画画，教大家A、B、C，炽热的太阳烘烤着，尘土飞旋。

11 在非洲，在第三世界国家，甚至世界的任何地方，我们看到太多对教育的渴望，那里的父母热切期望着教育能带他们的孩子逃脱贫穷。

12 大家可以想象一下，在南非某个正遭受着旱灾的穷困地方，在一家印度商店前面。一群人，大多数是妇女，排着队，拿着各种容器。这个商店每天下午从镇上运来一车水，这些人就在这里等那车宝贵的饮用水。

from the town, and here the people wait.

13 The Indian is standing with the heels of his hands pressed down on the counter, and he is watching a black woman, who is bending over a wadge of paper that looks as if it has been torn from a book. She is reading *Anna Karenin*. She is reading slowly, mouthing the words. It looks a difficult book. This is a young woman with two little children clutching at her legs. She is pregnant. The Indian is distressed, because the young woman's headscarf, which should be white, is yellow with dust. Dust lies between her breasts and on her arms. This man is distressed because of the lines of people, all thirsty. He doesn't have enough water for them. He is angry because he knows there are people dying out there, beyond the dust clouds. His older brother had been here holding the fort, but he had said he needed a break, had gone into town, really rather ill, because of the drought.

14 This man is curious. He says to the young woman, "What are you reading?"

15 "It is about Russia," says the girl.

16 "Do you know where Russia is?" He hardly knows himself.

17 The young woman looks straight at him, full of dignity, though her eyes are red from dust, "I was best in the class. My teacher said I was best."

18 The young woman resumes her reading. She wants to get to the end of the paragraph. The Indian looks at the two little children and reaches for some Fanta, but the mother says, "Fanta

13 印度老板双手撑在柜台上站着，他看着一位黑人妇女。那女人正躬身盯着地上的一沓纸，像是从一本书上撕下的。她在读《安娜·卡列尼娜》。她读得很慢，喃喃地念着，看来这本书有点难。女人身旁两个孩子紧紧地扯着她的裤腿。她还怀着身孕。印度人感到难过，因为这妇女的白头巾已经被尘土染黄了，胸口、胳膊上也都是灰尘。同时，让这老板难过的还有这排着长龙的人们，他们站在风尘中，个个口渴难忍，而他没有足够的水给他们喝。他感到愤慨，他知道远处——在这扑朔的尘土之外还有人因为口渴已经奄奄一息。他哥哥曾在这里帮他看守，但现在因为大旱他也病得很厉害，正在镇上休息。

14 这位老板很好奇，就问那妇女："你在读什么？"

15 "是关于俄国的，"她回答。

16 "你知道俄国在哪儿吗？"连他自己都不太清楚。

17 这妇女直视着他，瞪着被尘土磨红的双眼，充满自尊，义正词严："我是班里最好的学生，老师说了，我是最好的。"

18 说完，年轻的女人又开始读她的书。她想把这一段看完。印度人看了看两个小孩，给他们拿了些芬达，但妈妈却说："芬达只会让他们

makes them thirstier."

19　The Indian knows he shouldn't do this but he reaches down to a great plastic container beside him, behind the counter, and pours out two mugs of water, which he hands to the children. He watches while the girl looks at her children drinking, her mouth moving. He gives her a mug of water. It hurts him to see her drinking it, so painfully thirsty is she.

20　Now she hands him her own plastic water container, which he fills. The young woman and the children watch him closely so that he doesn't spill any.

21　She is bending again over the book. She reads slowly. The paragraph fascinates her and she reads it again.

22　"Varenka, with her white kerchief over her black hair, surrounded by the children and gaily and good-humouredly busy with them, and at the same visibly excited at the possibility of an offer of marriage from a man she cared for, looked very attractive. Koznyshev walked by her side and kept casting admiring glances at her. Looking at her, he recalled all the delightful things he had heard from her lips, all the good he knew about her, and became more and more conscious that the feeling he had for her was something rare, something he had felt but once before, long, long ago, in his early youth. The joy of being near her increased step by step, and at last reached such a point that, as he put a huge birch mushroom with a slender stalk and up-curling top into her basket, he looked into her eyes and, noting the flush of

更渴。"

19　印度人知道不应该这么做，但他还是在柜台旁边的塑料桶里倒出两小杯给孩子递了过去。他看见孩子喝水时，这妈妈看着，自己的嘴也不觉地在颤动。于是他给妈妈也倒了一杯。看着她喝水时渴得难受的样子，他觉得无比心痛。

20　这时她把自己的塑料桶递给这位印度老板，他又给她盛满了。盛水时妇女和孩子紧紧盯着他，生怕他把水洒了。

21　过后她再次俯身看起书来。她读得很慢。这段文字简直让她着迷，她又读了一遍。

22　"瓦莲卡的黑发上包着一条白头巾，显得很迷人，身边环绕着一群孩子，她正亲昵而快活地为他们忙着。显然，由于她钟爱的男子可能向她求婚，她兴奋不已，模样儿楚楚动人。科兹内舍夫和她并肩走着，不住地向她抛去爱慕的眼光。望着她，他回忆起她说过的一切动人的话语，和她的一切优点。他越来越意识到，他对她的感情是非常特殊的，这种感情，他在很久很久以前，在他的青年时代也只感受过一次。靠近她所产生的愉悦感不断加强，达到不同寻常的地步。当他发现一个茎秆并不粗壮、伞盖却很大的桦树菌时，他采摘下来放到她的提篮里，望着她的眼睛，看到她满脸又惊又喜的红晕，他自己也

glad and frightened agitation that suffused her face, he was confused himself, and in silence gave her a smile that said too much."

23 This lump of print is lying on the counter, together with some old copies of magazines, some pages of newspapers with pictures of girls in bikinis.

24 It is time for the woman to leave the haven of the Indian store, and set off back along the four miles to her village. Outside, the lines of waiting women clamour and complain. But still the Indian lingers. He knows what it will cost this girl—going back home, with the two clinging children. He would give her the piece of prose that so fascinates her, but he cannot really believe this splinter of a girl with her great belly can really understand it.

25 Why is perhaps a third of *Anna Karenin* here on this counter in a remote Indian store? It is like this.

26 A certain high official, from the United Nations as it happens, bought a copy of this novel in a bookshop before he set out on his journey to cross several oceans and seas. On the plane, settled in his business class seat, he tore the book into three parts. He looked around his fellow passengers as he did this, knowing he would see looks of shock, curiosity, but some of amusement. When he was settled, his seat belt tight, he said aloud to whomever could hear, "I always do this when I've a long trip. You don't want to have to hold up some heavy great book." The novel

感到一阵迷乱，便默默地向她微笑，这是无声胜有声的语言。"

23 这份读物摆在柜台上，上面还有一些旧杂志，几页报纸印着些穿比基尼的摩登女郎。

24 是时候离开这个避难所似的印度商店，返回几英里外她自己的村子了。外面排队等候的妇女们在叫喊、抱怨。但这位印度人还站在那里观望。他知道这个拖着两个孩子的女人回家的路程会有多艰难。他想把那半本令她着迷的小说送给她，却不知道这个挺着大肚子的瘦小女人能不能真正读懂。

25 那么这本可能只有三分之一的《安娜·卡列尼娜》是怎么出现在这个遥远的印度商店的柜台上的呢？事情是这样的。

26 联合国的一位高官在漂洋过海开始他的旅行之前，碰巧在书店里买了这本小说。飞机上，他进了商务舱后，就把这本书撕成了三份。他一边撕，一边看周围的乘客，他就知道会看到各种惊诧、好奇和觉得有趣的表情。坐稳系好安全带之后，他大声说，好像要所有人都能听到一样："我长途旅行的时候都会这样做。你们也不会想带这么重的大部头书的。"这本书是平装本，但确实，又厚又长。这个人已经习惯了自己说话时有

was a paperback, but, true, it is a long book. This man is well used to people listening when he spoke. "I always do this, travelling," he confided. "Travelling at all these days, is hard enough." And as soon as people were settling down, he opened his part of *Anna Karenin*, and read. When people looked his way, curiously or not, he confided in them. "No, it really is the only way to travel." He knew the novel, liked it, and this original mode of reading did add spice to what was after all a well known book.

27 When he reached the end of a section of the book, he called the air hostess, and sent the chapters back to his secretary, travelling in the cheaper seats. This caused much interest, condemnation, certainly curiosity, every time a section of the great Russian novel arrived, mutilated but readable, in the back part of the plane. Altogether, this clever way of reading *Anna Karenin* makes an impression, and probably no one there would forget it.

28 Meanwhile, in the Indian store, the young woman is holding on to the counter, her little children clinging to her skirts. She wears jeans, since she is a modern woman, but over them she has put on the heavy woollen skirt, part of the traditional dress of her people: her children can easily cling onto its thick folds.

29 She sends a thankful look to the Indian, whom she knew liked her and was sorry for her, and she steps out into the blowing clouds. The children are past crying, and their throats are full of dust.

人在听了。人们都坐下之后，他就打开他的那部分《安娜·卡列尼娜》开始读。当人们好奇或者随便怎样向他看一眼时，他就对他们说，"我经常旅行，"他承认，"长途旅行太难受了。但这是唯一的旅行方式了，不是吗？"他先前就知道这本小说，很喜欢，而且这种独特的阅读方式确实给这本名著添了不少色彩。

27 手上的这一部分读完了，他叫来乘务员，把这几章拿给他坐在经济舱里的秘书。每次这撕破的但尚可阅读的伟大的俄国小说到来时，就会引起经济舱里一阵骚动，有非议也有好奇。总之，用这种聪明的方法读《安娜·卡列尼娜》的确让人印象深刻，可能现场每个人都不会忘记。

28 而另一幅画面则是：在这个印度商店里，这位年轻的妇女靠着柜台，两个孩子紧紧地抓着她的裙摆。作为一个现代女性，她穿着牛仔裤，但在牛仔裤上又加了一层厚重的当地人传统羊绒短裙。这样孩子很容易就能抓住厚厚的裙褶。

29 她感激地看了印度老板一眼，她知道老板喜欢而且同情她。她走出店铺，踏进了大风吹起的漫天尘土里。孩子们不再哭泣，他们的喉咙里灌满了尘土。

30 This was hard, oh yes, it was hard, this stepping, one foot after another, through the dust that lay in soft *deceiving*⑨ mounds under her feet. Hard, but she was used to hardship, was she not? Her mind was on the story she had been reading. She was thinking: She is just like me, in her white headscarf, and she is looking after children, too. I could be her, that Russian girl. And the man there, he loves her and will ask her to marry him. She had not finished more than that one paragraph. Yes, she thinks, a man will come for me, and take me away from all this, take me and the children, yes, he will love me and look after me.

31 She steps on. The can of water is heavy on her shoulders. On she goes. The children can hear the water slopping about. Half way she stops, sets down the can. Her children are *whimpering*⑩ and touching it. She thinks that she cannot open it, because dust would blow in. There is no way she can open the can until she gets home.

32 "Wait," she tells her children, "wait."

33 She has to pull herself together and go on.

34 She thinks, my teacher said there is a library, bigger than the supermarket, a big building and it is full of books. The young woman is smiling as she moves on, the dust blowing in her face. I am clever, she thinks. Teacher said I am clever. The cleverest in the school—she

30 她一步一个脚印，走得很艰难，是的，步履维艰，穿行在那软绵绵的土堆里。艰难，但她已经习惯了，不是吗？她的心思还在刚读过的故事里。她在想着，她跟我一样呢，也戴着白头巾，也在照看孩子。我也可以成为她——那个俄国女孩——那样的。而书里的那个男人爱着她，要向她求婚。她只看到了这里。是的，她想，会有一个男人为我而来，带我远离这里，带着我的孩子，是的，他会爱我，照顾我。

31 她继续向前走。一罐水沉重地压在她肩膀上。但她仍然继续跋涉着。孩子们可以听见水在罐子里来回泼溅。走到一半时她停了下来，放下水罐。孩子在摸着水罐啜泣。但她知道她不能打开它，因为尘土会吹进去。不到家她绝不能打开罐子。

32 "等一等，"她对孩子说，"再等等吧。"

33 她强拖着自己站起来，继续前行。

34 她在想，老师说过有一个图书馆比超市还大，一个塞满了书的大房子。她一边走一边微笑，灰尘扑打着她的面颊。我很聪明，她想，老师也说了我很聪明。我是学校里最聪明的，这是她说的。我的孩子也会像我

---

⑨ deceive [dɪ'siːv] *vt.* 欺骗

⑩ whimper ['(h)wɪmpə] *vi.* 呜咽；啜泣；低声抱怨

said I was. My children will be clever, like me. I will take them to the library, the place full of books, and they will go to school, and they will be teachers—my teacher told me I could be a teacher. My children will live far from here, earning money. They will live near the big library and enjoy a good life.

35 You may ask how that piece of the Russian novel ever ended up on that counter in the Indian store?

36 It would make a pretty story. Perhaps someone will tell it.

37 On goes that poor girl, held upright by thoughts of the water she will give her children once home, and drink a little of herself. On she goes, through the dreaded dusts of an African drought.

38 We are a jaded lot; we are in our threatened world. We are good for irony and even cynicism. Some words and ideas we hardly use, so worn out have they become. But we may want to restore some words that have lost their potency.

39 We have a treasure-house of literature, going back to the Egyptians, the Greeks, the Romans. It is all there, this wealth of literature, to be discovered again and again by whoever is lucky enough to come upon it. A treasure. Suppose it did not exist. How impoverished, how empty we would be.

40 We own a legacy of languages, poems, histories, and it is not one that will ever be exhausted. It is there, always.

41 We have a bequest of stories, tales from

一样聪明的。我会带他们去图书馆，去那个到处都是书的地方，他们会上学，将来会当老师——我的老师说我可以成为一名教师的。他们要远离这里，去挣钱，去住在大图书馆附近，过上好日子。

35 你们可能会问，那本俄国小说的残片怎么就到了印度商店的柜台上?

36 这是一个动人的故事，将来会有人讲的。

37 这个可怜的妇女继续走着，满脑子都想着回家后她要给孩子喝水，自己也要喝一点。她走着，一步步穿过南非旱季可怕的沙尘。

38 在这个面临威胁的世界里，我们是疲惫不堪的一群人，我们擅长冷嘲热讽。有些词、有些思想我们很少提及，它们已经成了陈词滥调。但可能我们还是要恢复一些使用较少的词。

39 我们有一个珍贵的文学宝库，可以一直上溯到古埃及、古希腊和古代罗马时代。这文学的财富就在那里，等着被幸运儿一次又一次地发现。这真的是财富。试想如果没有这个宝库，生活将会多么贫乏，多么空虚。

40 我们拥有丰富的语言、诗歌和历史的遗产，它们始终都在那里，取之不竭。

41 还有从知名或不知名的老一

the old storytellers, some of whose names we know, but some not. The storytellers go back and back, to a clearing in the forest where a great fire burns, and the old shamans dance and sing, for our heritage of stories began in fire, magic, the spirit world. And that is where it is held, today.

42 Ask any modern storyteller and they will say there is always a moment when they are touched with fire, with what we like to call inspiration, and this goes back and back to the beginning of our race, to the great winds that shaped us and our world.

43 The storyteller is deep inside every one of us. The story-maker is always with us. Let us suppose our world is ravaged by war, by the horrors that we all of us easily imagine. Let us suppose floods wash through our cities, the seas rise. But the storyteller will be there, for it is our imaginations which shape us, keep us, create us—for good and for ill. It is our stories that will recreate us, when we are torn, hurt, even destroyed. It is the storyteller, the dream-maker, the myth-maker, that is our phoenix, that represents us at our best, and at our most creative.

44 That poor girl trudging through the dust, dreaming of an education for her children, do we think that we are better than she is—we, stuffed full of food, our cupboards full of clothes, stifling in our superfluities?

45 I think it is that girl, and the women who were talking about books and an education when they had not eaten for three days, that may yet define us.

辈人那里流传下来的故事盛宴。这些讲故事的人可以追溯到很久很久以前，可能是在一片森林里，人们点着篝火，古老的萨满巫师载歌载舞。因为我们这些故事的起源就与火、魔力和神灵有关。今天的一切也是从那里开始的。

42 询问现代讲故事的人，他们会说总有那么一瞬间，他们灵光一闪就触到了火焰，也就是我们说的灵感。而这要追溯到人类的起源，正是远古时代的伟大风气成就了今天的世界。

43 每个人内心深处都有一个讲故事的人。编故事的人随处可见。让我们展开想象，假如世界被战争践踏、被极易想象的恐怖事件破坏；或者洪水淹没了城市，海平面上升。不管怎样，讲故事的人一直都在，因为无论世界好坏，是我们的想象力在塑造、延续、创造着我们。当我们遭受重创，甚至毁灭时，这些故事使我们再生。这些讲故事的人、造梦者、编造神话传说的人是我们劫后不死的长生鸟，他们代表了人类的最佳状态，把人类的创造力发挥到了极致。

44 那个一路跋涉在黄沙尘土中的女孩，梦想着自己的孩子能接受教育。而我们除了衣食无忧，还享用着过剩的奢侈品——我们比她强吗？

45 我觉得，我们应该被那个尘土里的女孩和那些三天没有进食还在谈论书本和教育的妇女们重新定义。

独立的人格：以卓越思想启迪人生的诺贝尔奖大师演讲

演讲关键词 Practical Expressions

1. electric typewriter 电动打字机
2. new writer 文坛新秀
3. business class seat 商务舱座位
4. air hostess 空中小姐
5. a legacy of histories 历史遗产
6. be stuffed full of food, cupboards full of clothes 衣食无忧
7. dance and sing 载歌载舞

精华佳句

1. We own a legacy of languages, poems, histories, and it is not one that will ever be exhausted. It is there, always.

   我们拥有丰富的语言、诗歌和历史的遗产，它们始终都在那里，取之不竭。

2. I think it is that girl, and the women who were talking about books and an education when they had not eaten for three days, that may yet define us.

   我觉得，我们应该被那个尘土里的女孩和那些三天没有进食还在谈论书本和教育的妇女们重新定义。

诺贝尔奖背后的那些趣事

"蠢材" 也能得奖?

英国医学教授约翰·格登和日本医学教授山中伸弥是 2012 年诺贝尔医学奖得主。但成功却来得并不容易。

15 岁时，格登在英国著名贵族学校伊顿公学求学。当时，250 名学生当中，格登的生物成绩倒数第一，其他科目成绩也都不甚理想，他被同学讥笑为"科学蠢材"。在 1949 年的学校成绩报告单中，一名老师给格登的评语是这样的："我相信格登想成为科学家，但以他目前的学业表现，这个想法非常荒谬，他连简单的生物知识都学不会，根本不可能成为专家，对于他个人以及想教导他的人来说，这根本是浪费时间。"尽管饱受老师、同学的讥笑和打击，格登仍然坚持梦想，执着于自己对生物学的热爱。至今，这份成绩报告仍被格登放在自己的办公桌上，他时而以此自娱。

格登说："每当遇到什么麻烦，比如实验无法进行下去等情况时，我都会看看这份评价，来提醒自己要努力坚持，不然真的就被以前的老师说中了。"

Speech 3
What Desires Are Important?（Excerpt）
那些影响深远的欲望（节选）

—Speech by Bertrand Russell for the Nobel Prize in Literature in 1950
——多才多艺的天才学者伯特兰·罗素 1950 年诺贝尔文学奖获奖演讲

 名家速览 About the Author

诺贝尔奖大师	伯特兰·罗素
奖项归属	诺贝尔文学奖
获奖作品	《婚姻与道德》
获奖理由	表彰他所写的捍卫人道主义理想和思想自由的多种多样意义重大的作品。
知名演讲链接	伯特兰·罗素反核武器演讲

伯特兰·罗素（Bertrand Russell，1872—1970）是英国哲学家、数学家、逻辑学家、历史学家。他是 20 世纪西方最著名、影响最大的学者及和平主义社会活动家之一，他参与创建了分析哲学，此外他还在认识论、形而上学、伦理学、政治哲学和哲学史方面做出过贡献。他与怀特海合著的《数学原理》对逻辑学、数学、集合论、语言学和分析哲学有着巨大影响。1950 年，罗素获得诺贝尔文学奖，他的代表作品有《幸福之路》、《西方哲学史》、《数学原理》、《物的分析》等。罗素出生于英国一个辉格党贵族世家。其祖父约翰·罗素勋爵在维多利亚时代曾两度出任首相，并获封伯爵爵位。父亲安伯力·罗素是一位激进的自由主义者。4 岁时罗素失去双亲，由祖母抚养。祖母在道德方面对罗素要求极为严格，精神上无所畏惧，敢于蔑视习俗，曾将"不可随众行恶"（出自《圣经·旧约·出埃及记》23:2）题赠给罗素，这句话成为罗素一生的座右铭。作为一位哲学家，罗素在本篇演讲中就人类的欲望，以及这些欲望在政治领域发挥的强大作用发表了深刻的见解，他独到精辟的分析令人不禁叫绝。

演讲现场
Speech Script

精美译文
Suggested Translation

1 I have chosen this subject for my lecture tonight because I think that most current discussions of politics and political theory take insufficient account of psychology. Economic facts, population statistics, constitutional organization, and so on, are **set forth**① **minutely**②. There is no difficulty in finding out how many South Koreans and how many North Koreans there were when the Korean War began. If you will look into the right books you will be able to **ascertain**③ what was their average income per head, and what were the sizes of their respective armies. But if you want to know what sort of person a Korean is, and whether there is any appreciable difference between a North Korean and a South Korean; if you wish to know what they respectively want out of life, what are their discontents, what their hopes and what their fears; in a word, what it is that, as they say, "makes them tick", you will look through the reference books in vain. And so you cannot tell whether the South Koreans are enthusiastic about UNO, or would prefer union with their cousins in the North. Nor can you guess whether they are willing to **forgo**④ land reform for the privilege

1 用这个话题来做今晚的演讲，是因为据我所见，当今大多数关于政治及政治理论的讨论都没有充分考虑到心理学。经济情况、人口数据、宪法组织等，这些都能详尽地提出。要查明朝鲜战争时期韩国和朝鲜的人口数量并不难。而且只要你对了书，你就能确定当时这两个国家各自的人均收入和军队规模。但是如果你想通过查阅参考书了解朝鲜半岛的居民，知道朝鲜人和韩国人之间存在的差异，获悉他们各自的生活愿望，以及他们的嫌恶、期许和恐惧，还有一切构成了他们生活方式的东西，那只能是徒劳的。因此你不知道韩国人是更热心于联合国组织还是更喜欢与他们北边的兄弟联盟。你也无法获知他们是否愿意为了获取投票权而放弃土地改革，即使他们从未听说过那位需要他们选票的政治家。正是因为那些安坐在遥远首都的杰出人士忽视了这些问题，才会引发诸多令人失望的后果。要想使政治更加科学，更易掌控，我们就应该改变以往的政治思维，去探索人类行为背后的动机和缘由。饥饿

---

① set forth 阐述，提出　如：set forth one's view 陈述某人的观点

② minutely ['mɪnɪtlɪ] *adv.* 详细地，精密地

③ ascertain [ˌæsəˈteɪn] *vt.* 查明，断定　如：It's difficult to ascertain the coal deposits. 煤储量很难查明。

④ forgo [fɔːˈgəʊ] *vt.* 放弃，对……断念

of voting for some politician they have never heard of. It is neglect of such questions by the eminent men who sit in remote capitals, that so frequently causes disappointment. If politics is to become scientific, and if the event is not to be constantly surprising, it is *imperative* ⑤ that our political thinking should penetrate more deeply into the springs of human action. What is the influence of hunger upon slogans? How does their effectiveness fluctuate with the number of calories in your diet? If one man offers you democracy and another offers you a bag of grain, at what stage of starvation will you prefer the grain to the vote? Such questions are far too little considered. However, let us, for the present, forget the Koreans, and consider the human race.

2 All human activity is *prompted* ⑥ by desire. There is a wholly fallacious theory advanced by some earnest moralists *to the effect that* ⑦ it is possible to resist desire *in the interests of* ⑧ duty and moral principle. I say this is fallacious, not because no man ever acts from a sense of duty, but because duty has no hold on him unless he desires to be dutiful. If you wish to know what men will do, you must know not only, or principally, their material circumstances, but rather the whole system of their desires with their relative strengths.

对政治口号有何影响？政治宣言的有效性与人体内能量的变化有何关系？如果一个人给你民主，另一个人供你粮食，你在饥饿达到什么程度时才会舍民主而取食物呢？人们真的很少考虑这些问题。然而，现在，让我们暂时忘掉韩国人和朝鲜人来考虑一下整个人类吧。

2 所有的人类活动都由欲望驱使而产生。一些较真的道德家曾提出一个完全错误的论断，认为责任和道德准则有可能抵抗欲望的诱惑。我说这是一个谬误，并不是说没有人会出于责任而行动，而是因为如果没有履行责任的欲望，他也就不去行使责任了。如果你想知道人们将会做什么，你不仅或者说主要要了解他们的物质现状，更要清楚他们的欲望和相对力量构成的整个体系。

⑤ imperative [ɪmˈperətɪv] *adj.* 必要的，势在必行的

⑥ prompt [prɒmpt] *vt.* 激起，引起，促使　如：Her question was prompted by her worries about future. 她提那个问题是因为她对前途十分忧虑。

⑦ to the effect that... 意思是，大意是

⑧ in the interest of... 为了……

3 There are some desires which, though very powerful, have not, as a rule, any great political importance. Most men at some period of their lives desire to marry, but as a rule they can satisfy this desire without having to take any political action. There are, of course, exceptions; the rape of the Sabine women is a case in point. And the development of northern Australia is seriously impeded by the fact that the vigorous young men who ought to do the work dislike being wholly deprived of female society. But such cases are unusual, and in general the interest that men and women take in each other has little influence upon politics.

4 The desires that are politically important may be divided into a primary and a secondary group. In the primary group come the necessities of life: food and shelter and clothing. When these things become very scarce, there is no limit to the efforts that men will make, or to the violence that they will display, in the hope of securing them. It is said by students of the earliest history that, on four separate occasions, drought in Arabia caused the population of that country to overflow into surrounding regions, with immense effects, political, cultural, and religious. The last of these four occasions was the rise of Islam. The gradual spread of Germanic tribes from southern Russia to England, and thence to San Francisco, had similar motives. Undoubtedly the desire for food has been, and still is, one of the main causes of great political events.

5 **But man differs from other animals in**

3 有些欲望尽管很强大，但通常并无重要的政治意义。就像大多数人都会在他们人生的某个阶段很想结婚，但他们通常并不需要采取任何政治行为去满足这个欲望。当然也有例外，被掳拐的萨宾妇女就是一个例子。还有澳大利亚北部地区的发展严重受阻，就是因为本该去开荒拓土的男性不愿意离开女性社会。但是这种例子并不多，而且一般男女之间对彼此的兴趣也极少产生政治影响。

4 政治影响力巨大的欲望可以分为两个层次。第一层来自于生活基本需求：衣食住所需之物。一旦这些物品短缺，人们会竭尽全力、不惜一切代价去使它们得到保障，甚至会诉诸暴力。研究早期历史的学者们表示，在四个不同的历史时期，阿拉伯半岛的干旱导致其人口向周边地区外流，由此产生了极大的政治、文化和宗教影响。在这四次人口外流的最后一次中诞生了伊斯兰教。除此之外，俄国南部的日耳曼部落逐渐向英格兰扩散，继而向旧金山移民也是基于相同的原因。无疑，对食物的欲望一直都是重大政治事件的主要原因之一。

5 但是，人区别于动物的一个

one very important respect, and that is that he has some desires which are, so to speak, infinite, which can never be fully gratified, and which would keep him restless even in Paradise. The **boa constrictor** [9], when he has had an adequate meal, goes to sleep, and does not wake until he needs another meal. Human beings, for the most part, are not like this. When the Arabs, who had been used to living sparingly on a few dates, acquired the riches of the Eastern Roman Empire, and dwelt in palaces of almost unbelievable luxury, they did not, on that account, become inactive. Hunger could no longer be a motive, for Greek slaves supplied them with exquisite viands at the slightest nod. But other desires kept them active: four in particular, which we can label **acquisitiveness** [10], rivalry, vanity, and love of power.

6 Acquisitiveness—the wish to possess as much as possible of goods, or the title to goods— is a motive which, I suppose, has its origin in a combination of fear with the desire for necessaries. I once befriended two little girls from Estonia, who had narrowly escaped death from starvation in a famine. They lived in my family, and of course had plenty to eat. But they spent all their leisure visiting neighbouring farms and stealing potatoes, which they hoarded. Rockefeller, who in his infancy had experienced great poverty, spent his adult life in a similar manner. Similarly the Arab chieftains on their silken Byzantine divans could not forget the desert, and hoarded riches far beyond any possible physical need. But whatever

主要方面就在于，人的有些欲望是无止境的，可以说永远得不到满足，即使到了天堂也会让他焦虑不安。大蟒蛇在饱餐之后就会睡去，一直睡到需要再次进食才醒来。而人类在大多数情况下并非如此。比如，习惯了以几颗枣子节俭度日的阿拉伯人，在占领东罗马帝国，获得巨额财富，住进奢华至极的宫殿之后，他们并没有因此就懈怠懒惰起来。饥饿固然不再是动力了，因为只要稍稍一点头，希腊奴隶就会为他们奉上精致的食物。但是还有其他的欲望使他们保持活力，尤其是这四种，我们可以称之为占有欲、竞争欲、虚荣心和对权力的迷恋。

6 占有欲——总是希望尽可能多地拥有物品或其所有权——我认为这可能源于对必需品既渴望又恐惧的心理。我曾经帮助过两个从饥荒中勉强幸存的爱沙尼亚女孩。她们住在我家里，肯定有充足的食物。但是她们一有空闲时间就要去附近的农场参观，去偷些土豆储藏起来。洛克菲勒由于小时候饱受贫苦，成人后他也一直保持着与当年类似的生活方式。同样地，阿拉伯的酋长即使坐在东罗马柔软的丝绸长沙发里，也还对沙漠念念不忘，集聚的钱财远远超过所需。不管对占有欲进行怎样的心理分析，都无法否认它是人类最大的动力之

---

⑨ boa constrictor ['bəuə kən'striktə] n. 大蟒蛇   ⑩ acquisitiveness [ə'kwizitivnis] n. 占有欲

独立的人格：以卓越思想启迪人生的诺贝尔奖大师演讲

may be the psychoanalysis of acquisitiveness, no one can deny that it is one of the great motives—especially among the more powerful, for, as I said before, it is one of the infinite motives. However much you may acquire, you will always wish to acquire more; **_satiety_** [11] is a dream which will always elude you.

7 But acquisitiveness, although it is the mainspring of the capitalist system, is by no means the most powerful of the motives that survive the conquest of hunger. Rivalry is a much stronger motive. Over and over again in Mohammedan history, dynasties have come to grief because the sons of a sultan by different mothers could not agree, and in the resulting civil war universal ruin resulted. The same sort of thing happens in modern Europe. When the British Government very unwisely allowed the Kaiser to be present at a naval review at Spithead, the thought which arose in his mind was not the one which we had intended. What he thought was, "I must have a Navy as good as Grandmamma's". And from this thought have sprung all our subsequent troubles. The world would be a happier place than it is if acquisitiveness were always stronger than rivalry. But in fact, a great many men will cheerfully face impoverishment if they can thereby secure complete ruin for their rivals. Hence the present level of taxation.

8 Vanity is a motive of immense potency. Anyone who has much to do with children knows how they are constantly performing some antic,

———特别是比较强大的动力，因为正如我之前所说，占有欲也是无止境的动力。不管你拥有多少，你都还想占有更多；满足就像一个梦，一个永远也得不到的梦。

7 占有欲虽然是资本主义的主要推动力，但它绝不是能与饥饿相提并论的最强动机。竞争欲是更大的一个动机。在伊斯兰国家历史上，一个又一个王朝土崩瓦解，就是因为统治者那些同父异母的儿子之间意见不一，互不服输，导致内战爆发，从而造成了巨大灾难。类似的事情在现代欧洲也有发生。英国政府曾傻傻地邀请德国皇帝参加海上阅兵，但他在阅兵现场的想法与之前已经大相径庭了。他想的是，"我得拥有一支强大的军队，像当年祖母的军队那样威力无比。"就是这个想法引发了之后的一系列灾难。如果占有欲永远都比竞争欲强，这世界将会更加幸福快乐。然而事实却是，大多数人为了毁灭竞争对手而甘愿忍受贫穷。这也是现在税收居高不下的原因。

8 虚荣心也是一个威力巨大的动机。任何跟孩子接触较多的人都知道，他们总是不断地做出滑稽的动

---

⑪ satiety [səˈtaɪətɪ] *n.* 满足

and saying "Look at me". "Look at me" is one of the most fundamental desires of the human heart. It can take innumerable forms, from *buffoonery* ⑫ to the pursuit of posthumous fame. There was a Renaissance Italian princeling who was asked by the priest on his deathbed if he had anything to repent of. "Yes", he said, "there is one thing. On one occasion I had a visit from the Emperor and the Pope simultaneously. I took them to the top of my tower to see the view, and I neglected the opportunity to throw them both down, which would have given me immortal fame." History does not relate whether the priest gave him absolution. One of the troubles about vanity is that it grows with what it feeds on. The more you are talked about, the more you will wish to be talked about. The condemned murderer who is allowed to see the account of his trial in the press is indignant if he finds a newspaper which has reported it inadequately. And the more he finds about himself in other newspapers, the more indignant he will be with the one whose reports are meagre. Politicians and literary men are in the same case. And the more famous they become, the more difficult the press-cutting agency finds it to satisfy them. It is scarcely possible to exaggerate the influence of vanity throughout the range of human life, from the child of three to the potentate at whose frown the world trembles. Mankind have even committed the impiety of attributing similar desires to the Deity, whom they imagine *avid* ⑬

作，然后对别人说"看我，看我"。"看我"是人类内心最基本的欲望之一。它可能有无数种表现方式，从插科打诨博人欢笑到对身后名的不懈追求。曾经有一位文艺复兴时期的意大利王子，在临终时牧师问他是否还有什么事需要忏悔。"有的，"他说，"有一件事。有一次国王和大主教同时来拜访我，我带他们登到塔顶赏景，我真后悔没有抓住时机将他们两个都推下去，那样我就能享有不朽的名声了。"历史并没有记载牧师是否赦免了这位王子。关于虚荣心，麻烦之一就是，它会随着所依托之物增长。你的名气越大，你越是希望人们更多地谈论你。被判了刑的杀人犯，在公布自己罪行的发布会上若看见哪家报纸对他的报道不够充分，他也会愤愤不平。而且在其他报纸上看到关于自己的内容越多，他就对报道不足的报纸越憎恨。政治家和作家也一样。这些人名气越大，媒体越难满足他们。从三岁小儿到威震四方的当权者，虚荣心在人们生活中的影响力无论怎么夸大都不过分。人们侥幸地把这种虚荣心归根于上帝，毕竟我们的造物主也贪婪地享受着世人的赞美。

⑫ buffoonery [bə'fu:nərɪ] *n.* 打诨，滑稽
⑬ avid ['ævɪd] *adj.* 渴望的　如：avid for... 对……很渴望

for continual praise.

9 But great as is the influence of the motives we have been considering, there is one which outweighs them all. I mean the love of power. Love of power is closely akin to vanity, but it is not by any means the same thing. What vanity needs for its satisfaction is glory, and it is easy to have glory without power. The people who enjoy the greatest glory in the United States are film stars, but they can be put in their place by the Committee for Un-American Activities, which enjoys no glory whatever. In England, the King has more glory than the Prime Minister, but the Prime Minister has more power than the King. Many people prefer glory to power, but on the whole these people have less effect upon the course of events than those who prefer power to glory. When Blücher, in 1814, saw Napoleon's palaces, he said, "Wasn't he a fool to have all this and to go running after Moscow." Napoleon, who certainly was not destitute of vanity, preferred power when he had to choose. To Blücher, this choice seemed foolish. Power, like vanity, is insatiable. Nothing short of omnipotence could satisfy it completely. And as it is especially the vice of energetic men, the causal efficacy of love of power is out of all proportion to its frequency. It is, indeed, by far the strongest motive in the lives of important men.

10 Love of power is greatly increased by the experience of power, and this applies to petty power as well as to that of potentates. In the happy days before 1914, when well-to-do ladies

9 尽管以上考虑的这些因素影响力已经够大了，但还有一种动机比它们更威猛。那就是对权力的迷恋。迷恋权力跟虚荣心十分类似，但肯定不能将二者混为一谈。荣耀使虚荣心得以满足，但荣耀却并不需要权力来保障。在美国，电影明星享有最高荣耀，但他们的地位有时候却由非美活动委员会说了算，这个委员会可不享受什么荣誉。在英国，国王比首相享有更高荣耀，但首相比国王拥有更大的权力。比起权力，很多人更喜欢荣耀，但总体上这些人对大事的影响力可不如那些更迷恋权力的人。1814年，布吕歇尔看了拿破仑的宫殿后说道："拥有这么多了还去攻伐俄国，这个人是不是傻子？"拿破仑得到的虚荣并不少，但若要他选择，他则更向往权力。对布吕歇尔来说，这样的选择似乎很愚蠢。权力，就像虚荣心一样，是永远也无法彻底满足的。若没有超能力根本不可能满足它。通常精力充沛的人更迷恋权力，这一恶习也使得其发生频率与效力严重失衡。事实上，迄今为止它也是重要人物一生中最强大的动力。

10 权力无论大小，只要有过享受权力的经历，就会大大增加人们对其热爱的程度。在1914年前的欢乐岁月里，富贵人家的太太、小姐尚有

could acquire a host of servants, their pleasure in exercising power over the domestics steadily increased with age. Similarly, in any autocratic regime, the holders of power become increasingly tyrannical with experience of the delights that power can afford. Since power over human beings is shown in making them do what they would rather not do, the man who is actuated by love of power *is* more *apt to* [14] inflict pain than to permit pleasure. If you ask your boss for leave of absence from the office on some legitimate occasion, his love of power will derive more satisfaction from a refusal than from a consent. If you require a building permit, the petty official concerned will obviously get more pleasure from saying "No" than from saying "Yes". It is this sort of thing which makes the love of power such a dangerous motive.

11 But it has other sides which are more desirable. The pursuit of knowledge is, I think, mainly actuated by love of power. And so are all advances in scientific technique. In politics, also, a reformer may have just as strong a love of power as a despot. It would be a complete mistake to decry love of power altogether as a motive. Whether you will be led by this motive to actions which are useful, or to actions which are pernicious, depends upon the social system, and upon your capacities. If your capacities are theoretical or technical, you will contribute to

一大群仆人，她们在家政上行使权力的快感也会随着年龄增长而与日俱增。同样地，任何一个专制政权下，一旦掌权者体验了权力带来的快感之后都会变得更专横。权力行使在人身上就表现为迫使人们去做本来不愿意做的事情，因此对权力的迷恋更倾向于制造痛苦而非容忍欢乐。当你向老板请假时，即使你这么做完全正当，他也会因为贪恋权力而拒绝，因为拒绝能带给他行使权力的更大满足感。当你需要一张施工执照时，显然相关官员说"不行"比说"可以"能获得更多快感。正是这些东西使对权力的迷恋成了一个危险的动机。

11 但是它也有好的一面。我认为，对知识的追求就主要缘于迷恋权力。所有科技上的进步也是如此。同样，在政治上，改革者对权力的热爱并不亚于一个独裁者。对人类行为的动机之一——迷恋权力持完全否定态度，这本身就是一个极大的错误。能否利用好对权力的迷恋，做出有益之事而非误入歧途，取决于社会制度，也取决于你自己的能力。如果你有理论或技术上的能力，通常你就能为知识和科技贡献有用的力量；如果

[14] be apt to... 倾向于……，易于…… 如：Remember children will be apt to do what you do, not necessarily what you tell them to do. 别忘了，孩子会模仿你做事，而不是做那些你告诉他应该做的事。

knowledge or technique, and, as a rule, your activity will be useful. If you are a politician you may be actuated by love of power, but as a rule this motive will join itself on to the desire to see some state of affairs realized which, for some reason, you prefer to the status quo. A great general may, like Alcibiades, be quite indifferent as to which side he fights on, but most generals have preferred to fight for their own country, and have, therefore, had other motives besides love of power. The politician may change sides so frequently as to find himself always in the majority, but most politicians have a preference for one party to the other, and subordinate their love of power to this preference. Love of power as nearly pure as possible is to be seen in various different types of men. One type is the soldier of fortune, of whom Napoleon is the supreme example. Napoleon had, I think, no ideological preference for France over Corsica, but if he had become Emperor of Corsica he would not have been so great a man as he became by pretending to be a Frenchman. Such men, however, are not quite pure examples, since they also derive immense satisfaction from vanity. The purest type is that of the eminence grise—the power behind the throne that never appears in public, and merely hugs itself with the secret thought: "How little these puppets know who is pulling the strings. " Baron Holstein, who controlled the foreign policy of the German Empire from 1890 to 1906, illustrates this type to perfection. He lived in a slum; he never appeared in society;

你是一个政治家，这种对权力的迷恋就会发展成另外一种欲望——希望看到事态以你喜欢的方式发展。一个伟大的将军，像亚西比德（雅典杰出的军事家、政治家、演讲家），可能对为谁而战并不关心，但是大多数统帅还是更喜欢为自己的国家战斗，因此除了对权力的贪恋，他们还有其他动机。有的政客为了使自己永远处于多数党的地位会频繁改变自己的立场，但是大多数政治家在党派上有自己的偏爱，他们会使对权力的迷恋服从于这种偏爱。不同的人对权力纯粹迷恋的程度也不同。其中一种就是拥有财富的军人，拿破仑就是一个典型。我认为，拿破仑在意识形态上并非偏向法国而否定科西嘉，只是他即使做一个虚伪的法国人也比做科西嘉的皇帝要伟大得多。像拿破仑这样的人并不算是纯粹热爱权力的典型，因为他们在虚荣心上也得到了极大的满足。最纯粹的是那些幕后的权力操纵者。这些王位背后的权力操纵者从未露过面，他们仅靠一句话聊以自慰，那就是"木偶们啊，有几个知道是谁在操纵那些线啊？"从1890到1906年一直控制着德国对外政策的赫尔斯泰男爵，就是这一类人的完美典型。他住在贫民窟里，从不抛头露面；也避免与国王会面，只有一次在国王的强行要求下，推辞不过，才与之相见；他拒绝所有朝堂活动的邀请，借口是自己没有合适的朝服。他掌握的秘密足

he avoided meeting the Emperor, except on one single occasion when the Emperor's importunity could not be resisted; he refused all invitations to Court functions, on the ground that he possessed no court dress. He had acquired secrets which enabled him to blackmail the Chancellor and many of the Kaiser's intimates. He used the power of blackmail, not to acquire wealth, or fame, or any other obvious advantage, but merely to compel the adoption of the foreign policy he preferred.

...

以敲诈勒索德国总理和许多皇亲国戚。但他用这权力勒索的却不是财富、名誉或其他任何显而易见的利益，他只是强迫国家采用他喜欢的外交政策而已。

……

 演讲关键词 Practical Expressions

1. constitutional organization 宪法机构
2. average income per head 人均收入
3. the necessities of life 生活必需品
4. posthumous fame 身后名
5. autocratic regime 专制政权
6. state of affairs 事态
7. eminence grise 幕后操纵者

精华佳句

1. But man differs from other animals in one very important respect, and that is that he has some desires which are, so to speak, infinite, which can never be fully gratified, and which would keep him restless even in Paradise.
但是，人区别于动物的一个主要方面就在于，人的有些欲望是无止境的，可以说永远得不到满足，即使到了天堂也会让他焦虑不安。

独立的人格：以卓越思想启迪人生的诺贝尔奖大师演讲

2. Mankind have even committed the impiety of attributing similar desires to the Deity, whom they imagine avid for continual praise.

人们侥幸地把这种虚荣心归根于上帝，毕竟我们的造物主也贪婪地享受着世人的赞美。

诺贝尔奖背后的那些趣事

诺贝尔奖明星家庭

在诺贝尔奖的舞台上，不仅有"上阵父子兵"，也有"比翼双飞夫妻档"。大家耳熟能详的当然是居里家族。居里家族是迄今为止唯一有连续两代夫妻都获得诺贝尔奖的家庭。除此之外，还有一些杰出夫妻们也因双双获得诺贝尔奖而美名远扬。1947年的诺贝尔生理学和医学奖在同一天授予了同一年出生、考进同一所大学的科里夫妇。而来自瑞典的米达尔夫妇，丈夫摘得1974年诺贝尔经济学奖，妻子则荣获1982年诺贝尔和平奖。都说"军功章里有我的一半，也有你的一半"，那这两块沉甸甸的奖牌可真是够他们"分"的了。

Speech 4

Let Us Put an End to It
终结这一切

—Speech by Malala Yousafzai for the Nobel Peace Prize on December 10, 2014
——巴基斯坦少年巾帼斗士马拉拉·优素福扎伊 2014 年 12 月 10 日诺贝尔
和平奖获奖演讲

名家速览 **About the Author**

诺贝尔奖大师	马拉拉·优素福扎伊
奖 项 归 属	诺贝尔和平奖
获 奖 理 由	为受剥削的儿童及年轻人、为所有孩子的受教育的权利抗争。
相关演讲链接	2013 年 16 岁的马拉拉在联合国大会上的演讲

　　马拉拉·优素福扎伊，女，1997 年 7 月 12 日出生于巴基斯坦西北边境省一个普什图穆斯林家庭，是一名中学生，也是一名女权主义者，以争取妇女接受教育的权利而闻名。除此之外，马拉拉因致力于斯瓦特地区的和平而备受赞誉。虽然塔利班禁止斯瓦特地区的女性接受教育，但是马拉拉在自己的抗争下不仅继续学习，还为外媒写稿件，为巴基斯坦妇女和儿童争取权益。由于反对塔利班的恐怖统治，2012 年 10 月 9 日，她乘校车回家时遭到枪击，伤势严重，经过治疗，于 2013 年 1 月 4 日出院，并在英国伯明翰就近入学埃德巴斯通女子高中。马拉拉被巴基斯坦政府授予"国家青年和平奖"，是这一奖项的首位得主。2012 年 11 月 10 日，为表彰马拉拉不畏塔利班威胁、积极为巴基斯坦女童争取受教育权利所做的杰出贡献，联合国表示，将当年的 7 月 12 日（马拉拉的生日）定为"马拉拉日"。2014 年，她与印度的凯拉什·萨蒂亚尔希共同获得诺贝尔和平奖，成为该奖项最年轻的得主。本篇演讲中，马拉拉谈到了世界各地，尤其是巴基斯坦、印度等地的儿童，特别是女童被剥夺受教育权的问题。她呼吁世界和平，号召世界人民为每一个儿童能享受到平等的优质教育而奋斗。

独立的人格：以卓越思想启迪人生的诺贝尔奖大师演讲

演讲现场
Speech Script

精美译文
Suggested Translation

1 Your Majesties, Your royal highnesses, distinguished members of the Norweigan Nobel Committee, dear sisters and brothers,

2 Today is a day of great happiness for me. I am humbled that the Nobel Committee has selected me for this precious award.

3 Thank you to everyone for your continued support and love. Thank you for the letters and cards that I still receive from all around the world. Your kind and encouraging words strengthens and inspires me.

4 I would like to thank my parents for their unconditional love. Thank you to my father for not clipping my wings and for letting me fly. Thank you to my mother for inspiring me to be patient and to always speak the truth— which we strongly believe is the true message of Islam. And also thank you to all my wonderful teachers, who inspired me to believe in myself and be brave.

5 I am proud, well in fact, I am very proud to be the first Pashtun, the first Pakistani, and the youngest person to receive this award. Along with that, along with that, I am pretty certain that I am also the first recipient of the Nobel Peace Prize who still fights with her younger brothers. I want there to be peace everywhere, but my brothers and I are still working on that.

6 I am also honoured to receive this award together with Kailash Satyarthi, who has been a champion for children's rights for a long time. Twice as long, in fact, than I have been alive. I

1 尊敬的国王和王后陛下，尊敬的殿下，尊敬的挪威诺贝尔委员会的成员们，亲爱的兄弟姐妹们：

2 今天对我来说是值得开心的一天。感谢诺贝尔奖委员会将这个珍贵无比的奖项授予我，对此我受宠若惊。

3 感谢你们每一个人的支持和关爱，直到今天我还能收到从世界各地寄来的信件和贺卡。你们热心鼓励的话语给了我力量，使我倍受鼓舞。

4 我想感谢我的父母，他们给予我无条件的关爱。多谢我的父亲没有折断我的翅膀，使我能继续飞翔。多谢我的母亲激励我要耐心，不管怎样都要讲真话，我强烈地相信这就是伊斯兰教的真谛。还要感谢我所有优秀的老师们，是你们教会我相信自己，教我勇敢。

5 我感到骄傲，真的。我非常自豪自己是第一个获得诺贝尔和平奖的普什图人，也是第一个获此奖的巴基斯坦人，还是此奖项最年轻的获得者。除此之外，我相信我还是仍在同兄弟姐妹们一起为和平斗争的人中的第一位得主。我希望世界各地充满和平，但今天我和我的同胞还在为此奋斗。

6 能与凯拉什·萨蒂亚尔希同获此奖我深感荣幸，为争取儿童权利他已经奋战了很长时间，事实上，比我活过的年份还要多一倍。能和他一起

am proud that we can work together, we can work together and show the world that an Indian and a Pakistani, they can work together and achieve their goals of children's rights.

7 Dear brothers and sisters, I was named after the inspirational Malalai of Maiwand who is the Pashtun Joan of Arc. The word Malalai means "grief stricken, sad", but in order to lend some happiness to it, my grandfather would always call me Malala—the happiest girl in the world and today I am very happy that we are together fighting for an important cause.

8 This award is not just for me. It is for those forgotten children who want education. It is for those frightened children who want peace. It is for those voiceless children who want change.

9 I am here to stand up for their rights, to raise their voice… it is not time to pity them. It is not time to pity them. It is time to take action so it becomes the last time, the last time, so it becomes the last time that we see a child deprived of education.

10 I have found that people describe me in many different ways.

11 Some people call me the girl who was shot by the Taliban.

12 And some, the girl who fought for her rights.

13 Some people, call me a "Nobel Laureate" now.

14 However, my brothers still call me that annoying **bossy**① sister. As far as I know, I am

工作我感到骄傲，我们向世界展示一个印度人和一个巴基斯坦人可以为了儿童的权利一起奋战。

7 亲爱的兄弟姐妹们，我的名字取自梅万地区的马莱拉的名字，她是普什图人的圣女贞德。"马莱拉"这个词意味着"被悲伤击中"，但是为了使它听起来不那么悲伤，我的祖父总是叫我"马拉拉"——世界上最快乐的女孩。今天，我们能一起为一项重要的事业而奋斗，我感到很快乐。

8 这个奖项不是给我一个人的。它是给那些被遗忘了的、渴望教育的孩子们的，是给那些感到恐惧、渴望和平的孩子们的，更是给那些没有话语权却想为此做出改变的孩子们的。

9 我站在这里代表的是他们的权利，是为了提高他们的呼声。现在不是同情他们的时候，不是同情他们的时候。现在是该做出行动的时候了，让这成为我们最后一次、最后一次、最后一次看见一个孩子被剥夺受教育权。

10 我发现人们用很多不同的方式描述我。

11 有些人把我称作"一个遭受塔利班枪击的女孩"。

12 有些人叫我"为自己的权利斗争的女孩"。

13 现在，又有人叫我"诺贝尔奖得主"了。

14 但我的弟弟仍然把我当作那个烦人的专横姐姐。就我自己来说，

---

① bossy ['bɒsɪ] *adj.* 专横的，爱指挥人的

just a committed and even stubborn person who wants to see every child getting quality education, who wants to see women having equal rights and who wants peace in every corner of the world.

15 Education is one of the blessings of life—and one of its necessities. That has been my experience during the 17 years of my life. In my paradise home, Swat, I always loved learning and discovering new things. I remember when my friends and I would decorate our hands with henna on special occasions. And instead of drawing flowers and patterns we would paint our hands with mathematical formulas and equations.

16 We had a thirst for education, we had a thirst for education because our future was right there in that classroom. We would sit and learn and read together. We loved to wear neat and tidy school uniforms and we would sit there with big dreams in our eyes. We wanted to make our parents proud and prove that we could also excel in our studies and achieve those goals, which some people think only boys can.

17 But things did not remain the same. When I was in Swat, which was a place of tourism and beauty, suddenly changed into a place of terrorism. I was just ten that more than 400 schools were destroyed. Women were *flogged* ②. People were killed. And our beautiful dreams turned into nightmares.

18 Education went from being a right to being a crime.

我只是一个尽心竭力甚至固执己见的人，想看到每一位孩子都能享受到优质教育，每一位妇女都能享受平等的权利，想让和平充满世界每一个角落。

15 教育是生活中的一项福利，也是生活的必需品之一。这是我有限的17年生命中得来的经验。在我天堂般的家乡——斯瓦特，我一直都酷爱学习和发现新事物。我还记得在一些特殊场合，我和我的小伙伴们会用指甲花修饰我们的双手。我们不画花卉和图案，我们把双手都涂满了数学公式和方程式。

16 我们渴望教育，我们渴望教育是因为那间教室里有我们的未来。在那里我们将坐下来一起学习和阅读。我们喜欢穿着干净整洁的校服，眼睛里写满了梦想。我们想让父母为我们感到骄傲，证明我们也可以成为学习上的佼佼者，也可以实现我们的目标，而不是像有些人想的那样，只有男孩可以做到。

17 但是事情并不是这样发展的。我所在的斯瓦特地区曾经是一个美丽的旅游胜地，但是突然就变成了一个恐怖主义集结之地。400多所学校被毁时，我才刚刚十岁。妇女遭受鞭打，无辜的人遭到杀害。我们的美丽梦想瞬间就变成了噩梦。

18 教育从一项权利变成一种罪行。

② flog [flɒg] *vt.* 鞭打　如：He was publicly flogged for breaking the country's alcohol laws. 他因违反国家的酒法而被当众处以鞭刑。

19 Girls were stopped from going to school.

20 When my world suddenly changed, my priorities changed too.

21 I had two options. One was to remain silent and wait to be killed. And the second was to speak up and then be killed.

22 I chose the second one. I decided to speak up.

23 We could not just stand by and see those injustices of the terrorists denying our rights, ruthlessly killing people and misusing the name of Islam. We decided to raise our voice and tell them: Have you not learnt, have you not learnt that in the Holy *Quran* Allah says: if you kill one person it is as if you kill the whole humanity?

24 Do you not know that Mohammad, peace be upon him, the prophet of mercy, he says, do not harm yourself or others?

25 And do you not know that the very first word of the Holy *Quran* is the word "Iqra", which means "read"?

26 The terrorists tried to stop us and attacked me and my friends who are here today, on our school bus in 2012, but neither their ideas nor their bullets could win.

27 We survived. And since that day, our voices have grown louder and louder.

28 I tell my story, not because it is unique, but because it is not.

29 It is the story of many girls.

30 Today, I tell their stories too. I have brought with me some of my sisters from Pakistan, from Nigeria and from Syria, who share this story. My brave sisters Shazia and Kainat

19 女孩从此不能再继续上学。

20 我的世界突然发生了改变，事情的轻重缓急也就随之改变了。

21 我面临两个选择。一个是继续保持沉默，等着被杀害。另一个是为权利高呼，然后被杀害。

22 我选择了第二个，我决定说出来。

23 我们不能只是袖手旁观，看着那些恐怖分子错用伊斯兰教的名义来剥夺我们的权利，残忍地屠杀人民。我们决定高声告诉他们：你们不知道吗？你们难道不知道《古兰经》里真主安拉说过：你杀一个人，就是杀害整个人类吗？

24 你们难道不知道，穆罕默德，我们的先知，以和平与同情的名义说过，不要伤害你自己和他人吗？

25 你们难道不知道，《古兰经》里的第一个字就是"Iqra"，意思是"阅读"吗？

26 2012年，恐怖分子试图攻击、阻止我和今天在座的我的朋友们，但是他们的阴谋和子弹都没有得逞。

27 我们幸存下来了。从那天开始，我们的呼声就越来越大。

28 我讲我的故事，并不是因为它很特别，而是因为它很普遍。

29 这是许多女孩的故事。

30 今天，我也在讲她们的故事。我带来了我巴基斯坦的姐妹们，还有来自尼日利亚和叙利亚的姐妹们，这也是她们的故事。我勇敢的姐

who were also shot that day on our school bus. But they have not stopped learning. And my brave sister Kainat Soomro who went through severe abuse and extreme violence, even her brother was killed, but she did not *succumb* [3].

31 Also my sisters here, whom I have met during my Malala Fund campaign. My 16-year-old courageous sister, Mezon from Syria, who now lives in Jordan as *refugee* [4] and goes from tent to tent encouraging girls and boys to learn. And my sister Amina, from the North of Nigeria, where Boko Haram threatens, and stops girls and even *kidnaps* [5] girls, just for wanting to go to school.

32 Though I appear as one girl, though I appear as one girl, one person, who is 5 foot 2 inches tall, if you include my high heels. (It means I am 5 foot only.) I am not a lone voice; I am not a lone voice; I am many.

I am Malala. But I am also Shazia.

I am Kainat.

I am Kainat Soomro.

I am Mezon.

33 I am Amina. I am those 66 million girls who are *deprived* [6] of education. And today I am not raising my voice, it is the voice of those 66 million girls.

妹萨佳和坎纳特那天也在校车上被击中。但她们并没有中断学习。我勇敢的姐妹坎纳特·苏姆罗经历了严重的暴力虐待，她的弟弟也被杀害了，但是她自己却并没有屈服。

31 这里还有我另一位姐妹，是我在马拉拉基金活动中遇见的，以及我 16 岁的姐妹，来自叙利亚的麦隆，她以难民的身份住在约旦，走进一间间帐篷鼓励孩子们学习。阿米娜来自尼日利亚北部地区，那里遭受着博科圣地组织的威胁，不仅不让女孩接受教育，还绑架那些想去上学的女孩。

32 尽管我是以一个女孩的身份出现在这里，一个人，一个带上鞋跟只有 5 英尺 2 英寸高的女孩（也就是说我自己只有 5 英尺高），但我的声音并不孤单，我不是一个人在呼喊，我代表着很多人。

我是马拉拉，但我也是萨佳。

我是坎纳特。

我是坎纳特·苏姆罗。

我是麦隆。

33 我是阿米娜。我是那 6600 万被剥夺受教育权的女孩们。今天我不是为我自己高呼，而是为那 6600 万女童呐喊。

③ succumb [səˈkʌm] *vi.* 屈服　如：succumb to temptation 受惑

④ refugee [ˌrefju(ː)ˈdʒiː] *n.* 难民

⑤ kidnap [ˈkɪdnæp] *vt.* 绑架，劫持　如：Two businessmen have been kidnapped by terrorists. 两名商人遭恐怖分子绑架。

⑥ deprived [dɪˈpraɪvd] *adj.* 缺乏足够教育的，贫乏的　如：She was deprived of schooling at ten. 她 10 岁时就失学了。

34 Sometimes people like to ask me why should girls go to school, why is it important for them. But I think the more important question is why shouldn't they, why shouldn't they have this right to go to school.

35 Dear sisters and brothers, today, in half of the world, we see rapid progress and development. However, there are many countries where millions still suffer from the very old problems of war, poverty, and injustice.

36 We still see conflicts in which innocent people lose their lives and children become orphans. We see many people becoming refugees in Syria, Gaza and Iraq. In Afghanistan, we see families being killed in suicide attacks and bomb blasts.

37 Many children in Africa do not have access to education because of poverty. And as I said, we still see, we still see girls who have no freedom to go to school in the north of Nigeria.

38 Many children in countries like Pakistan and India, as Kailash Satyarthi mentioned, many children, especially in India and Pakistan are deprived of their right to education because of social *taboos* [⑦], or they have been forced into child marriage or into child labour.

39 One of my very good school friends, the same age as me, who had always been a bold and confident girl, dreamed of becoming a doctor. But her dream remained a dream. At the age of 12, she was forced to get married. And then soon she had a son, she had a child when she herself was still a child—only 14. I know that she could have been a

34 有时人们会问我为什么女孩要上学，这对她们为什么那么重要。但我想更重要的问题应该是：为什么不呢？为什么她们不能有接受教育的权利呢？

35 亲爱的兄弟姐妹们，今天，在世界上一半的地区我们都可以看到进步与发展。但是，很多国家却仍然遭受着古老的灾难：战争、贫困和非正义。

36 我们仍然能看到无辜的人丢掉性命，儿童成为孤儿。在叙利亚、加沙和伊拉克，许多人沦为难民。在阿富汗，许多家庭在自杀式袭击和爆炸中丧生。

37 非洲许多儿童因为贫穷而没有机会接受教育。还有，如我所说，尼日利亚北部很多女童被剥夺上学的权利和自由。

38 像萨蒂亚尔希提到的，在巴基斯坦和印度这样的国家，尤其是在巴基斯坦和印度，很多儿童因为社会禁忌要么没有受教育的权利，要么被迫成为儿童婚姻和童工的牺牲品。

39 我在学校有一位非常好的朋友，和我一样的年纪，她非常大胆也很自信，梦想成为一名医生。但是她的梦想也只能是梦想了。12 岁时，她就被逼结婚。不久就有了一个儿子，14 岁——在她自己都还是一个孩子的时候就有了孩子。我知道她本

---

⑦ taboo [təˈbuː] *n.* 禁忌　如：a taboo subject 一个忌讳的话题

very good doctor.

40　But she couldn't... because she was a girl.

41　Her story is why I dedicate the Nobel Peace Prize money to the Malala Fund, to help give girls quality education, everywhere, anywhere in the world and to raise their voices. The first place this funding will go to is where my heart is, to build schools in Pakistan—especially in my home of Swat and Shangla.

42　In my own village, there is still no secondary school for girls. And it is my wish and my commitment, and now my challenge to build one so that my friends and my sisters can go there to school and get quality education and to get this opportunity to fulfil their dreams.

43　This is where I will begin, but it is not where I will stop. I will continue this fight until I see every child, every child in school.

44　Dear brothers and sisters, great people, who brought change, like Martin Luther King, Nelson Mandela, Mother Teresa and Aung San Suu Kyi, once stood here on this stage. I hope the steps that Kailash Satyarthi and I have taken so far and will take on this journey will also bring change—lasting change.

45　My great hope is that this will be the last time, this will be the last time we must fight for education. Let's solve this once and for all.

46　We have already taken many steps. Now it is time to take a leap.

47　It is not time to tell the world leaders to realise how important education is—they already

来可以成为一名出色的医生的。

40　但是这不可能……因为她是一个女孩。

41　她的故事就是我要用诺贝尔奖奖金建立马拉拉基金的原因——为了帮助她们获得平等的受教育权，帮助世界各地的女童提高她们的呼声。这笔基金的第一笔款项将被投放在我心之所系的祖国巴基斯坦，尤其是我的家乡斯瓦特和香拉。

42　我所在的村里仍然没有女子中学。因此我希望，我承诺，现在也是我面临的挑战——在这里建立女子中学，让我的朋友们、姐妹们能够进入学校，接受素质教育，抓住机会实现她们的梦想。

43　这是我开始要做的，但这并不是终点。我会继续斗争，直到看到每一位孩子，每一位孩子都能进入学校。

44　亲爱的兄弟姐妹们，像马丁·路德·金、纳尔逊·曼德拉、特雷莎修女和昂山素季这些使世界发生改变的伟人们都曾站在这个台上。我希望我和萨蒂亚尔希所做的事，以及将要做的事情也能为这个世界带来改变——持续长久的改变。

45　我有一个很大的期望，我希望这是我们最后一次，最后一次为受教育权而奋战。让我们为此打响最后一役吧!

46　我们已经走了很多步了，现在该勇敢一跃了。

47　是时候告诉世界各国的领导人，要意识到教育的重要性了——他

改变世界的力量：诺贝尔奖大师演讲精选

know it—their own children are in good schools. Now it is time to call them to take action for the rest of the world's children.

48 We ask the world leaders to unite and make education their top priority.

49 Fifteen years ago, the world leaders decided on a set of global goals, the Millennium Development Goals. In the years that have followed, we have seen some progress. The number of children out of school has been halved, as Kailash Satyarthi said. However, the world focused only on primary education, and progress did not reach everyone.

50 In year 2015, representatives from all around the world will meet in the United Nations to set the next set of goals, the Sustainable Development Goals. This will set the world's ambition for the next generations.

51 The world can no longer accept, the world can no longer accept that basic education is enough. Why do leaders accept that for children in developing countries, only basic literacy is sufficient, when their own children do homework in algebra, mathematics, science and physics?

52 Leaders must seize this opportunity to guarantee a free, quality, primary and secondary education for every child.

53 Some will say this is impractical, or too expensive, or too hard. Or maybe even impossible. But it is time the world thinks bigger.

54 Dear sisters and brothers, the so-called world of adults may understand it, but we children

们已经知道了——因为他们自己的孩子就在很好的学校里接受教育。现在是他们采取行动，为剩下的孩子们争取权利的时候了。

48 我们呼吁世界各国领导人团结起来，把教育当作当务之急。

49 15年前，世界各国领导人制定出一系列全球目标——"千禧年发展目标"。接下来的这些年，我们已经取得了巨大进展。如萨蒂亚尔希所说，失学儿童已经减少了一半。然而，世界只关注了初级教育，而且这些进展也并没有普及到每个人。

50 2015年，世界各国的代表会相聚在联合国来制定下一套发展目标——可持续发展目标。这是为下一代人设立的雄心壮志。

51 世界不能接受，不能接受仅基础教育就已足够。为什么领导人能接受发展中国家的儿童享有基本的识字教育就已足够，而他们自己的孩子却在学习代数、数学、科学和物理？

52 世界各国领导人必须抓住这次机会保证让每个孩子都能享受到免费、优质的初级和中级教育。

53 有些人可能觉得这太不现实，要付出太过昂贵的代价，也太难了，或者甚至都是不可能完成的。但是世界也该有一个大点的理想了。

54 亲爱的兄弟姐妹们，可能所谓的大人们的世界能够理解，但我们

140

don't. Why is it that countries which we call "strong" are so powerful in creating wars but are so weak in bringing peace? Why is it that giving guns is so easy but giving books is so hard? Why is it, why is it that making tanks is so easy, but building schools is so hard?

55 We are living in the modern age and we believe that nothing is impossible. We have reached the moon 45 years ago and maybe will soon land on Mars. Then, in this 21st century, we must be able to give every child quality education.

56 Dear sisters and brothers, dear fellow children, we must work… not wait. Not just the politicians and the world leaders, we all need to contribute. Me. You. We. It is our duty.

57 Let us become the first generation to decide to be the last, let us become the first generation that decides to be the last that sees empty classrooms, lost childhoods, and wasted potentials.

58 Let this be the last time that a girl or a boy spends their childhood in a factory.

59 Let this be the last time that a girl is forced into early child marriage.

60 Let this be the last time that a child loses life in war.

61 Let this be the last time that we see a child out of school.

62 Let this end with us.

63 Let's begin this ending… together… today… right here, right now. Let's begin this ending now.

64 Thank you so much.

孩子却不能。为什么那个所谓的"强国"强大到能制造战争却不能带来和平？为什么发出一支枪那么容易而发放课本却那么难？为什么？为什么制造坦克那么简单，而建学校却如此困难？

55 我们生活在现代，我们相信一切皆有可能。我们45年前就登上了月球，或许不久就要登陆火星。那么，在此21世纪我们也一定要给每一个孩子平等的教育。

56 亲爱的兄弟姐妹们，亲爱的伙伴们，我们必须行动……不能再等待了。不只是政治家和全世界的领导人们，我们所有人都需要贡献力量。我，你，我们。这是我们的责任。

57 让我们下定决心做第一代决定我们命运的人，让我们做最后遭受不幸的人，让自己不再看到空荡的教室、流失的童年和浪费的潜能。

58 这是最后一次女童或男童在工厂里度过童年。

59 这是最后一次女童被迫走入过早的儿童婚姻。

60 这是最后一次儿童在战争中失去生命。

61 这是最后一次我们看到儿童失学。

62 让这些从我们开始结束。

63 让我们开始结束这些……共同……今天……就在此时此地。让我们现在开始结束这一切！

64 谢谢大家。

演讲关键词 Practical Expressions

1. quality education 优质教育
2. school uniforms 校服
3. suicide attack 自杀式袭击
4. social taboos 社会禁忌
5. be honored to... 对……深感荣幸
6. deprived of education 被剥夺受教育权

 精华佳句

1. This award is not just for me. It is for those forgotten children who want education. It is for those frightened children who want peace. It is for those voiceless children who want change.

这个奖项不是给我一个人的。它是给那些被遗忘了的、渴望教育的孩子们的，是给那些感到恐惧、渴望和平的孩子们的，更是给那些没有话语权却想为此做出改变的孩子们的。

2. Education is one of the blessings of life—and one of its necessities.

教育是生活中的一项福利，也是生活的必需品之一。

 诺贝尔奖背后的那些趣事

抢占先机的重要性

　　2004 年的诺贝尔物理学奖由三位美国物理学家——格罗斯、维尔切克和波利策共同获得，因为他们在 1973 年发现了物质的最基本粒子夸克有一种所谓"渐近自由"的特性。而得知获奖消息后，另外两位物理学家却不仅笑不起来，还后悔莫及。一位是美国物理学家特霍夫特，另一位是华裔美国物理学家徐一鸿。徐一鸿在 1972 年春天就想到了"渐近自由"，但是这样的想法在当时新颖得简直不可思议，因此他没敢再往下想。特霍夫特则更可惜，在 1972 年的一次会议上他就曾对德国物理学家西曼尼谈起，他可以证明"渐近自由"符合现有的理论。西曼尼还鼓励他："倘若你是对的，那么你应该马上发表这一结果，因为这会十分重要！"可惜的是，特霍夫特当时忙于另外一项研究，一定程度上忽略了西曼尼的建议。到 1973 年格罗斯、维尔切克和波利策发表他们的发现以后，特霍夫特把肠子都悔青了，但没办法，为时已晚，大奖就这样与他失之交臂了。

Chapter 3

共建未来世界：捍卫人类家园的诺贝尔奖大师演讲

Speech 1

To Unite for a Better Future
团结共赴美好未来

—Nobel Lecture by Kofi Annan for the Nobel Peace Prize on December 10, 2001
——带领联合国跨越两个世纪的秘书长科菲·安南 2001 年 12 月 10 日诺贝尔和平奖获奖演讲

 名家速览 About the Author

诺贝尔奖大师	科菲·安南
奖 项 归 属	诺贝尔和平奖。
获 奖 理 由	为他们对更有组织与和平的世界做出的努力。
相关演讲链接	安南在北京大学的演讲《构建更加和谐的世界秩序》(*Toward a More Harmonious World Order*)

科菲·安南（1938 年 4 月 8 日—），加纳库马西人，联合国第七任秘书长。他出生于库马西的一个名门望族，家境优越，在当地也颇有地位，这为安南提供了良好的学习成长环境。后来，他到美国和瑞士留学，掌握英语、法语及多种非洲语言。他先后获得经济学学士学位和麻省理工学院管理硕士学位。安南 1962 年进入联合国工作，先后在多个部门及地区担任职位，为世界和平与发展做出了不懈努力。1996 年第 51 届联合国大会任命安南为联合国秘书长。他在担任秘书长期间的贡献是国际社会有目共睹的，数年间他和他的团队穿梭于世界各地，竭力调和世界争端，维护世界和平，促进发展。在非洲战乱、中东危机、南亚克什米尔争端、东帝汶暴乱、阿富汗战争和其他极度敏感的政治危机中，安南和他所在的联合国对于事件的和平解决都起到了重大作用。本篇演讲中，安南依然不忘他的使命和责任，在演讲开头即谈到阿富汗地区人们的生存状况，全文呼吁世界各国和各国人民团结一致，对抗不和平因素，与贫困、战争和疾病做斗争，共同为一个更美好的未来而努力。

演讲现场
Speech Script

精美译文
Suggested Translation

1 Today, in Afghanistan, a girl will be born. Her mother will hold her and feed her, comfort her and care for her—just as any mother would anywhere in the world. In these most basic acts of human nature, humanity knows no divisions. But to be born a girl in today's Afghanistan is to begin life centuries away from the prosperity that one small part of humanity has achieved. It is to live under conditions that many of us in this hall would consider inhuman.

2 I speak of a girl in Afghanistan, but I might equally well have mentioned a baby boy or girl in Sierra Leone. No one today is unaware of this divide between the world's rich and poor. No one today can claim ignorance of the cost that this divide imposes on the poor and dispossessed who are no less deserving of human dignity, fundamental freedoms, security, food and education than any of us. The cost, however, is not borne by them alone. <u>Ultimately, it is borne by all of us—North and South, rich and poor, men and women of all races and religions.</u>

3 Today's real borders are not between nations, but between powerful and powerless, free and fettered, privileged and humiliated. Today, no walls can separate humanitarian or human rights crises in one part of the world from national security crises in another.

1 今天，一个女孩将出生在阿富汗。她的母亲会像世界其他地方的任何一位母亲一样，抱她，喂养她，安抚她，照顾她。这些是人类的天性，并无人与人之间的差别。但是今天在阿富汗出生的这个女孩，她将开始的生活与小部分人类已经获得的富足生活相差甚远，简直是落后了几个世纪。那里的生存条件，在今天坐在这个大厅里的人看来，是野蛮的、不人道的。

2 我讲到了一个阿富汗女孩，但其实我也可以讲一个有着差不多境况的塞拉利昂男孩或女孩。今天没有谁还对世界的贫富差距一无所知。也没有谁敢说对贫困人群要为之付出的额外代价一无所知，这些一穷二白的人们同样应该享有人类尊严、基本的自由、安全、食物和教育。而承担代价的人绝不只是他们。<u>从根本上来说，我们所有人——不论来自南半球还是北半球，贫穷还是富有，也不论人种、宗教和性别差异，都要承担此代价。</u>

3 今天，真正的界限不在国家之间，而在强弱之间，在自由和压制之间，在特权阶级和受辱人群之间。今天，也没有任何高墙能够将一个地方的人权危机与另一个地方的国家安全危机隔离开来。

4 Scientists tell us that the world of nature is so small and interdependent that a butterfly flapping its wings in the Amazon rainforest can generate a violent storm on the other side of the earth. This principle is known as the "Butterfly Effect". Today, we realize, perhaps more than ever, that the world of human activity also has its own "Butterfly Effect"—for better or for worse.

5 Ladies and Gentlemen,

6 We have entered the third millennium through a gate of fire. If today, after the horror of 11 September, we see better, and we see further— we will realize that humanity is indivisible. New threats make no distinction between races, nations or regions. A new insecurity has entered every mind, regardless of wealth or status. A deeper awareness of the bonds that bind us all—in pain as in prosperity—has gripped young and old.

7 In the early beginnings of the 21st century— a century already violently *disabused* ① of any hopes that progress towards global peace and prosperity is inevitable—this new reality can no longer be ignored. It must be confronted.

8 The 20th century was perhaps the deadliest in human history, devastated by innumerable conflicts, untold suffering, and unimaginable crimes. Time after time, a group or a nation *inflicted* ② extreme violence on another, often

4 科学家告诉我们，自然界很小而且相互依存。亚马逊雨林的一只蝴蝶震动几下翅膀就可能引发地球另一端的一场风暴。这就是著名的"蝴蝶效应"。今天，我们比以往任何时候都清楚，人类活动也有自己的"蝴蝶效应"——有的引发良性结果，有的却让事态更糟。

5 女士们，先生们，

6 通过一道火焰之门，我们已经进入第三个千年。在9·11恐怖袭击之后的今天，如果我们能更好地、更有远见地审视这个世界，就会意识到人类本为一体，不可分割。在新的威胁面前，并无人种、国家或地区之分。不论贫富差异和地位高低，新的不安全感已经渗透到每个人内心。不论年龄长幼，人们都对——无论是在苦难中，还是处于富饶时——将大家团结在一起的凝聚力有了更深的认识。

7 人们曾怀着在世界和平繁荣之路上继续前进的希望进入21世纪，但在本世纪初，暴力已经惊扰了这一美梦。这是不容忽略的事实。我们必须面对。

8 20世纪可能是人类历史上死难最惨重的一个世纪。数不清的冲突，无限的苦难，难以想象的罪行让这个世纪几近毁灭。一次又一次，在非理性的仇恨和猜疑，不受控制的傲

① disabuse [ˌdɪsəˈbjuːz] *vt.* 使省悟，纠正　如：disabuse foolish prejudices 纠正愚昧的偏见
② inflict [ɪnˈflɪkt] *vt.* 使遭受（损伤、痛苦等）　如：The attack has inflicted heavy losses on the enemy. 这次攻击给敌人造成了极大损失。

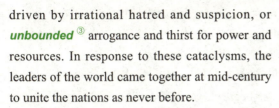
driven by irrational hatred and suspicion, or **unbounded** ③ arrogance and thirst for power and resources. In response to these cataclysms, the leaders of the world came together at mid-century to unite the nations as never before.

9 A forum was created—the United Nations—where all nations could join forces to affirm the dignity and worth of every person, and to secure peace and development for all peoples. Here States could unite to strengthen the rule of law, recognize and address the needs of the poor, restrain man's brutality and greed, conserve the resources and beauty of nature, sustain the equal rights of men and women, and provide for the safety of future generations.

10 We thus inherit from the 20th century the political, as well as the scientific and technological power, which—if only we have the will to use them—give us the chance to **vanquish** ④ poverty, ignorance and disease.

11 In the 21st Century I believe the mission of the United Nations will be defined by a new, more profound, awareness of the **sanctity** ⑤ and dignity of every human life, regardless of race or religion. This will require us to look beyond the framework of States, and beneath the surface of nations or communities. We must focus, as never before, on improving the conditions of the individual men and women who give the state or

慢和对权势与资源的贪婪驱使下，一个个群体或国家用极端暴力对待着彼此。为应对这些灾难，20 世纪中叶世界各国元首走到一起，让世界空前团结起来。

9 于是一个世界论坛——联合国诞生了。在这里，所有的国家都协力团结以确保每个世界公民的尊严和价值，保障每个国家人民的安全和发展。在这里，各国共同致力于加强法治，发现并满足贫民的需要，控制人类的残酷与贪婪，保护自然资源，维护人权（包括女权），为后代提供安全基础。

10 所以说，我们从 20 世纪继承了政治、科学和技术力量，只要我们愿意使用这些力量，就会有征服贫困、无知和疾病的可能。

11 我相信，在 21 世纪不分种族、宗教的，对全人类尊严更深刻的认识将重新定义联合国的使命。这要求我们超越国家界限，从民族、团体的表象下看到本质问题。我们必须比以往任何时候都更集中精力改善个人的生存条件，因为正是这些个人赋予了国家丰富内涵和民族性格。从这个阿富汗女孩开始，我们必须认识到

③ unbounded [ʌnˈbaʊndɪd] *adj.* 极大的，无限的　如：unbounded space 无边无际的空间

④ vanquish [ˈvæŋkwɪʃ] *vt.* 征服，击败，克服　如：Success vanquished their fears. 成功战胜了他们的恐惧。

⑤ sanctity [ˈsæŋktɪtɪ] *n.* 尊严，神圣不可侵犯性

nation its richness and character. We must begin with the young Afghan girl, recognizing that saving that one life is to save humanity itself.

12 Over the past five years, I have often recalled that the *United Nations' Charter* begins with the words: "We the peoples." What is not always recognized is that "we the peoples" are made up of individuals whose claims to the most fundamental rights have too often been sacrificed in the supposed interests of the state or the nation.

13 A genocide begins with the killing of one man—not for what he has done, but because of who he is. A campaign of "ethnic cleansing" begins with one neighbour *turning on* [6] another. Poverty begins when even one child is denied his or her fundamental right to education. What begins with the failure to uphold the dignity of one life, all too often ends with a *calamity* [7] for entire nations.

14 In this new century, we must start from the understanding that peace belongs not only to states or peoples, but to each and every member of those communities. The sovereignty of States must no longer be used as a shield for gross violations of human rights. Peace must be made real and tangible in the daily existence of every individual in need. Peace must be sought, above all, because it is the condition for every member of the human family to live a life of dignity and security.

拯救这样一个生命就是在拯救人类自己。

12 过去这五年，我常常想起《联合国宪章》是以"我联合国人民"这几个字开头的。但是人们常常意识不到"我联合国人民"是由个人组成的，而个人最基本的权利却经常要为所谓的国家或民族利益做出牺牲。

13 种族灭绝开始时杀一个人不是因为他的所作所为，而是因为他是某个人种或属于某个族群。一场"种族清洗"运动开始往往因为邻居互相攻击。而贫困甚至从剥夺一个孩子的基本受教育权开始。开始时是一个生命的尊严没有得到维护，而结果往往是整个民族的灾难。

14 在新世纪，我们必须从理解这样的道理开始：和平不只属于整个国家或国民，更属于这些团体中的每一个人。国家主权绝不能再成为严重违反人权的挡箭牌。和平必须是真实的，对每一个生活穷困的人都有实际的好处。首先，人们必须追求和平，因为它是人类社会每一个成员能过上有尊严和安全生活的前提条件。

---

⑥ turn on (sb.) 突然攻击　如：The dogs suddenly turned on each other. 那两条狗突然互相撕咬了起来。

⑦ calamity [kə'læmɪtɪ] *n.* 灾难，不幸

15 The rights of the individual are of no less importance to immigrants and minorities in Europe and the Americas than to women in Afghanistan or children in Africa. They are as fundamental to the poor as to the rich; they are as necessary to the security of the developed world as to that of the developing world.

16 From this vision of the role of the United Nations in the next century flow three key priorities for the future: eradicating poverty, preventing conflict, and promoting democracy. Only in a world that is rid of poverty can all men and women make the most of their abilities. Only where individual rights are respected can differences be channelled politically and resolved peacefully. Only in a democratic environment, based on respect for diversity and dialogue, can individual self-expression and self-government be secured, and freedom of association be upheld.

17 Throughout my term as Secretary-General, I have sought to place human beings at the centre of everything we do—from conflict prevention to development to human rights. Securing real and lasting improvement in the lives of individual men and women is the measure of all we do at the United Nations.

18 It is in this spirit that I humbly accept the Centennial Nobel Peace Prize. Forty years ago today, the Prize for 1961 was awarded for the first time to a Secretary-General of the United Nations—posthumously, because Dag Hammarskjöld had already given his life for peace in Central Africa. And on the same day, the

15 从个人权利的重要性上看，欧洲和美国的移民或少数民族的权力与阿富汗女孩或非洲儿童的同等重要。人权的根本性没有富人和穷人之分；其必要性也没有发展中国家和发达国家之分。

16 从这一角度看联合国的作用，下一世纪联合国将有三大当务之急：消除贫困、遏止冲突和促进民主。只有在一个远离贫困的世界里，人们才能充分发挥自己的能力。只有在一个尊重人权的社会里，才能和平消除政治分歧。只有在一个民主的环境下，在最终多样性和对话的基础上，个人表达和自治才能得到保障，自由结社的权利才能得以维护。

17 在我任联合国秘书长期间，我一直设法将人置于我们所有工作的核心——从化解冲突到人权的发展。联合国所有工作的衡量标准就是确保个人生活得到实在而持续的改善。

18 正是本着这种精神我谦卑地接受诺贝尔百年和平奖。40 年前的今天，1961 年诺贝尔和平奖第一次授予联合国秘书长，却是在当事人逝世之后，因为达格·哈马舍尔德已经将他的生命献给了中非的和平事业。同样在这一天，1960 年，此奖第一

Prize for 1960 was awarded for the first time to an African—Albert Luthuli, one of the earliest leaders of the struggle against *apartheid* [8] in South Africa. For me, as a young African beginning his career in the United Nations a few months later, those two men set a standard that I have sought to follow throughout my working life.

19 This award belongs not just to me. I do not stand here alone. On behalf of all my colleagues in every part of the United Nations, in every corner of the globe, who have devoted their lives—and in many instances risked or given their lives in the cause of peace—I thank the Members of the Nobel Committee for this high honour. My own path to service at the United Nations was made possible by the sacrifice and commitment of my family and many friends from all continents— some of whom have passed away—who taught me and guided me. To them, I offer my most profound gratitude.

20 In a world filled with weapons of war and all too often words of war, the Nobel Committee has become a vital agent for peace. Sadly, a prize for peace is a rarity in this world. Most nations have monuments or memorials to war, bronze salutations to heroic battles, archways of triumph. But peace has no parade, no pantheon of victory.

21 What it does have is the Nobel Prize— a statement of hope and courage with unique resonance and authority. Only by understanding

次授予一位非洲人——艾伯特·卢图利，他是同南非种族隔离做斗争的最早的领导人之一。而我，一位几个月后在联合国开始职业生涯的非洲青年，将毕生追随两位伟人的脚步，以他们为榜样努力做好我的工作。

19 这个奖不只属于我。我不是独自一个人站在这里。还有在联合国各个部门和岗位，在世界各个角落工作的同仁们，他们致力于和平事业——在很多情况下冒着付出生命的危险，我代表这些同志感谢诺贝尔奖委员会的成员们授予我们这项至高的荣誉。没有我的家人和来自各大洲朋友的尽职尽责和做出的牺牲，我自己不可能走上为联合国服务的道路。他们教导、引领了我——尽管这些人中有些已经离世了。为此我要向他们致以最深厚的感激。

20 在一个充斥着战争武器和战争言论的世界，诺贝尔奖委员会已然成为一个对和平至关重要的机构。可悲的是，为和平设奖在这个世界却是罕事。大部分国家为战争设立了纪念馆、纪念仪式，铸造铜雕向英勇的战役致礼，为凯旋胜利建造歌功颂德的拱门。但是和平却没有游行庆祝，没有胜利殿堂。

21 和平拥有的是诺贝尔奖——是希望与勇气的宣言，而且有着独一无二的反响和权威。只有理解并解决

⑧ apartheid [əˈpɑːt(h)aɪt] *n.* 种族隔离制度

and addressing the needs of individuals for peace, for dignity, and for security can we at the United Nations hope to live up to the honour *conferred* [9] today, and fulfill the vision of our founders. This is the broad mission of peace that United Nations staff members carry out every day in every part of the world.

22 A few of them, women and men, are with us in this hall today. Among them, for instance, are a Military Observer from Senegal who is helping to provide basic security in the Democratic Republic of the Congo; a Civilian Police Adviser from the United States who is helping to improve the rule of law in Kosovo; a UNICEF Child Protection Officer from Ecuador who is helping to secure the rights of Colombia's most vulnerable citizens; and a World Food Programme Officer from China who is helping to feed the people of North Korea.

23 Distinguished guests,

24 The idea that there is one people in possession of the truth, one answer to the world's ills, or one solution to humanity's needs, has done untold harm throughout history—especially in the last century. Today, however, even amidst continuing ethnic conflict around the world, there is a growing understanding that human diversity is both the reality that makes dialogue necessary, and the very basis for that dialogue.

25 We understand, as never before, that each of us is fully worthy of the respect and dignity essential to our common humanity. We

人类对和平、尊严和安全的需要，我们才能不负今天的这项荣誉，才能完成联合国的设立者最初的愿景。这项关于和平的重大使命，联合国的成员们每天都在世界各地执行着。

22 他们中一小部分人，男士女士们，今天也在这大厅里。他们中间有塞内加尔的军事观察员，正在帮助刚果共和国提供基本的安全保障；有美国的民警顾问，正在帮助改善科索沃地区的法治建设；有来自厄瓜多尔的联合国儿童基金会的儿童保护官，正致力于保障哥伦比亚弱势群体的权力；还有来自中国的世界粮食计划署的工作人员在帮助朝鲜人民摆脱饥饿。

23 尊敬的来宾，

24 只有一类人掌握着真理，只有一种方法能治愈疾病或者只有一种方案能解决人类需求。这些说法在整个历史进程中——尤其是在上个世纪，已经给人类造成了无数灾难。然而，今天，在世界各地持续不断的民族冲突中，人们已经越来越多地认识到人类多样性既使对话成为一种必要，也是这种对话的基础。

25 我们前所未有地理解了，每个人都值得享有对共同的人性来说必不可少的尊重和尊严。我们认识到，

---

⑨ confer [kən'fɜː] *vt.* 授予　如：confer a medal on the hero 授予英雄一枚勋章

recognize that we are the products of many cultures, traditions and memories; that mutual respect allows us to study and learn from other cultures; and that we gain strength by combining the foreign with the familiar.

26 In every great faith and tradition one can find the values of tolerance and mutual understanding. The *Qur'an*, for example, tells us that "We created you from a single pair of male and female and made you into nations and tribes, that you may know each other." Confucius urged his followers, "When the good way prevails in the state, speak boldly and act boldly. When the state has lost the way, act boldly and speak softly." In the Jewish tradition, the *injunction* [10] to "love thy neighbour as thyself", is considered to be the very essence of the Torah.

27 This thought is reflected in the Christian Gospel, which also teaches us to love our enemies and pray for those who wish to persecute us. Hindus are taught that "truth is one, the sages give it various names." And in the Buddhist tradition, individuals are urged to act with compassion in every facet of life.

28 Each of us has the right to take pride in our particular faith or heritage. But the notion that what is ours is necessarily in conflict with what is theirs is both false and dangerous. It has resulted in endless enmity and conflict, leading men to commit the greatest of crimes in the name of a higher power.

29 It need not be so. People of different

众多文化、传统和历史记忆塑造了不同的我们，只有互相尊重才能学习吸收其他文化的长处，只有将异质文化与我们自己熟悉的东西结合才能增强力量。

26 在所有伟大的信仰和传统中都有包容与相互理解这类价值观的体现。例如，《古兰经》中曾说："我确已从一男一女创造你们，我使你们成为许多民族和部落，以便你们互相认识。"孔子劝导自己的弟子，说道："邦有道，危言危行；邦无道，危行言孙。"犹太教中，关于"爱邻如爱己"的训谕被誉为犹太律法的精华。

27 基督教的福音书也反映了这种思想，它教导人们要爱自己的敌人，为那些要迫害你的人祈祷。印度教认为"真理唯一，哲人以不同名义谓之。"在佛教传统中，也倡导个人要在生活的各方面都以慈悲为怀。

28 每个人都有权以自己独特的信仰或文化遗产为荣。我们的信仰一定与别人的冲突，这样的想法是错误的，也是危险的。这已经造成了无尽的仇恨和冲突，导致人们以更高权势的名义犯下滔天罪行。

29 不一定要这样的。不同文化

---

⑩ injunction [ɪn'dʒʌŋkʃən] *n.* 训谕，诫训

religions and cultures live side by side in almost every part of the world, and most of us have overlapping identities which unite us with very different groups. We can love what we are, without hating what—and who—we are not. We can thrive in our own tradition, even as we learn from others, and come to respect their teachings.

30 This will not be possible, however, without freedom of religion, of expression, of assembly, and basic equality under the law. Indeed, the lesson of the past century has been that where the dignity of the individual has been trampled or threatened—where citizens have not enjoyed the basic right to choose their government, or the right to change it regularly—conflict has too often followed, with innocent civilians paying the price, in lives cut short and communities destroyed.

31 The obstacles to democracy have little to do with culture or religion, and much more to do with the desire of those in power to maintain their position at any cost. This is neither a new phenomenon nor one confined to any particular part of the world. People of all cultures value their freedom of choice, and feel the need to have a say in decisions affecting their lives.

32 The United Nations, whose membership comprises almost all the States in the world, is founded on the principle of the equal worth of every human being. It is the nearest thing we have to a representative institution that can address the interests of all states, and all peoples. Through this universal, indispensable instrument of human

和宗教的人们在世界几乎每个角落比邻而居，而我们大多数人拥有的多重身份将不同的群体团结在一起。我们可以爱我们自己，但也不会因此恨那些与我们不同的人。即使我们学习他人，尊重他们的文化，我们也能在自己的文化传统中发展繁荣。

30 然而，没有宗教、言论和集会自由，以及法律面前基本的平等，这些都不可能实现。事实上，过去一个世纪的教训已经证明，哪里的个人尊严遭到践踏或威胁，哪里的公民不能享有选择或定期更换政府的基本权利，哪里就会经常发生冲突，无辜平民就要为此付出代价，生命将遭受摧残，社会将遭到摧毁。

31 阻碍民主的因素与文化或者宗教几乎没有关系，而与当权者不惜一切代价维持自己权力的欲望关系甚大。这既不是什么新现象，也不局限在特定地区。所有文化的人们都很珍视选择的自由，他们认为需要在影响他们生活的决策上拥有发言权。

32 联合国建立在人人价值平等的原则之上，其成员国包括世界上几乎全部国家。它是我们为各国和各国人民的利益服务的再好不过的代表性组织。这个全球性的、不可或缺的组织代表着人类进步，通过这个组织各国可以认识到并协力追求彼此的共同

progress, States can serve the interests of their citizens by recognizing common interests and pursuing them in unity. No doubt, that is why the Nobel Committee says that it "wishes, in its *centenary* [11] year, to proclaim that the only negotiable route to global peace and cooperation goes by way of the United Nations".

33 I believe the Committee also recognized that this era of global challenges leaves no choice but cooperation at the global level. When States undermine the rule of law and violate the rights of their individual citizens, they become a menace not only to their own people, but also to their neighbours, and indeed the world. What we need today is better governance—legitimate, democratic governance that allows each individual to flourish, and each State to thrive.

34 Your Majesties, Excellencies, Ladies and Gentlemen, You will recall that I began my address with a reference to the girl born in Afghanistan today. Even though her mother will do all in her power to protect and sustain her, there is a one-in-four risk that she will not live to see her fifth birthday. Whether she does is just one test of our common humanity—of our belief in our individual responsibility for our fellow men and women. But it is the only test that matters.

35 Remember this girl and then our larger aims—to fight poverty, prevent conflict, or cure disease—will not seem distant, or impossible. Indeed, those aims will seem very near, and very achievable—as they should. Because beneath the

利益，从而为各自的国民服务。无疑，这也就是为什么诺贝尔奖委员会称，"在这百年之际将这个奖颁给联合国，以此宣告，联合国是通过谈判实现世界和平与合作的唯一道路"。

33 我相信诺贝尔奖委员会也认识到，在这个充满挑战的时代，我们除了合作别无选择。那些破坏法治、违反公民权利的国家不仅是对本国人民的威胁，也是对邻国，实际上是对整个世界的威胁。今天我们需要的是更好的统治——是法律之下的民主管理，在这种管理下每个公民、每个国家都能发展繁荣。

34 尊敬的陛下、各位阁下、女士们、先生们，还记得我今天在演讲开始时谈到一个出生在阿富汗的女孩吧。尽管她的母亲会尽全力去保护和抚养她，但仍然有四分之一的危险性使她可能活不到五岁。能不能活过五岁，这仅仅是对我们全人类的一个考验，考验我们是否坚信我们对其他人类同胞负有责任。但这确实是唯一重要的考验。

35 记住这个女孩，那么我们更大的目标——战胜贫穷、遏制冲突或者治愈疾病就会显得不再遥远，就有可能实现。事实上，这些目标似乎会变得非常近，很容易达成，就像它们

---

① centenary [sen'ti:nəri] *adj.* 一百年的 如：the centenary year 一百周年纪念

surface of states and nations, ideas and language, lies the fate of individual human beings in need. Answering their needs will be the mission of the United Nations in the century to come.

36 Thank you very much.

本应该的那样。因为在国家与民族、思想与语言的表象下，是处于困境中的人类个人命运。应对这些困境就是联合国在新世纪的任务。

36 多谢大家。

演讲关键词 Practical Expressions

1. human dignity 人类尊严
2. *United Nations' Charter*《联合国宪章》
3. ethnic conflict 民族冲突
4. overlapping identities 多重身份
5. common interests 共同利益
6. prevent conflict 遏制冲突
7. vulnerable citizens 弱势群体
8. basic security 基本安全保障

1. Ultimately, it is borne by all of us—North and South, rich and poor, men and women of all races and religions.

从根本上来说，我们所有人——不论来自南半球还是北半球，贫穷还是富有，也不论人种、宗教和性别差异，都要承担此代价。

2. They are as fundamental to the poor as to the rich; they are as necessary to the security of the developed world as to that of the developing world.

人权的根本性没有富人和穷人之分；其必要性也没有发展中国家和发达国家之分。

颁奖典礼上的讲究

根据诺贝尔的遗嘱，诺贝尔和平奖的颁奖典礼在挪威首都奥斯陆举行。除此之外，其他诺贝尔奖奖项的颁发都在瑞典首都斯德哥尔摩举行。每年的颁奖仪式都是既隆重又简约的，而仪式的流程和所用设备及装饰都有特别的惯例或规定。这些都完美体现了对诺贝尔的纪念和尊敬。比如，颁奖仪式中用到的白花和黄花都必须从当年诺贝尔去世的城市——意大利的圣莫雷空运过来。在颁奖典礼上，出席的男士要穿燕尾服，女士要穿正式晚礼服。如果有人想穿本民族特色的传统服装，还得提前与组委会沟通，在正式性不受影响的前提下他们会给予许可。但是，据说无论那天穿得多么光芒四射，都很难有人可以媲美瑞典王后西尔维娅，她那顶价值几百万瑞典克朗的精致珠宝王冠和同样华丽的礼服让她光彩夺目。

Speech 2
Striving for Common Happiness and Welfare
为共同的福祉而奋斗

—Nobel Lecture by Nelson Mandela on December 10, 1993
——南非国父纳尔逊·曼德拉 1993 年 12 月 10 日诺贝尔和平奖获奖演讲

名家速览 About the Author

诺贝尔奖大师	纳尔逊·曼德拉
奖 项 归 属	诺贝尔和平奖
获 奖 理 由	表彰他们为和平终结种族隔离制度所做的贡献，他们的工作为一个新的民主南非的产生奠定了基础。
相关演讲链接	1990 年 2 月 11 日纳尔逊·曼德拉出狱演讲

纳尔逊·曼德拉（Nelson Mandela）于 1918 年 7 月 18 日出生于南非特兰斯凯，2013 年 12 月 6 日在约翰内斯堡的住所去世。他本人获得了文学学士学位和律师资格。曼德拉在 1994 至 1999 年间任南非总统，作为首位黑人总统，他被尊称为南非国父。曼德拉一生致力于废除南非的种族隔离制度，为此做出了巨大  的贡献和牺牲。在他领导暴力民主运动的时候，南非当局曾以密谋推翻政府等罪名将其逮捕关押达 27 年之久。1990 年出狱后，他发表演讲，转而支持以和平协商的方式同种族隔离斗争。因一生为争取南非人民的民主自由平等所做的杰出贡献，他曾获得很多荣誉。1992 年他在访华期间还获得了北京大学授予的法学荣誉博士学位。本文是曼德拉 1993 年获得诺贝尔和平奖时所做的演讲，他在其中说明了诺贝尔和平奖的意义，列举了数年来为世界和平、民主、平等、自由而奋战的数位诺贝尔和平奖获得者，同时讲述了南非人民的民主之路，号召世界人民团结起来，共同追求美好平等的未来。

1 Your Majesty the King,

2 Your Royal Highness,

3 Esteemed Members of the Norwegian Nobel Committee,

4 Honourable Prime Minister, Madame Gro Harlem Brundtland, Ministers, Members of Parliament and Ambassadors, Fellow Laureate, Mr. F.W. de Klerk,

5 Distinguished Guests, Friends, Ladies and Gentlemen,

6 I am indeed humble to be standing here today to receive this year's Nobel Peace Prize.

7 I extend my heartfelt thanks to the Norwegian Nobel Committee for elevating us to the status of a Nobel Peace Prize winner.

8 I would also like to take this opportunity to congratulate my compatriot and fellow laureate, State President F.W. de Klerk, on his receipt of this high honour.

9 Together, we join two distinguished South Africans, the *late* ① Chief Albert Lutuli and His Grace Archbishop Desmond Tutu, to whose *seminal* ② contributions to the peaceful struggle against the evil system of apartheid you paid well-deserved tribute by awarding them the Nobel Peace Prize.

---

1 尊敬的国王陛下，

2 各位阁下，

3 尊敬的挪威诺贝尔奖委员会的成员们，

4 尊敬的首相及格罗·哈莱姆·布伦特兰首相夫人，尊敬的各位部长、议员和大使，同为诺贝尔奖得主的德克勒克先生，

5 尊敬的来宾、朋友们、女士们、先生们，

6 事实上，我是怀着无比谦卑的心情在此接受今年的诺贝尔和平奖的。

7 我由衷地感谢挪威诺贝尔奖委员会将和平奖授予我们。

8 借此机会，我想祝贺我的同胞——总统德克勒克先生也获得这项至高荣誉。

9 还有另外两位杰出的南非人士——已故的领袖阿尔伯特·卢图利和德斯蒙德·图图大主教——他们也因对和平反抗罪恶的种族隔离制度所做的重大贡献，获得了诺贝尔和平奖。

---

① late [leɪt] *adj.* 已故的　如：in memory of the late Premier 纪念已故的总理

② seminal ['siːmɪnl] *adj.* 影响深远的，有重大意义的　如：a seminal article 有巨大影响的文章

10 It will not be ***presumptuous*** ③ of us if we also add, among our predecessors, the name of another outstanding Nobel Peace Prize winner, the late African American statesman and internationalist Rev Martin Luther King Jr. He, too, ***grappled*** ④ with and died in the effort to make a contribution to the just solution of the same great issues of the day which we have had to face as South Africans.

11 We speak here of the challenge of the dichotomies of war and peace, violence and non-violence, racism and human dignity, oppression and repression and liberty and human rights, poverty and freedom from want.

12 We stand here today as nothing more than a representative of the millions of our people who dared to rise up against a social system whose very essence is war, violence, racism, oppression, repression and the impoverishment of an entire people.

13 I am also here today as a representative of the millions of people across the globe, the anti-apartheid movement, the governments and organisations that joined with us, not to fight against South Africa as a country or any of its peoples, but to oppose an inhuman system and sue for a speedy end to the apartheid crime against humanity.

14 These countless human beings, both

10 在我们的前辈中，我还要提到另一位和平奖获得者——已故的非裔美籍政治家和国际主义者马丁·路德·金牧师。他也曾面临时下南非人民面临的问题，他为此努力斗争，寻求解决办法，也为此献出了生命。

11 我们在这里谈论的是一些对立的挑战：战争与和平，暴力与非暴力，种族歧视与人类尊严，压迫、镇压与自由、人权，贫困与富足。

12 今天我们仅作为成百上千万人的代表站在这里，我们敢于站起来同一个充斥着战争、暴力、种族歧视、压迫与贫困的社会制度做斗争。

13 同时，在此我还代表着全世界成百上千万人，代表着反种族隔离运动和那些同我们站在一起的政府和组织。我们并不反对南非这个国家或者它的人民，我们控诉的是非人道的制度，希望快速结束这违反人道的种族隔离罪行。

14 不管是南非本国还是国外，

③ presumptuous [prɪˈzʌmptjʊəs] *adj.* 冒昧的，放肆的   如：It is too presumptuous for him to do so. 他这样做太放肆了。

④ grapple [ˈgræpl] *vi.* 努力解决某事   如：The new government has yet to grapple with the problem of air pollution. 新政府还需尽力解决空气污染问题。

inside and outside our country, had the nobility of spirit to stand in the path of tyranny and injustice, without seeking selfish gain. They recognised that an injury to one is an injury to all and therefore acted together in defense of justice and a common human decency.

15 Because of their courage and persistence for many years, we can, today, even set the dates when all humanity will join together to celebrate one of the outstanding human victories of our century.

16 When that moment comes, we shall, together, rejoice in a common victory over racism, apartheid and white minority rule.

17 That triumph will finally bring to a close a history of five hundred years of African colonisation that began with the establishment of the Portuguese empire.

18 Thus, it will mark a great step forward in history and also serve as a common pledge of the peoples of the world to fight racism, wherever it occurs and whatever guise it assumes.

19 At the southern tip of the continent of Africa, a rich reward in the making, an invaluable gift is in the preparation for those who suffered in the name of all humanity when they sacrified everything—for liberty, peace, human dignity and human fulfillment.

20 This reward will not be measured in money. Nor can it be reckoned in the collective price of the rare metals and precious stones that rest in the bowels of the African soil we tread in the footsteps of our ancestors. It will and must

无数人怀着崇高的精神无私地反对暴政和非正义行为。他们意识到了，对一个人的伤害就是伤害所有人，因此只有一起行动才能维护正义和人类共同的尊严。

15 正是因为他们的勇气和多年坚持不懈的努力，我们今天在这里才敢畅想，有朝一日世界人民会共同庆祝本世纪人类的伟大胜利。

16 当那一刻到来时，我们会一起庆祝共同的胜利，我们战胜了种族歧视、种族隔离和少数白人的统治。

17 到那时，一段以西班牙政权的建立为始的长达500年的非洲殖民史将画上一个句号。

18 因此，不管种族主义在何处以何种面目出现，这一胜利将是人类历史上的一大进步，是全人类反对种族主义的共同誓言。

19 在非洲的最南端，当那些人以全人类的名义牺牲所有为自由、和平、人类尊严和人类自我实现做斗争的时候，他们将获得无价的荣誉和回报。

20 这份回报是不能用钱来衡量的，也不能用稀少的奖牌或者栖息在我们祖先脚下非洲土壤里的珍贵钻石来衡量。它必须以儿童的快乐和幸福来衡量，在任何时候，任何社会，儿

be measured by the happiness and welfare of the children, at once the most vulnerable citizens in any society and the greatest of our treasures.

21 The children must, at last, play in the open veld, no longer tortured by the ***pangs*** ⑤ of hunger or ***ravaged*** ⑥ by disease or threatened with the ***scourge*** ⑦ of ignorance, ***molestation*** ⑧ and abuse, and no longer required to engage in deeds whose gravity exceeds the demands of their tender years.

22 In front of this distinguished audience, we commit the new South Africa to the relentless pursuit of the purposes defined in the World Declaration on the Survival, Protection and Development of Children.

23 The reward of which we have spoken will and must also be measured by the happiness and welfare of the mothers and fathers of these children, who must walk the earth without fear of being robbed, killed for political or material profit, or spat upon because they are beggars. They too must be relieved of the heavy burden of despair which they carry in their hearts, born of hunger, homelessness and unemployment.

24 The value of that gift to all who have suffered will and must be measured by the happiness and welfare of all the people of our country, who will have torn down the inhuman walls that divide them.

童都是最易受伤害的人群，也是我们最大的财富。

21 最终孩子们要能在开阔的大草原上玩耍，不再承受饥饿的折磨，不再遭受疾病的蹂躏或无知造成的灾难的威胁，也不再忍受性骚扰和虐待，或者被逼迫做超出他们那个脆弱年纪承受范围的事情。

22 面对诸位杰出的听众，我们保证新南非将坚持不懈地追求"世界儿童生存、保护和发展宣言"中制定的目标。

23 前面提到的回报也必须以这些孩子们父母的福祉来衡量，他们不必担心走路遭抢劫，也不必担心因政治或物质利益被杀害，或者因为他们的乞丐身份而遭人唾弃。还要释放他们内心绝望的重担，改变他们生而贫穷、无家可归和失业的现状。

24 对于所有遭受苦痛的人们来说，那份回报的价值必须用我们国家所有人的幸福来衡量，是他们推翻了隔离我们的非人道的高墙。

⑤ pang [pæŋ] *n.* 痛苦　如：the pang of the toothache 一阵阵的牙痛

⑥ ravage ['rævɪdʒ] *vt.* 破坏，蹂躏　如：A tornado ravaged the countryside. 一阵龙卷风摧毁了乡村。

⑦ scourge [skɜːdʒ] *n.* 祸害，灾祸　如：the scourge of war 战争之苦

⑧ molestation [ˌməʊlesˈteɪʃən] *n.* (对儿童) 性骚扰

25 These great masses will have turned their backs on the grave insult to human dignity which described some as masters and others as servants, and transformed each into a predator whose survival depended on the destruction of the other.

26 The value of our shared reward will and must be measured by the joyful peace which will triumph, because the common humanity that bonds both black and white into one human race, will have said to each one of us that we shall all live like the children of paradise.

27 Thus shall we live, because we will have created a society which recognises that all people are born equal, with each entitled in equal measure to life, liberty, prosperity, human rights and good governance.

28 Such a society should never allow again that there should be prisoners of conscience nor that any person's human right should be violated.

29 Neither should it ever happen that once more the avenues to peaceful change are blocked by usurpers who seek to take power away from the people, in pursuit of their own, *ignoble* ⑨ purposes.

30 In relation to these matters, we appeal to those who govern Burma that they release our fellow Nobel Peace Prize laureate, Aung San Suu Kyi, and engage her and those she represents in serious dialogue, for the benefit of all the people of Burma.

31 We pray that those who have the power to do so will, without further delay, permit that she uses her talents and energies for the greater good of the

25 广大民众会反抗这种对人类尊严的侮辱——将一些人作为主人，其他人沦为仆人，将所有人都变成要靠毁灭他人生存的掠夺者。

26 我们共同的回报也将而且必须以和平的胜利来衡量，因为将白人和黑人团结起来的人道主义精神将告诉我们每一个人，我们都会像天堂里的孩子般生活。

27 我们将那样生活，因为我们将创造一个人人平等的社会，每个人在生命、自由、财富、人权和良好的统治上都将被赋予同等权利。

28 这样的社会里，绝不能再允许有良心的罪犯，也不能容忍任何人的权利遭到侵犯。

29 也绝不能让篡位者阻挡和平之路，夺走属于人民的权利来达到他们自己肮脏的目的。

30 与此同时，我们也呼吁缅甸的执政者释放同为诺贝尔和平奖获得者的昂山素季；为了所有缅甸人的利益，与昂山素季以及她所代表的人们进行严肃认真的对话。

31 我们祈求当权者别再推延，允许昂山素季为了她国家的人民和全人类的福祉发挥她的天赋和能力。

---

⑨ ignoble [ɪɡˈnəʊbl] *adj.* 不光彩的，卑鄙的　如：ignoble thoughts 可耻的想法

people of her country and humanity as a whole.

32 Far from the rough and tumble of the politics of our own country. I would like to take this opportunity to join the Norwegian Nobel Committee and *pay tribute to* ⑩ my joint laureate. Mr. F.W. de Klerk.

33 He had the courage to admit that a terrible wrong had been done to our country and people through the imposition of the system of apartheid.

34 He had the foresight to understand and accept that all the people of South Africa must through negotiations and as equal participants in the process, together determine what they want to make of their future.

35 But there are still some within our country who wrongly believe they can make a contribution to the cause of justice and peace by clinging to the shibboleths that have been proved to spell nothing but disaster.

36 It remains our hope that these, too, will be blessed with sufficient reason to realise that history will not be denied and that the new society cannot be created by reproducing the repugnant past, however refined or enticingly repackaged.

37 We would also like to take advantage of this occasion to pay tribute to the many formations of the democratic movement of our country, including the members here of our Patriotic Front, who have themselves played a central role in bringing our country as close to the democratic transformation as it is today.

38 We are happy that many representatives

32 暂且抛开我们自己国家政治上的坎坷不说，我也希望借此机会同挪威诺贝尔委员会一道向同为诺贝尔和平奖获得者的德克勒先生致以崇高的敬意。

33 他勇敢地承认，种族隔离制度是强加在我们的国家和人民身上的严重错误。

34 他深谋远虑，认为南非人民必须通过平等参与谈判过程，共同决定他们想要的未来。

35 但是我们国家还有一些人错误地相信，他们可以守着那些只能引发灾难的信仰为正义与和平的事业做出贡献。

36 但是我们仍怀有希望，希望他们能认识到历史不能被否认，不管我们如何改造和包装过去，新社会都不能靠复制苦难的过去而诞生。

37 我们也希望借此机会向国内各种形式的民主运动组织致以崇高的敬意。"爱国前线"的成员们发挥他们的关键作用，使我们国家尽可能地迈向了今天的民主改革进程。

38 我们非常高兴，这些组织的

⑩ pay tribute to... 赞颂，称赞

of these formations, including people who have served or are serving in the "homeland" structures, came with us to Oslo. They too must share the accolade which the Nobel Peace Prize confers.

39 <u>We live with the hope that as she battles to remake herself, South Africa, will be like a microcosm of the new world that is striving to be born.</u>

40 This must be a world of democracy and respect for human rights, a world freed from the horrors of poverty, hunger, deprivation and ignorance, relieved of the threat and the scourge of civil wars and external aggression and unburdened of the great tragedy of millions forced to become refugees.

41 The processes in which South Africa and Southern Africa as a whole are engaged, beckon and urge us all that we take this tide at the flood and make of this region as a living example of what all people of conscience would like the world to be.

42 We do not believe that this Nobel Peace Prize is intended as a commendation for matters that have happened and passed.

43 We hear the voices which say that it is an appeal from all those, throughout the universe, who sought an end to the system of apartheid. We understand their call, that we devote what remains of our lives to the use of our country's unique and painful experience to demonstrate, in practice, that the normal condition for human existence is democracy, justice, peace, non-racism, non-sexism, prosperity for everybody, a healthy

代表，以及那些曾经或正在为"家园"组织服务的人们，也同我们一起来到了奥斯陆。他们也必须共享诺贝尔奖所赋予的崇高荣誉。

39 我们满怀希望地看到，为重塑自己而奋战的南非就是人们为之奋斗的新世界的缩影。

40 这必将是一个尊重人权的民主世界，是一个远离贫穷与饥饿、困乏与无知，免受内战与外侮，以及威胁之苦的世界，这个世界里不会有成百上千万人一起沦为难民的悲剧发生。

41 南非以及整个非洲南部并肩作战的这一过程，呼唤并促使我们每一个人融入这一潮流中，使这一地区成为全世界有良知的人民心目中美好世界的典型。

42 我们不相信诺贝尔奖仅仅是为了表彰过去发生的事情。

43 我们听到了来自全人类的要终结种族隔离制度的呼声。我们理解他们的呼吁，我们将不遗余力地用我们国家自身独特的苦痛经历来证明——人类生存的正常条件是民主、正义、和平、无种族歧视、无性别歧视、人人富足，以及一个健康、平等、团结一致的社会环境。

environment and equality and solidarity among the peoples.

44 Moved by that appeal and inspired by the eminence you have thrust upon us, we undertake that we too will do what we can to contribute to the renewal of our world so that none should, in future, be described as the "wretched of the earth".

45 Let it never be said by future generations that indifference, cynicism or selfishness made us fail to live up to the ideals of humanism which the Nobel Peace Prize *encapsulates*[①].

46 Let the strivings of us all, prove Martin Luther King Jr. to have been correct, when he said that humanity can no longer be tragically bound to the starless midnight of racism and war.

47 Let the efforts of us all, prove that he was not a mere dreamer when he spoke of the beauty of genuine brotherhood and peace being more precious than diamonds or silver or gold.

48 Let a new age be born!

49 Thank you.

44 这些呼吁以及你们授予的荣誉既感动着我们，也使我们倍受鼓舞。我们承诺，我们会尽一切所能为世界的繁荣复兴贡献力量，希望将来没有人成为在这个世界上受苦的人。

45 希望我们的后代永远也没有机会说：因为冷漠、玩世不恭或自私自利，我们辜负了诺贝尔和平奖所倡导的人道主义理想。

46 让我们用所有的奋战证明马丁•路德•金是正确的——人类不能再悲剧地困在种族歧视和战争的茫茫黑夜中。

47 让我们用所有的努力证明，当他说真诚的手足情义与和平之美比钻石和黄金、白银更珍贵时，他不只是一个纯粹的梦想家。

48 让一个崭新的时代诞生吧！

49 谢谢大家！

 演讲关键词 Practical Expressions

1. social system 社会制度
2. anti-apartheid movement 反种族隔离运动
3. democratic transformation 民主改革
4. the ideals of humanism 人道主义理想
5. the system of apartheid 种族隔离制度
6. devote what remains of our lives 不遗余力

① encapsulate [ɪnˈkæpsjʊleɪt] *vt.* 概括，包括　如：The poems encapsulates many of the central themes of her writing. 这首诗是对她多年著作的核心主题的概括。

1. They recognised that an injury to one is an injury to all and therefore acted together in defense of justice and a common human decency.

他们意识到了，对一个人的伤害就是伤害所有人，因此只有一起行动才能维护正义和人类共同的尊严。

2. We live with the hope that as she battles to remake herself, South Africa, will be like a microcosm of the new world that is striving to be born.

我们满怀希望地看到，为重塑自己而奋战的南非就是人们为之奋斗的新世界的缩影。

奖牌曾遭溶解

德国科学家劳厄和弗兰克·赫兹分别获得1914年和1925年的物理学奖。第二次世界大战期间，德国纳粹政府要没收他们的诺贝尔奖奖牌。两位科学家为了保护奖牌辗转至丹麦，请他们的丹麦同行——1922年诺贝尔物理奖得主波尔帮忙保存奖牌。不料，1940年纳粹德国占领丹麦，波尔心急如焚，害怕奖牌在此濒危。就在此时匈牙利化学家赫维西想出了一个好办法：他们将奖牌放入"王水"(即硫酸与硝酸混合液)中，纯金奖牌便溶解了。战争结束后，他们将溶液瓶里的黄金还原后送到了斯德哥尔摩，并按当年的样子重新铸造，1949年奖牌得以完璧归赵。

Speech 3
Cooperate to Build a Mine-Free World
携手共建无雷世界

—Speech by Jody Williams for the Nobel Peace Prize in 1997
——国际禁雷运动大使乔迪·威廉姆斯 1997 年诺贝尔和平奖获奖演讲

名家速览 About the Author

诺贝尔奖大师	乔迪·威廉姆斯
奖 项 归 属	诺贝尔和平奖
获 奖 理 由	因为他们为禁止和清除地雷所做的努力。
主 要 成 就	带领开展"国际禁雷运动"，号召所有国家积极进行"禁止地雷"工作

　　乔迪·威廉姆斯（Jody Williams），女，生于 1950 年 10 月
9 日。乔迪自小就对不公平正义的事情怀有深深的憎恶，常为
身患残疾的哥哥打抱不平。她长大后成为一名教师，积极投身
于国际人道主义事业，为解决人道主义危机和援助做出了极大
贡献。深埋于地下的地雷在战场上伤害的是士兵，却也很有可
能在默默等待着无辜的平民百姓，只要他们不小心触碰到雷
区，马上就会被炸得粉身碎骨。第一次世界大战末期，地雷开
始大量投入使用。之后的战争中地雷技术不断改进，不仅成了
防御武器，更显示出进攻的优势。但是其让人毫无防备的杀伤
性也让参战士兵，尤其是平民百姓深受其害。为了取缔这种惨
无人道的杀伤性武器，乔迪全心全意地投入到了这项史无前例的国际事业中。她组织"国际
禁雷运动"，联合其他非政府间组织和支持禁雷的国家政府协商签署了《国际禁雷公约》。本
篇演讲中，乔迪详细讲述了该国际条约的签署过程和禁雷运动的发展，阐明了禁雷运动的意
义，号召世界各国团结起来为建立一个无雷的未来世界而奋斗。

演讲现场
Speech Script

精美译文
Suggested Translation

1 Your Majesties, Honorable Members of the Norwegian Nobel Committee, Excellencies and Honored Guests,

2 It is a privilege to be here today, together with other representatives of the International Campaign to Ban Landmines, to receive jointly the 1997 Nobel Peace Prize. Our appreciation goes to those who nominated us and to the Nobel Committee for choosing this year to recognize, from among so many other nominees who have worked diligently for peace, the work of the International Campaign.

3 I am deeply honored—but whatever personal recognition derives from this award, I believe that this high tribute is the result of the truly historic achievement of this humanitarian effort to rid the world of one indiscriminate weapon. In the words of the Nobel Committee, the International Campaign "started a process which in the space of a few years changed a ban on *antipersonnel* ① mines from a vision to a *feasible* ② reality".

4 Further, the Committee noted that the Campaign has been able to "express and mediate a broad range of popular commitment in an unprecedented way. With the governments of several small and medium-sized countries taking the issue up... this work has grown into

1 尊敬的国王和王后陛下，尊敬的挪威诺贝尔委员会的成员们，各位阁下，尊敬的来宾们：

2 今天能站在这里同国际禁雷运动的成员们一起接受 1997 年的诺贝尔和平奖，我感到非常荣幸。感谢那些提名我们获此奖项的人们，也感谢诺贝尔委员会今年从那么多为和平奋斗的被提名者中选中了我们，对我们在国际禁雷运动中所做的工作给予充分肯定。

3 我确实深感荣幸——但是不管我个人从这个奖项中得到何种认可，我都相信这项至高荣誉之所以能够存在，是因为人们在摆脱一种杀伤性武器的运动中取得了历史性成就。用诺贝尔奖委员会的话来说就是，国际禁雷运动"开启了禁止杀伤性武器的进程，使得关于杀伤性地雷的禁令在几年内由幻想变成可行的现实"。

4 诺贝尔奖委员会进一步说这项运动"以前所未有的方式表达并调和了很多同样重要的义务。几个小国的政府首先承担起了这个责任……现在这项工作已经发展成为追求和平方面的典范。"

① antipersonnel ['ænti,pɜːsə'nel] *adj.* 杀伤性的　如：antipersonnel bombs 杀伤性炸弹
② feasible ['fiːzəbl] *adj.* 可行的　如：a feasible plan 可行的计划

a convincing example of an effective policy for peace."

5 The desire to ban landmines is not new. In the late 1970s, the International Committee of the Red Cross, along with a handful of nongovernmental organizations (NGOs), pressed the world to look at weapons that were particularly injurious and/or indiscriminate. One of the weapons of special concern was landmines. People often ask why the focus on this one weapon. How is the landmine different from any other conventional weapon?

6 Landmines distinguish themselves because once they have been sown, once the soldier walks away from the weapon, the landmine cannot tell the difference between a soldier or a civilian—a woman, a child, a grandmother going out to collect firewood to make the family meal. The *crux* ③ of the problem is that while the use of the weapon might be militarily justifiable during the day of the battle, or even the two weeks of the battle, or maybe even the two months of the battle, once peace is declared the landmine does not recognize that peace. The landmine is eternally prepared to take victims. In common parlance, it is the perfect soldier, the "eternal *sentry* ④". The war ends, the landmine goes on killing.

7 Since World War II most of the conflicts in the world have been internal conflicts. The weapon of choice in those wars has all too often been landmines—to such a degree that what

5 人类禁止地雷的愿望已经不是一两天的事了。早在 20 世纪 70 年代末，国际红十字会和其他一些非政府间组织就已经开始呼吁世界重新审视那些具有特别杀伤力的武器。其中，地雷就是人们最关心的武器之一。人们经常会问：为什么要关注这一种武器呢？地雷与其他常规武器有什么不同吗？

6 地雷的不同之处在于，一旦它们被埋在了地下，不管是士兵还是平民，抑或是妇女、儿童和外出捡柴为家人烧饭的老奶奶，对它们来说都没有什么区别了。问题的关键在于，地雷的使用在战争时期，在战斗当天、两周内或者甚至在战争期间的两个月内可能都是合理的，可是一旦宣告和平，地雷却意识不到战争已经结束。它们仍然随时准备着残害人们。照一般的说法，它就是一个完美的士兵，是"永远的哨兵"。战争结束了，它还继续着杀害。

7 第二次世界大战以后，世界上大多数战争都是民族内部冲突。在武器使用上，这些战争经常付诸地雷，以至于我们今天发现的上千万的

---

③ crux [krʌks] *n.* 难题，关键 　如：the crux of the matter 事件的关键

④ sentry ['sentrɪ] *n.* 哨兵

we find today are tens of millions of landmines contaminating approximately 70 countries around the world. The overwhelming majority of those countries are found in the developing world, primarily in those countries that do not have the resources to clean up the mess, to care for the tens of thousands of landmine victims. The end result is an international community now faced with a global humanitarian crisis.

8 Let me take a moment to give a few examples of the degree of the *epidemic* ⑤. Today Cambodia has somewhere between four and six million landmines, which can be found in over 50 percent of its national territory. Afghanistan is littered with perhaps nine million landmines. The US military has said that during the height of the Russian invasion and ensuing war in that country, up to 30 million mines were scattered throughout Afghanistan. In the few years of the fighting in the former Yugoslavia, some six million landmines were sown throughout various sections of the country—Angola nine million, Mozambique a million, Somalia a million—I could go on, but it gets tedious. Not only do we have to worry about the mines already in the ground, we must be concerned about those that are stockpiled and ready for use. Estimates range between one and two hundred million mines in stockpiles around the world.

9 When the ICRC pressed in the 1970s for the governments of the world to consider increased

地雷还在残害着世界上近 70 个国家。这些国家大多数都是发展中国家，它们大部分都没有资源去清理混乱的战场，关爱成千上万的地雷受害者。结果就是国际社会现在要面临世界性的人道主义危机。

8 请允许我花一点时间举例说明一下事态有多严重。今天柬埔寨有 400 到 600 万颗地雷分布在全国超过 50% 的土地上。阿富汗可能散落着 900 万颗地雷。据美国军方数据，在俄罗斯入侵阿富汗期间以及这个国家之后的战争中，超过 3 000 万颗地雷被丢在了全国各地。在前南斯拉夫联盟短暂的几年战争期间，全国留下了约 600 万颗地雷。除此之外，安哥拉 900 万颗，莫桑比克 100 万颗，索马里 100 万颗——我还可以继续列举，但不免冗长单调。我们不仅要担心那些已经埋藏在世界各地的地雷，那些储藏在仓库里随时准备投入使用的地雷同样令人担忧。据粗略估计，世界各地存储的地雷数量可达 1 亿到 2 亿颗。

9 20 世纪 70 年代，当世界红十字会呼吁各国政府考虑对特别具有伤

---

⑤ epidemic [ˌepɪˈdemɪk] n. 蔓延，盛行   如：an epidemic of crime in the inner cities 市内中心区犯罪活动盛行

restrictions or elimination of particularly injurious or indiscriminate weapons, there was little support for a ban of landmines. The end result of several years of negotiations was the 1980 *Convention on Conventional Weapons* (CCW). What that treaty did was attempt to regulate the use of landmines. While the Convention tried to tell commanders in the field when it was okay to use the weapon and when it was not okay to use the weapon, it also allowed them to make decisions about the applicability of the law in the midst of battle. Unfortunately, in the heat of battle, the laws of war do not exactly come to mind. When you are trying to save your skin you use anything and everything at your disposal to do so.

10 Throughout these years the Cold War raged on, and internal conflicts that often were ***proxy*** ⑥ wars of the Super Powers proliferated. Finally, with the collapse of the Soviet Bloc, people began to look at war and peace differently. Without the overarching threat of nuclear ***holocaust*** ⑦, people started to look at how wars had actually been fought during the Cold War. What they found was that in the internal conflicts fought during that time, the most ***insidious*** ⑧ weapon of all was the antipersonnel landmine— and that it contaminated the globe in epidemic proportion.

11 As relative peace broke out with the end of the Cold War, the UN was able to go into these nations that had been torn by internal strife,

害性的武器增加限制或者彻底取缔的时候，几乎没有几个国家支持禁雷。经过多年谈判协商，终于达成了1980年的《常规武器公约》。这个公约旨在规范地雷的使用。它尝试告诉战场上的领袖们，什么时候可以用武器，什么时候不能用，但同时它也允许这些领袖有权自主决定此法律在战争中的适用性。不幸的是，在战争处于白热化阶段时，人们不一定能考虑到这些战争法。当你想活命时，就会用尽一切手段。

10 冷战对峙的这些年间，那些民族内部冲突的双方常常是世界超级大国势力的延伸和代理。最终，随着苏联的解体，人们开始以不同的态度看待战争与和平。独当一面的核武器大屠杀的威胁散去后，人们开始重新审视冷战期间的战争形式。人们发现，在那段时间的内部冲突中，最阴险残酷的武器就是极具杀伤力的地雷——它大规模泛滥于整个世界。

11 冷战的结束带来了世界的相对和平，使得联合国能够深入到那些深受内部冲突伤害的国家。他们发现

---

⑥ proxy ['prɒksɪ] *n.* 代理人   ⑦ holocaust ['hɒləkɔːst] *n.* 大屠杀
⑧ insidious [ɪn'sɪdɪəs] *adj.* 暗中为害的，阴险的   如：insidious disease 暗疾

and what they found when they got there were millions and millions of landmines which affected every aspect of peacekeeping, which affected every aspect of post-conflict reconstruction of those societies. You know, if you are in Phnom Penh in Cambodia, and you are setting up the peacekeeping operations, it might seem relatively easy. But when you want to send your troops out into the hinterlands where four or six million landmines are, it becomes a problem, because the main routes are mined. Part of the peace agreement was to bring the hundreds of thousands of refugees back into the country so that they could participate in the voting, in the new democracy being forged in Cambodia. Part of the plan to bring them back included giving each family enough land so that they could be self-sufficient, so they wouldn't be a drain on the country, so that they could contribute to reconstruction. What they found? So many landmines they couldn't give land to the families. What did they get? Fifty dollars and a year's supply of rice. That is the impact of landmines.

12 It was the NGOs, the nongovernmental organizations, who began to seriously think about trying to deal with the root of the problem—to eliminate the problem, it would be necessary to eliminate the weapon. The work of NGOs across the board was affected by the landmines in the developing world. Children's groups, development organizations, refugee organizations, medical and humanitarian relief groups—all had to make huge adjustments in their programs to try

这些地方成百上千万的地雷影响着维护和平进程的方方面面，也影响着这些地区的战后重建。在柬埔寨的金边做维和工作会相对容易。但是如果你想使兵力深入到埋有 400 万到 600 万颗地雷的冲突腹地的话，就是一个大问题了，因为主要路段都掩埋了地雷。缅甸和平协定的部分内容就是让成千上万的难民回归祖国，让他们参与组建缅甸新民主政府的投票。而接难民回国的计划中，要保证给每个家庭足够的土地使他们能够自给自足，不至于成为这个国家的拖累，从而为重建贡献力量。但联合国人员发现：这些遍布地雷的土地根本不能分给那些家庭。那他们能得到什么呢？只能得到 50 美元和一年大米的供给。这就是地雷带来的影响。

12 而非政府间组织开始严肃地思考从根源解决问题的办法——要彻底解决问题，就必须根除这种武器。非政府间组织的工作深受发展中国家地雷问题的影响。儿童组织、发展组织、难民组织、医疗和人道主义救济组织——所有这些组织都要对自己的工作做出巨大调整，试图解决当地的地雷危机及其对那些深受地雷危害的受助群体的影响。正是在这个进程中

to deal with the landmine crisis and its impact on the people they were trying to help. It was also in this period that the first NGO humanitarian demining organizations were born—to try to return contaminated land to rural communities.

13 It was a handful of NGOs, with their roots in humanitarian and human rights work, which began to come together, in late 1991 and early 1992, in an organized effort to ban antipersonnel landmines. In October of 1992, Handicap International, Human Rights Watch, Medico International, Mines Advisory Group, Physicians for Human Rights and Vietnam Veterans of America Foundation came together to issue a *Joint Call to Ban Antipersonnel Landmines*. These organizations, which became the steering committee of the International Campaign to Ban Landmines called for an end to the use, production, trade and stockpiling of antipersonnel landmines. The call also pressed governments to increase resources for humanitarian mine clearance and for victim assistance.

14 From this inauspicious beginning, the International Campaign has become an unprecedented coalition of 1,000 organizations working together in 60 countries to achieve the common goal of a ban of antipersonnel landmines. And as the Campaign grew, the steering committee was expanded to represent the continuing growth and diversity of those who had come together in this global movement. We added the Afghan and Cambodian Campaigns and Rädda Barnen in 1996, and the South African

诞生了世界上第一个反地雷的非政府间组织，这个组织旨在恢复地雷区正常的农村生活。

13 1991 年年底至 1992 年年初，大批致力于人道主义和人权工作的非政府间组织齐聚一堂，开始为禁雷运动努力。1992 年 10 月，国际助残组织、人权监察站、国际医疗组织、排雷咨询组织、人权医生组织和美国越战老兵基金会联合发布了一项《禁雷联合声明》。这些组织都成了国际禁雷运动坚定的成员，他们联合呼吁结束使用、制造、买卖和存储地雷。这些呼声迫使各国政府增加资源开展人道主义的清雷工作，为受害者提供援助。

14 从那时开始，国际禁雷运动就成了一个联合 60 多个国家的 1 000 多家组织的史无前例的联盟，他们的共同目标就是禁止地雷。随着运动的不断发展壮大，指导委员会也随之扩大以适应这个不断有新组织加入的国际运动。1996 年柬埔寨和阿富汗组织以及瑞典的拯救儿童组织加入了我们；今年，正当我们为目标努力的时候，南非和肯尼亚的组织也随之加入。用了 6 年时间，我们做到了。今

Campaign and Kenya Coalition early this year as we continued to press toward our goal. And in six years we did it. In September of this year, 89 countries came together—here in Oslo—and finished the negotiations of a ban treaty based on a draft drawn up by Austria only at the beginning of this year. Just last week in Ottawa, Canada, 121 countries came together again to sign that ban treaty. And as a clear indication of the political will to bring this treaty into force as soon as possible, three countries ratified the treaty upon signature—Canada, Mauritius and Ireland.

15　In its first years, the International Campaign developed primarily in the North—in the countries which had been significant producers of antipersonnel landmines. The strategy was to press for national, regional and international measures to ban landmines. Part of this strategy was to get the governments of the world to review the CCW and in the review process—try to get them to ban the weapon through that convention. We did not succeed. But over the two and one-half years of the review process, with the pressure that we were able to generate—the heightened international attention to the issue—began to raise the stakes, so that different governments wanted to be seen as leaders on what the world was increasingly recognizing as a global humanitarian crisis.

16　The early lead had been taken in the United States, with the first legislated ***moratorium*** ⑨

年 9 月份，89 个国家在奥斯陆结束了关于奥地利今年年初起草的禁雷条约的谈判。上周在加拿大的渥太华，121 个国家再次共同签署了这项条约。为表明尽快使此条约付诸实施的政治决心，加拿大、毛里求斯和爱尔兰三个国家签字批准了条约。

15　在最初几年，国际禁雷运动主要是在北半球——那些曾经的地雷制造大国。我们的策略是给国家、地区和国际社会施加压力，采取禁雷措施。其中一种办法就是使各国政府重修《常规武器公约》，在重修的过程中使他们通过此公约禁止相关武器。但是我们并未成功。但是在两年半重审公约的过程中，在我们制造的压力下，越来越多的关注开始往这方面集中，大大增加了成功的可能性。很多政府见势就想在正在上升的世界人道主义危机上扮演领头人的角色。

16　最先领头的就是美国，1992 年美国率先立法中止了地雷出口。而

---

⑨　moratorium [ˌmɒrəˈtɔːrɪəm] *n.* 禁止　如：a moratorium on the testing of atomic bombs 原子弹试验的禁止

on exports in 1992. And while the author of that legislation, Senator Leahy, has continued to fight tirelessly to ban the weapon in the US, increasingly other nations far surpassed that early leadership. In March of 1995, Belgium became the first country to ban the vise, production, trade and stockpiling domestically. Other countries followed suit: Austria, Norway, Sweden, and others. So even as the CCW review was ending in failure, increasingly governments were calling for a ban. What had once been called a Utopian goal of NGOs was gaining in strength and momentum.

17　While we still had that momentum, in the waning months of the CCW review, we decided to try to get the individual governments which had taken action or had called for a ban to come together in a self-identifying bloc. There is, after all, strength in numbers. So during the final days of the CCW we invited them to a meeting and they actually came. A handful of governments agreed to sit down with us and talk about where the movement to ban landmines would go next. Historically, NGOs and governments have too often seen each other as adversaries, not colleagues, and we were shocked that they came. Seven or nine came to the first meeting, 14 to the second, and 17 to the third. By the time we had concluded the third meeting, with the conclusion of the Review Conference on May 3rd of 1996, the Canadian government had offered to host a governmental meeting in October of last year, in which pro-ban governments would come together

禁雷法的起草者参议员莱希随后还继续不知疲倦地为美国禁雷事业奋斗，越来越多的其他国家开始超越最初的领导人在禁雷方面做出了杰出的成就。1995年3月，比利时成为第一个在国内禁止签发、制造、买卖和存储地雷的国家。其他紧跟其后的还有：奥地利、挪威、瑞典等。所以，尽管重修"常规武器公约"以失败告终，但越来越多的政府正在呼吁禁止地雷。这个曾经被称作非政府间组织的乌托邦梦想的目标，获得了发展的力量和势头。

17　我们现在还保持着同样的势头，在重修"公约"的几个月运动声势减弱，但我们决定试着使每个采取行动或呼吁禁止地雷的国家团结起来，形成一个有共同身份的集团。毕竟团结力量大。所以在修订公约的最后日子里，我们邀请各国参会，他们确实也到场了。许多国家同意坐下来和我们一起讨论禁雷运动接下来的发展方向。历史上，非政府间组织和政府不是同志式的关系，而且经常互相怀有敌意，所以我们很惊讶他们真的会来。第一次会议只有八九个国家参加，第二次就到了14个，而第三次又增至17个。到第三次会议的尾声时，在1996年5月3日的会议回顾上，加拿大政府主动提出主持去年十月的政府间会议，组织支持禁雷的国家一起为禁令的生成出谋划策。重修"常规武器公约"的过程没有产生

and strategize about how to bring about a ban. The CCW review process had not produced the results we sought, so what do we do next?

18 From the third to the fifth of October we met in Ottawa. It was a very fascinating meeting. There were 50 governments there as full participants and 24 observers. The International Campaign was also participating in the conference. The primary objectives of the conference were to develop an Ottawa Declaration, which states would sign signalling their intention to ban landmines, and an "Agenda for Action", which outlined concrete steps on the road to a ban. We were all prepared for that, but few were prepared for the concluding comments by Lloyd Axworthy, the Foreign Minister of Canada. Foreign Minister Axworthy stood up and congratulated everybody for formulating the Ottawa Declaration and the Agenda for Action, which were clearly seen as giving teeth to the ban movement. But the Foreign Minister did not end with congratulations. He ended with a challenge. The Canadian government challenged the world to return to Canada in a year to sign an international treaty banning antipersonnel landmines.

19 Members of the International Campaign to Ban Landmines erupted into cheers. The silence of the governments in the room was defeaning. Even the truly pro-ban states were horrified by the challenge. Canada had stepped outside of diplomatic process and procedure and put them between a rock and a hard place. They had said

我们理想的结果，那么接下来该怎么办呢？

18 今年 10 月 3 日到 5 日我们在渥太华再次召开会议。这次会议非常令人满意。到场的有 50 个完全成员国和 24 个观察国的政府。国际禁雷运动也参与了此次会议。这次会议的首要目标就是达成"渥太华宣言"，发出他们禁雷的信号，同时落定"行动纲领"，为禁令达成铺平道路。我们都为此做好了准备，但加拿大外交部部长阿克斯沃希的总结陈述却是很多人始料未及的。他起身祝贺大家达成了"渥太华宣言"和"行动纲领"，无疑，这对禁雷运动来说是如虎添翼。但是部长并没有以祝贺结束讲话，他在最后提出了一项挑战。加拿大政府呼吁世界各国在一年内相约加拿大，签署禁止地雷的国际条约。

19 于是，国际禁雷运动的成员们爆发出一阵欢呼。但是会议室里的沉默也是显而易见的，甚至连真正支持禁令的国家也被这个挑战吓坏了。加拿大跳过了外交过程和程序，直接使大家陷于进退两难之境地。他们曾说过他们支持禁令。他们也来到了

they were pro-ban. They had come to Ottawa to develop a road map to create a ban treaty and had signed a Declaration of intent. What could they do? They had to respond. It was really breath-taking. We stood up and cheered while the governments were moaning. But once they recovered from that initial shock, the governments that really wanted to see a ban treaty as soon as possible, rose to the challenge and negotiated a ban treaty in record time.

20 What has become known as the Ottawa Process began with the Axworthy Challenge. The treaty itself was based upon a ban treaty drafted by Austria and developed in a series of meetings in Vienna, in Bonn, in Brussels, which culminated in the three-week long treaty negotiating conference held in Oslo in September. The treaty negotiations were historic. They were historic for a number of reasons. For the first time, smaller and middle-sized powers had come together, to work in close cooperation with the nongovernmental organizations of the International Campaign to Ban Landmines, to negotiate a treaty which would remove from the world's *arsenals* [10] a weapon in widespread use. For the first time, smaller and middle-sized powers had not yielded ground to intense pressure from a superpower to weaken the treaty to accommodate the policies of that one country. Perhaps for the first time, negotiations ended with a treaty stronger than the draft on which the negotiations were based!

21 The Oslo negotiations gave the world a

渥太华，为禁雷条约画了蓝图，签署了表明意向的宣言。他们还能做什么呢？他们需要响应这宣言。这简直是惊人的。我们站起来欢呼的同时各国政府却在抱怨。但是很快他们就从那最初的震惊中恢复过来，那些真正想要看到禁雷条约尽快诞生的政府决定接受挑战，约定时间一起协商禁雷条约。

20 著名的渥太华条约是以阿克斯沃希挑战开始的。而基于奥地利起草的禁雷条约本身，它在维也纳、波恩、布鲁塞尔的一系列会议中发展形成，以9月份在奥斯陆举行的为期三周的协商会议作为结束。这次协约谈判由于种种原因而颇具历史性意义。中小国家首次团结携手与国际禁雷运动的非政府间组织亲密合作，为根除一种广泛使用的武器进行协商。这些中小国家也是首次没有屈于大国压力而找借口削弱条约来适应某一大国的政策。也是第一次，诞生了一项比作为谈判基础的草稿更强有力的协约！

21 奥斯陆谈判最终产生了一项

---

⑩ arsenal ['ɑːsɪnl] *n.* 军械库　如：a naval arsenal 海军军工厂

treaty banning antipersonnel landmines which is remarkably free of *loopholes* [11] and exceptions. It is a treaty which bans the use, production, trade and stockpiling of antipersonnel landmines. It is a treaty which requires states to destroy their stockpiles within four years of its entering into force. It is a treaty which requires mine clearance within ten years. It calls upon states to increase assistance for mine clearance and for victim assistance. It is not a perfect treaty—the Campaign has concerns about the provision allowing for antihandling devices on antivehicle mines; we are concerned about mines kept for training purposes; we would like to see the treaty directly apply to nonstate actors and we would like stronger language regarding victim assistance. But, given the close cooperation with governments which resulted in the treaty itself, we are certain that these issues can be addressed through the annual meetings and review conferences provided for in the treaty.

22　As I have already noted, last week in Ottawa, 121 countries signed the treaty. Three ratified it simultaneously—signalling the political will of the international community to bring this treaty into force as soon as possible. It is remarkable. Landmines have been used since the US Civil War, since the Crimean War, yet we are taking them out of arsenals of the world. It is amazing. It is historic. It proves that civil society and governments do not have to see themselves as adversaries. It demonstrates that small and

毫无漏洞和例外的禁雷协约——禁止使用、制造、买卖和存储地雷。协约要求存有地雷的各国在协约付诸实施的四年内销毁存储，要求十年内扫除各地掩埋的地雷。它呼吁世界各国增加对扫雷工作的支援和对受害者的帮助。但是这个协约并不完美——它允许针对反车辆地雷设置反拆装置。我们还担心那些保存下来用于训练目的的地雷。我们希望看到这项协约对那些无国界人士也能直接适用，希望听到更多为受害者提供帮助的呼声。但是鉴于同各国政府合作才达成了这项协约，我们坚信这些问题也都可以通过年度会议和协约的修订会议得到解决。

22　如我所说，上周在渥太华，121 个国家签署了禁雷公约。其中三个国家还签字批准以表明希望它尽快投诸实施的政治决心。这是一次标志性事件。自美国内战和克里米亚战争以来，人们就开始使用地雷，而现在我们正在将它逐出世界军械库。这也是具有重大历史意义的事件。它表明民间团体和政府间组织没有必要拿彼此当敌人；也表明中小国家可以和民间组织团结合作，以惊人的速度解决

⑪ loophole ['luːphəʊl] *n.* 漏洞，空子　如：a legal loophole 法律漏洞

middle powers can work together with civil society and address humanitarian concerns with breathtaking speed. It shows that such a partnership is a new kind of "superpower" in the post-Cold War world.

23 It is fair to say that the International Campaign to Ban Landmines made a difference. And the real prize is the treaty. What we are most proud of is the treaty. It would be foolish to say that we are not deeply honored by being awarded the Nobel Peace Prize. Of course, we are. But the receipt of the Nobel Peace Prize is recognition of the accomplishment of this Campaign. It is recognition of the fact that NGOs have worked in close cooperation with governments for the first time on an arms control issue, with the United Nations, with the International Committee of the Red Cross. Together, we have set a precedent. Together, we have changed history. The closing remarks of the French ambassador in Oslo to me were the best. She said, "This is historic not just because of the treaty. This is historic because, for the first time, the leaders of states have come together to answer the will of civil society."

24 For that, the International Campaign thanks them—for together we have given the world the possibility of one day living on a truly mine-free planet.

25 Thank you.

世界人道主义危机；还表明了这样一种合作关系是冷战结束后世界上新的"超级力量"。

23 国际禁雷运动使这个世界产生了好的改变，这么说是很公平的。而真正的奖励就是禁雷公约，这也是最值得我们骄傲的。说我们不为这个奖项深感荣耀是很愚蠢的。我们当然为此自豪。接受诺贝尔和平奖是对禁雷运动的肯定。它也肯定了非政府组织与各国政府、联合国和国际红十字会首次在控制武器问题上密切合作。我们共同开创了一个先例，共同改变了历史。法国大使在奥斯陆会议上的总结发言在我看来再好不过了。她说："意义重大并不在于这个协约，而在于国家领导人首次一起回应了民间组织的呼声。"

24 为此，国际禁雷运动谢谢他们——因为我们一起使未来的无雷世界成为可能。

25 感谢大家。

演讲关键词 Practical Expressions

1. indiscriminate weapon 滥杀滥伤武器
2. nongovernmental organizations 非政府间组织
3. conventional weapon 常规武器
4. international community 国际社会
5. humanitarian crisis 人道主义危机
6. the International Committee of the Red Cross 国际红十字会
7. the International Campaign to Ban Landmines 国际禁雷运动

精华佳句

1. Landmines distinguish themselves because once they have been sown, once the soldier walks away from the weapon, the landmine cannot tell the difference between a soldier or a civilian—a woman, a child, a grandmother going out to collect firewood to make the family meal.

   地雷的不同之处在于，一旦它们被埋在了地下，不管是士兵还是平民，抑或是妇女、儿童和外出捡柴为家人烧饭的老奶奶，对它们来说都没有什么区别了。

2. This is historic not just because of the treaty. This is historic because, for the first time, the leaders of states have come together to answer the will of civil society

   意义重大并不在于这个协约，而在于国家领导人首次一起回应了民间组织的呼声。

诺贝尔奖背后的那些趣事

诺贝尔奖，想说"终于等到你"

对于科学家们来说，用一年时间发表论文获奖，就已经称得上是奇迹了。因此至今除了杨振宁、李政道之外，绝大多数诺贝尔奖得主都难逃时间的折磨。美国物理学家盖尔曼获奖时，国际物理学界早就已经开始抱怨"这是等了6年多的事情"。所以，1969年诺贝尔物理奖得主是盖尔曼的消息公布后，大家都毫不意外，因为他们都认定"这奖早就应该颁给盖尔曼了"。同盖尔曼一样，等待有些年头的人物还有发现了X射线的德国物理学家伦琴，发现一系列放射性元素的卢瑟福，以及提出了原子结构的量子轨道理论的玻尔。相比之下，发现了蜜蜂跳圆圈舞的佛里斯的人生可能更为惨淡，他等待了半个多世纪才等到属于他的诺贝尔奖，他的蜜蜂也才随他出了名。

Chapter 4

和平的使者：点燃和平希望的
诺贝尔奖大师演讲

Speech 1

The Quest for Peace and Justice（1）
对和平与正义的不懈追求（1）

——Speech by Martin Luther King Jr. for the Nobel Peace Prize on December 11, 1964

——美国黑人运动领袖马丁·路德·金 1964 年 12 月 11 日诺贝尔和平奖获
奖演讲

名家速览 About the Author

诺贝尔奖大师	马丁·路德·金
奖 项 归 属	诺贝尔和平奖
突 出 成 就	美国民权运动领袖
相关演讲链接	1963 年在林肯纪念堂前发表演讲《我有一个梦想》

马丁·路德·金（Martin Luther King Jr., 1929 年 1 月 15 日——
1968 年 4 月 4 日）是 20 世纪 60 年代美国著名的民权运动领
袖。他出生于佐治亚州亚特兰大市，母亲是一名教师，父亲和
祖父都是牧师，他本人后来也成了一名浸信会牧师。他的家族
成员是非洲裔的美国人。他求学期间成绩优异，先后获得文学
学士和神学博士学位。1956 年他开始领导蒙哥马利市的黑人反
对当地公共汽车上的种族隔离制度，并获得成功。1959 年他到
印度游历，进一步研究并发展了圣雄甘地的非暴力策略。20 世
纪 60 年代，作为南方黑人领袖，马丁·路德·金带领美国黑人
展开了争取种族平等、民主自由的斗争，历史上称作"民权运动"。此后，他又发起了一系
列对抗经济问题的穷人运动。1968 年 4 月 4 日晚，他在田纳西州孟菲斯市洛林汽车旅店被种
族主义分子暗杀，终年 39 岁。本文节选自马丁·路德·金的诺贝尔获奖演讲，其中谈到了现
代社会人类面临的三大紧迫问题之一——种族不平等，他论证了种族歧视的非正义性，阐述
了美国的种族歧视状况，并号召用非暴力策略解决问题。

和平的使者：点燃和平希望的诺贝尔奖大师演讲

演讲现场
Speech Script

精美译文
Suggested Translation

1 It is impossible to begin this lecture without again expressing my deep appreciation to the Nobel Committee of the Norwegian Parliament for bestowing upon me and the civil rights movement in the United States such a great honor. Occasionally in life there are those moments of unutterable fulfillment which cannot be completely explained by those symbols called words. Their meaning can only be articulated by the *inaudible* ① language of the heart. Such is the moment I am presently experiencing. I experience this high and joyous moment not for myself alone but for those devotees of nonviolence who have moved so courageously against the *ramparts* ② of racial injustice and who in the process have acquired a new estimate of their own human worth. Many of them are young and cultured. Others are middle aged and middle class. The majority are poor and untutored. But they are all united in the quiet conviction that it is better to suffer in dignity than to accept segregation in humiliation. These are the real heroes of the freedom struggle: they are the noble people for whom I accept the Nobel Peace Prize.

2 This evening I would like to use this lofty and historic platform to discuss what appears to me to be the most pressing problem confronting mankind today. Modern man has brought this

1 在演讲开始前，我必须要向挪威议会诺贝尔奖委员会表达我由衷的感谢，谢谢你们将此至高荣誉授予我和美国的民权运动。生活中有一些经历是不能完全用语言表达出来的，这些经历的意义只能用心去体会，而我此时就在经历这样的时刻。但我并不是一个人在经历这令人欢欣鼓舞的时刻，我代表着那些非暴力运动的信徒们，他们勇敢地与种族歧视的壁垒抗争，在这个过程中他们找回了属于自己的人类尊严和价值。他们中许多人都是受过教育的年轻人，也有一些中年人和中产阶级。但是大部分人都是贫穷没有受过教育的。但是他们都怀着坚定的信念团结在一起，宁可有尊严地承受痛苦，也不接受屈辱下的种族隔离。他们是自由斗争的真正英雄，我为他们接受这崇高的诺贝尔和平奖。

2 今晚，我想借这个崇高的、具有深刻历史意义的平台来讨论一下当今人类面临的最紧迫的问题。整个世界在现代人的带领下来到了一个令

---

① inaudible [ɪn'ɔːdəbl] *adj.* 听不见的　如：His voice was almost inaudible. 他的声音几乎听不见。

② rampart ['ræmpɑːt] *n.* 壁垒

whole world to an *awe-inspiring* ③ threshold of the future. He has reached new and astonishing peaks of scientific success. He has produced machines that think and instruments that peer into the *unfathomable* ④ ranges of interstellar space. He has built gigantic bridges to span the seas and *gargantuan* ⑤ buildings to kiss the skies. His airplanes and spaceships have dwarfed distance, placed time in chains, and carved highways through the stratosphere. This is a dazzling picture of modern man's scientific and technological progress.

3　Yet, in spite of these spectacular strides in science and technology, and still unlimited ones to come, something basic is missing. There is a sort of poverty of the spirit which stands in glaring contrast to our scientific and technological abundance. The richer we have become materially, the poorer we have become morally and spiritually. We have learned to fly the air like birds and swim the sea like fish, but we have not learned the simple art of living together as brothers.

4　Every man lives in two realms, the internal and the external. The internal is that realm of spiritual ends expressed in art, literature, morals, and religion. The external is that complex of devices, techniques, mechanisms, and

人惊叹的未来之门前。人类在科学上已经大获成功，达到一个又一个不可思议的新高峰。他们创造出了可以思考的机器，以及可以探索星际空间的仪器。他们还造出了横跨海面的大桥、高耸入云的楼群。飞机和宇宙飞船缩小了时间和空间的距离，在高空平流层上快速行驶。这是一幅令人眩晕的现代人科技进步的图景。

3　尽管我们在科学技术上取得了如此大的进步，甚至还将有无止境的进展即将到来，然而，有些基本的东西我们却遗失了。一种精神上的匮乏同我们科技上的富足形成了鲜明的对比。我们物质上越富裕，精神和道德上就变得越贫穷。我们能像鸟儿一样在天空飞翔，像鱼儿一样遨游于海底，但是却没有掌握"与人如兄弟般相处"这样简单的生存之道。

4　每个人都生活在内心世界和外在世界两个领域中。内心世界是以艺术、文学、道德和宗教的形式传达的精神归属，而外在世界是人们赖以生存的设备、技术、机制和工具。今

---

③ awe-inspiring ['ɔːɪnˌspaɪərɪŋ] *adj.* 使人惊叹的　如：The building was awe-inspiring in size and design. 这座建筑的规模和设计气势恢宏。

④ unfathomable [ʌnˈfæðəməbl] *adj.* 深奥的，深不可测的　如：unfathomable theories 高深莫测的理论

⑤ gargantuan [gɑːˈgæntjʊən] *adj.* 巨大的　如：a gargantuan meal 丰盛的大餐

instrumentalities by means of which we live. Our problem today is that we have allowed the internal to become lost in the external. We have allowed the means by which we live to *outdistance* ⑥ the ends for which we live. So much of modern life can be summarized in that arresting dictum of the poet Thoreau: "Improved means to an unimproved end." This is the serious predicament the deep and haunting problem confronting modern man. If we are to survive today, our moral and spiritual "lag" must be eliminated. Enlarged material powers spell enlarged peril if there is not proportionate growth of the soul. When the "without" of man's nature subjugates the "within", dark storm clouds begin to form in the world.

5 This problem of spiritual and moral lag, which constitutes modern man's chief dilemma, expresses itself in three larger problems which grow out of man's ethical infantilism. Each of these problems, while appearing to be separate and isolated, is inextricably bound to the other. I refer to racial injustice, poverty, and war.

6 The first problem that I would like to mention is racial injustice. The struggle to eliminate the evil of racial injustice constitutes one of the major struggles of our time. The present upsurge of the Negro people of the United States grows out of a deep and passionate determination to make freedom and equality a reality "here" and "now". In one sense the civil rights movement in the United States is a special

天我们的问题在于内心世界在外在世界中逐渐迷失。我们已经让外在的生存法则超越了内心世界的归属。太多的现代生活可以用梭罗那句警世格言概括："外在的手段进步了，而目标却没有随之进步。"这就是现代人无法摆脱的窘境。但是今天我们要想生存，就必须摒弃精神和道德上的落后。如果心灵世界不随之进步，那么不断增长的物质力量只能招致更多的危难。如果人类的外在世界超越了内在，整个世界就会被阴云覆盖。

5 作为人类的主要困境，精神和道德的落后问题表现在三个方面，而这三个方面都源于人类道德上的不成熟。这三个问题看似相互分离，实则关系密切，它们就是：种族不平等、贫穷和战争。

6 我要说的第一个问题就是种族不平等。消除种族歧视的斗争已经成为我们时代最主要的斗争之一。现在美国黑人情绪高涨，是因为他们怀着深沉而强烈的决心要使自由平等成为现实，就从"此时"、"此地"开始。从某种程度上来说，美国的民权运动是一种特殊的美国现象，必须从历史角度看待，根据美国的实际情况

⑥ outdistance [aut'dɪstəns] *vt.* 大大超越　如：Their latest computers outdistanced all their rivals. 他们最新的计算机超越了所有的竞争对手。

American phenomenon which must be understood in the light of American history and dealt with in terms of the American situation. But on another and more important level, what is happening in the United States today is a relatively small part of a world development.

7　We live in a day, says the philosopher Alfred North Whitehead, "when civilization is shifting its basic outlook: a major turning point in history where the presuppositions on which society is structured are being analyzed, sharply challenged, and profoundly changed." What we are seeing now is a freedom explosion, the realization of "an idea whose time has come", to use Victor Hugo's phrase. The deep rumbling of discontent that we hear today is the thunder of disinherited masses, rising from *dungeons* ⑦ of oppression to the bright hills of freedom, in one majestic chorus the rising masses singing, in the words of our freedom song, "Ain't gonna let nobody turn us around." All over the world, like a fever, the freedom movement is spreading in the widest liberation in history. The great masses of people are determined to end the exploitation of their races and land. They are awake and moving toward their goal like a tidal wave. You can hear them rumbling in every village street, on the docks, in the houses, among the students, in the churches, and at political meetings. Historic movement was for several centuries that of the nations and societies of Western Europe out into the rest of the world in "conquest" of various

来解决。但是从另一种更重要的层面上讲，今天在美国发生的事件相对来说却是世界发展进程中的一小部分。

7　正如哲学家阿尔弗雷德·诺斯·怀特海德所说，我们生活的时代"文明正在改变它基本的面貌：这是一个历史的转折点，原来那一套用以组织社会的预想受到前所未有的分析和严苛的挑战，正在经历着深刻的变革。"我们现在看见的是自由爆炸的时代，是用维克多·雨果的话来说"思想的时代到来了"。我们今天听到被剥夺了继承权的民众发出深沉的如雷般的不满之声，他们从压迫的地牢中升至光明的自由之巅，奋起的民众用庄严的大合唱表达着自由之声——"绝不让任何人改变我们"。全世界都陷入了自由的狂热之中，自由主义运动获得了历史上前所未有的解放。人民大众决心要终结对他们种族和土地的剥削。他们如梦初醒般，像大潮中的巨浪朝着目标前进。在每一条乡村街道上、码头上、房间里、学校里、教堂里和政治会议上，在每一个地方都能听到他们呼喊的声音。历史性运动数世纪以来一直在西欧国家发生，现在却以各种形式扩展到了曾经被"征服"的世界其他地方。那段殖民时代已经结束。东方世界开始对峙西方世

⑦ dungeon ['dʌndʒən] *n.* 地牢

sorts. That period, the era of colonialism, is at an end. East is meeting West. The earth is being redistributed. Yes, we are "shifting our basic outlooks".

8　These developments should not surprise any student of history. Oppressed people cannot remain oppressed forever. The yearning for freedom eventually manifests itself. The *Bible* tells the thrilling story of how Moses stood in Pharaoh's court centuries ago and cried, "Let my people go." This is a kind of opening chapter in a continuing story. The present struggle in the United States is a later chapter in the same unfolding story. Something within has reminded the Negro of his birthright of freedom, and something without has reminded him that it can be gained. Consciously or unconsciously, he has been caught up by the Zeitgeist, and with his black brothers of Africa and his brown and yellow brothers in Asia, South America, and the Caribbean, the United States Negro is moving with a sense of great urgency toward the promised land of racial justice.

9　Fortunately, some significant strides have been made in the struggle to end the long night of racial injustice. We have seen the magnificent drama of independence unfold in Asia and Africa. Just thirty years ago there were only three independent nations in the whole of Africa. But today thirty-five African nations have risen from colonial bondage. In the United States we have witnessed the gradual ***demise*** [8] of the system of

界。世界力量开始重新分配。是的，我们"正在改变世界基本的样子"。

8　这些发展变化对历史系的学生来说并不稀奇。受压迫的人们不可能永远受压迫。自由的呼声终于开始显现了。《圣经》记载了一个令人毛骨悚然的故事：几个世纪以前摩西站在法老的朝廷之下，哭求着"放了我的人民吧。"这只是一个连续故事的开端。而美国现在进行的斗争则是同一个故事的续集。内心世界的某些东西提醒了黑人他与生俱来的自由权利，而外在世界的一些东西则告诉他这种权利可以获得。于是有意或无意地，美国的黑人逐渐被时代精神所感染，同他的非洲兄弟、棕色或黄色皮肤的亚洲、南美洲和加勒比地区的兄弟一道，他们怀着极大的紧迫感向承诺的种族平等前行。

9　所幸，在结束种族不平等的漫漫长夜中我们已经取得了一些进展。独立运动的大幕在亚洲和非洲已经拉开。30 年前非洲才只有三个独立国家，但今天那里已经有 35 个国家摆脱了殖民统治的束缚。在美国，我们也已看到种族隔离制度正在逐渐终止。1954 年最高法院判决公立学校的种族隔离违法，这给整套"隔离

---

⑧ demise [dɪ'maɪz] *n.* 终止，失败　如：the demise of an idea 失败的想法

racial segregation. The Supreme Court's decision of 1954 outlawing segregation in the public schools gave a legal and constitutional deathblow to the whole doctrine of separate but equal. The Court decreed that separate facilities are inherently unequal and that to segregate a child on the basis of race is to deny that child equal protection of the law. This decision came as a beacon light of hope to millions of disinherited people. Then came that glowing day a few months ago when a strong Civil Rights Bill became the law of our land. This bill, which was first recommended and promoted by President Kennedy, was passed because of the overwhelming support and perseverance of millions of Americans, Negro and white. It came as a bright interlude in the long and sometimes turbulent struggle for civil rights: the beginning of a second emancipation proclamation providing a comprehensive legal basis for equality of opportunity. Since the passage of this bill we have seen some encouraging and surprising signs of compliance. I am happy to report that, by and large, communities all over the southern part of the United States are obeying the *Civil Rights Law* and showing remarkable good sense in the process.

10 Another indication that progress is being made was found in the recent presidential election in the United States. The American people revealed great maturity by overwhelmingly rejecting a presidential candidate who had become identified with extremism, racism, and retrogression. The voters of our nation rendered

却平等"的信条送去致命一击。最高法院颁布法令声明，区分基础设施是不平等的表现，而将孩子们按种族分类隔离其实是否定法律对儿童的同等保护。这个决议对成百上千万被剥夺了权利的人来说就像黑夜里的灯塔，让人们看到了希望。几个月前我们又经历了光辉的一天——强有力的民权法案成了我们国家法律的一部分。这项法案首先得到了肯尼迪总统的推荐和支持，接着在千万美国白人和黑人的鼎力支持和不懈努力下得以通过。这是民权运动漫长动荡的斗争中一段光明的插曲，这是第二份解放宣言的开始，这份宣言将为平等的机会提供广泛的法律基础。自法案颁布以来，我们已经看到了一些令人惊讶但又鼓舞人心的服从迹象。我很高兴，总体上南部美国的大部分地区都在遵守《民权法案》，在整个过程中表现良好。

10 另一个进步的表现就是最近美国的总统选举。大多数美国人民都否定了那些怀有极端主义、种族主义和落后思想的总统候选人，这是我们思想成熟的表现。我们的投票人显然有效地打击了那些激进右派。他们战胜了社会中寻求白人对抗黑人，将

a telling blow to the radical right. They defeated those elements in our society which seek to pit white against Negro and lead the nation down a dangerous Fascist path.

11 Let me not leave you with a false impression. The problem is far from solved. We still have a long, long way to go before the dream of freedom is a reality for the Negro in the United States. To put it figuratively in biblical language, we have left the dusty soils of Egypt and crossed a Red Sea whose waters had for years been hardened by a long and piercing winter of massive resistance. But before we reach the majestic shores of the Promised Land, there is a frustrating and bewildering wilderness ahead. We must still face *prodigious* [9] hilltops of opposition and gigantic mountains of resistance. But with patient and firm determination we will press on until every valley of despair is exalted to new peaks of hope, until every mountain of pride and irrationality is made low by the leveling process of humility and compassion; until the rough places of injustice are transformed into a smooth plane of equality of opportunity; and until the crooked places of prejudice are transformed by the straightening process of bright-eyed wisdom.

12 What the main sections of the civil rights movement in the United States are saying is that the demand for dignity, equality, jobs, and citizenship will not be abandoned or *diluted* [10] or

国家引向法西斯危险道路的那些不良因素。

11 希望我没有给你们留下错误的印象。其实问题还远远没有解决。在美国黑人自由梦想成真之前，我们还有很长很长的一段路要走。用圣经中的话打比方就是，我们离开了埃及布满灰尘的土地，跨越了数年来漫长寒冬笼罩、充满艰难险阻的红海。但是在到达那宏伟庄严的乐土之前，我们还要走一段无比坎坷迷茫的蛮荒之路。我们仍然要面对惊人的阻碍和顽固抵抗。然而，我们还要怀着坚定的耐心和决心继续前行，直到每一个绝望之谷都上升为希望之峰；直到每一座傲慢和不合理的山峰都在谦逊和怜悯面前变得渺小，直到那些艰难坎坷的地方都变成充满平等机会的平原，直到被充满偏见歪曲的地方在智慧与远见的熏陶下都恢复正直。

12 美国民权运动的主要呼声就是，人们对尊严、平等、工作机会、公民权的需要不能被放弃、削弱或推迟。如果这意味着抵抗和冲突，那我

---

⑨ prodigious [prə'dɪdʒəs] *adj.* 巨大的，惊人的　如：a prodigious achievement 惊人的成就

⑩ dilute [daɪ'ljuːt] *vt.* 削弱　如：Large classes dilute the quality of education that children receive.
大班上课会降低孩子所受教育的质量。

postponed. If that means resistance and conflict we shall not flinch. We shall not be cowed. We are no longer afraid.

13　The word that symbolizes the spirit and the outward form of our encounter is nonviolence, and it is doubtless that factor which made it seem appropriate to award a peace prize to one identified with struggle. Broadly speaking, nonviolence in the civil rights struggle has meant not relying on arms and weapons of struggle. It has meant noncooperation with customs and laws which are institutional aspects of a regime of discrimination and enslavement. It has meant direct participation of masses in protest, rather than reliance on indirect methods which frequently do not involve masses in action at all.

14　Nonviolence has also meant that my people in the agonizing struggles of recent years have taken suffering upon themselves instead of inflicting it on others. It has meant, as I said, that we are no longer afraid and cowed. But in some substantial degree it has meant that we do not want to instill fear in others or into the society of which we are a part. The movement does not seek to liberate Negroes at the expense of the humiliation and enslavement of whites. It seeks no victory over anyone. It seeks to liberate American society and to share in the self-liberation of all the people.

15　Violence as a way of achieving racial justice is both impractical and immoral. I am not unmindful of the fact that violence often brings about momentary results. Nations have frequently

们不会畏缩。我们不会因受到威吓就害怕和后退。

13　能代表我们的精神和外在遭遇的词就是"非暴力运动"。无疑，这也是将和平奖授予一个斗争者的合适理由。从广义上说，民权斗争中的非暴力运动是指不依靠武器的斗争。它意味着对长久以来怀有歧视和实施奴役的社会中那些习俗与法律采取不合作态度。它意味着民众直接参与抗议，而不是依靠通常不让民众参与的间接斗争。

14　非暴力也意味着近年来这些参与艰难斗争的人们自己承受痛苦，而非将其转嫁给他人。如我所说，它意味着我们不再害怕，不再畏缩。但很大程度上，也意味着我们不想把恐惧灌输给他人，灌输给我们身在其中的社会。非暴力运动并不追求以羞辱和奴役白人来换取黑人解放。它的胜利不凌驾于任何人之上。它的目的是解放美国社会，共享所有人的自我解放。

15　企图通过暴力达到种族平等，这既不现实也不符合道义。我并非没有注意到暴力经常带来短暂的成果。很多国家频繁通过战争赢得独

won their independence in battle. But in spite of temporary victories, violence never brings permanent peace. It solves no social problem: it merely creates new and more complicated ones. Violence is impractical because it is a descending spiral ending in destruction for all. It is immoral because it seeks to humiliate the opponent rather than win his understanding: it seeks to *annihilate* [①] rather than convert. Violence is immoral because it thrives on hatred rather than love. It destroys community and makes brotherhood impossible. It leaves society in monologue rather than dialogue. Violence ends up defeating itself. It creates bitterness in the survivors and brutality in the destroyers.

16 In a real sense nonviolence seeks to redeem the spiritual and moral lag that I spoke of earlier as the chief dilemma of modern man. It seeks to secure moral ends through moral means. Nonviolence is a powerful and just weapon. Indeed, it is a weapon unique in history, which cuts without wounding and ennobles the man who wields it.

17 I believe in this method because I think it is the only way to reestablish a broken community. It is the method which seeks to implement the just law by appealing to the conscience of the great decent majority who through blindness, fear, pride, and irrationality have allowed their consciences to sleep.

18 The nonviolent resisters can summarize their message in the following simple terms: we

立。但是它带来的只是短暂的胜利，暴力绝不能收获持久和平。暴力不能解决社会问题，它只能制造更多更复杂的新问题。暴力不切实际，因为它是一个上升的螺旋，最终只能以毁坏所有来结尾。而且它不符合道义，因为它企图羞辱对手，而非争取对手的理解，企图歼灭而非改变对手。暴力不道德还因为它的斗争是基于仇恨而非爱意。它摧毁一个个群体，也摧毁了兄弟般友爱的可能性。它留给社会的是独白而非对话。暴力的结果是打败自己。它给幸存者的是痛苦，给毁灭者的是残忍。

16 实际上，非暴力寻求挽回我之前所说的现代人面临的主要困境——精神和道德上的落后。它寻求用道德方法来保护道德底线。非暴力是强大而正义的武器。事实上，它在历史上也是一个独特的武器，它划过而不留下伤痕，使用它的人也显得高贵。

17 我坚信非暴力的方法，因为它是唯一一条可以重建破碎家园的路。多数正派人的良知因为盲目、恐惧、傲慢和不理性而沉睡着，非暴力方法则通过实施公正的法律来唤醒人们的良知。

18 非暴力抵抗者的宗旨可以用以下句子简单概括：即使政府和官方

① annihilate [əˈnaɪəleɪt] *vt.* 消灭，歼灭　如：annihilate the enemies 歼灭敌人

will take direct action against injustice despite the failure of governmental and other official agencies to act first. We will not obey unjust laws or submit to unjust practices. We will do this peacefully, openly, cheerfully because our aim is to persuade. We adopt the means of nonviolence because our end is a community at peace with itself. We will try to persuade with our words, but if our words fail, we will try to persuade with our acts. We will always be willing to talk and seek fair compromise, but we are ready to suffer when necessary and even risk our lives to become witnesses to truth as we see it.

19 This approach to the problem of racial injustice is not at all without successful precedent. It was used in a magnificent way by Mohandas K. Gandhi to challenge the might of the British Empire and free his people from the political domination and economic exploitation inflicted upon them for centuries. He struggled only with the weapons of truth, soul force, non-injury, and courage.

20 In the past ten years unarmed gallant men and women of the United States have given living testimony to the moral power and efficacy of nonviolence. By the thousands, faceless, anonymous, relentless young people, black and white, have temporarily left the ivory towers of learning for the barricades of bias. Their courageous and disciplined activities have come as a refreshing oasis in a desert sweltering with the heat of injustice. They have taken our whole nation back to those great wells of democracy

机构不先行动，我们也会直接参与对抗非正义的斗争。我们不遵守非正义的法律，也不向非正义的行为屈服。我们会和平、公开、精神高昂地去行动，因为我们的目的是说服。我们采取非暴力的方法是因为我们的目的是创造一个内部和平的家园。我们将尝试用言语说服；但如果言语失败，我们会用行动去说服，我们愿意随时对话，寻求公平的妥协，但是我们也随时准备着必要时承受痛苦，甚至冒着生命危险去为我们眼中的事实作见证。

19 用这种办法应对种族歧视并非没有成功的先例。莫罕达斯·甘地就曾用此方法挑战大英帝国的权威，使印度人民摆脱了几个世纪以来强加在他们身上的政治控制和经济剥削。他只用真相、灵魂力量、无伤亡和勇气做武器来斗争。

20 过去的十年间，那些英勇的美国人已经证明了道德的力量和非暴力的功效。成千上万匿名的年轻人，包括白人和黑人，已经暂时离开象牙塔，开始为扫除偏见歧视等障碍斗争。他们勇敢而有序的行动，对不公正的社会来说，就像沙漠里一片令人重新振作的绿洲。我们的开国元勋们制定宪法，写下《独立宣言》，为我们挖出一眼民主的深井。现在这些人的行动将我们重新带回到伟大的民主

which were dug deep by the founding fathers in the formulation of the Constitution and the *Declaration of Independence*. One day all of America will be proud of their achievements.

21 I am only too well aware of the human weaknesses and failures which exist, the doubts about the efficacy of nonviolence, and the open advocacy of violence by some. But I am still convinced that nonviolence is both the most practically sound and morally excellent way to grapple with the age-old problem of racial injustice.

之井旁。终有一天，所有美国人都会为他们的成就感到骄傲。

21 我对人类的弱点和失败一清二楚，包括有些人对非暴力有效性的怀疑和对暴力的公开拥护。但我仍然坚信，非暴力才是同古老的种族不平等问题做斗争的正确方式，它既实际可靠，又符合道德要求。

 演讲关键词 Practical Expressions

1. interstellar space 星际空间
2. scientific and technological progress 科技进步
3. racial injustice 种族不平等
4. presidential election 总统选举
5. nonviolence movement 非暴力运动
6. *Declaration of Independence*《独立宣言》
7. political domination 政治控制
8. economic exploitation 经济剥削

精华佳句

1. There is a sort of poverty of the spirit which stands in glaring contrast to our scientific and technological abundance.
   一种精神上的匮乏同我们科技上的富足形成了鲜明的对比。

2. Enlarged material powers spell enlarged peril if there is not proportionate growth of the soul.
   如果心灵世界不随之进步，那么不断增长的物质力量只能招致更多的危难。

年龄不是问题

　　纵观诺贝尔奖历史，获奖者既有大器晚成型的，又有少年得志型的和平步青云型的。历史上最年长的诺贝尔奖获得者是明尼苏达大学的里奥尼德·赫维茨教授。他于 2007 年获得诺贝尔经济学奖，在那一年他已 90 高龄，获奖半年后他便离开了人世。因为身体原因，他无法坐飞机前往瑞典领奖，于是诺贝尔奖委员会专程派人到他所在的大学发奖。与此相比，史上最年轻的诺贝尔奖得主则是获得 1915 年诺贝尔物理学奖的英国人劳伦斯·布拉格，他在获奖时只有 25 岁。

Speech 2
The Quest for Peace and Justice (2)
对和平与正义的不懈追求 (2)

—Speech by Martin Luther King Jr. for the Nobel Peace Prize on December 11, 1964

——美国黑人运动领袖马丁•路德•金 1964 年 12 月 11 日诺贝尔和平奖获奖演讲

名家速览 About the Author

诺贝尔奖大师	马丁•路德•金
职　　业	牧师、民权运动领导人
著　名　作　品	《迈向自由：蒙哥马利的故事》、《爱的力量》
主　要　理　念	非暴力、民主自由平等

　　马丁•路德•金是将"非暴力"和"直接行动"作为社会变革方法的最为突出的倡导者之一。他一生致力于民权运动，带领广大黑人和白人为种族平等做斗争。20 世纪五六十年代，他组织发起了一系列反对种族隔离和不平等的非暴力运动。继蒙哥马利公共汽车事件胜利之后，为了推进民权运动的发展，马丁•路德•金和其他的南部黑人领袖于 1957 年建立了南方基督教领袖会议制度。1963 年 8 月 28 日，在林肯纪念馆的台阶上，马丁•路德•金发表了《我有一个梦想》的著名演讲。1963 年马丁•路德•金成为《时代周刊》的年度人物，并于 1964 年获得诺贝尔和平奖。2011 年 8 月 28 日，马丁•路德•金的纪念雕像在华盛顿国家广场揭幕。1986 年起，美国政府将每年 1 月的第 3 个星期一，定为马丁•路德•金全国纪念日。本篇为马丁•路德•金诺贝尔和平奖演讲的第二部分。他在文中论述了当今世界人类面临的另外两个紧迫问题——贫困和战争。他指出了富裕国家的贫富差距问题和世界性的普遍贫困问题，号召富国向贫困地区伸出援助之手。同时，他呼吁人类停止战争，用非暴力代替战争，换取爱与和平。

演讲现场
Speech Script

精美译文
Suggested Translation

1 A second evil which plagues the modern world is that of poverty. Like a monstrous octopus, it projects its nagging, *prehensile* [1] tentacles in lands and villages all over the world. Almost two-thirds of the peoples of the world go to bed hungry at night. They are undernourished, ill-housed, and shabbily clad. Many of them have no houses or beds to sleep in. Their only beds are the sidewalks of the cities and the dusty roads of the villages. Most of these poverty-stricken children of God have never seen a physician or a dentist. This problem of poverty is not only seen in the class division between the highly developed industrial nations and the so-called underdeveloped nations; it is seen in the great economic gaps within the rich nations themselves. Take my own country for example. We have developed the greatest system of production that history has ever known. We have become the richest nation in the world. Our national gross product this year will reach the astounding figure of almost 650 billion dollars. Yet, at least one-fifth of our fellow citizens—some ten million families, comprising about forty million individuals—are bound to a miserable culture of poverty. In a sense the poverty of the poor in America is more frustrating than the poverty of Africa and Asia. The misery of the poor in Africa and Asia is shared misery, a fact of life for the vast majority;

1 困扰当今世界的第二大问题是贫困。它就像一只巨大的章鱼，将它那可伸缩的烦人触角伸向全世界的土地和村庄。世界上几乎三分之二的人在晚上饿着睡觉。他们营养不良，房屋简陋，衣衫褴褛。他们中的许多人甚至没有可供睡觉的房子或床。他们唯一的床就是城市的人行道和农村尘土飞扬的道路旁。同为上帝的子民，这些为贫穷所困的孩子大多数都从未看过医生或牙医。贫困问题不仅存在于高度发达、阶级区分明显的工业化国家以及那些所谓的欠发达国家，贫富差距巨大的富裕国家本身也存在这个问题。就拿我自己的国家来说吧。我们拥有有史以来最大的生产体系。我们已经成为世界上最富有的国家。今年我们的国民生产总值将达到惊人的 6 500 亿美元。然而，我们却有至少五分之一的国民——大约 1 000 万个家庭，4 000 万人——陷在贫困圈内不能自拔。从某种程度上来说，美国的贫困比非洲和亚洲的贫困更令人沮丧。非洲和亚洲人民的贫困是普遍的，是大多数人的生活现实；他们共同承受的贫困是由常年的剥削和落后造成的。不幸的是，与之对比，美国的穷人却知道他们生活在世界上最富裕的国家，甚至他们将在贫

① prehensile [prɪˈhensaɪl] *adj.* 可伸缩的

they are all poor together as a result of years of exploitation and underdevelopment. In sad contrast, the poor in America know that they live in the richest nation in the world, and that even though they are perishing on a lonely island of poverty they are surrounded by a vast ocean of material prosperity. Glistening towers of glass and steel easily seen from their slum dwellings spring up almost overnight. Jet liners speed over their ghettoes at 600 miles an hour; satellites streak through outer space and reveal details of the moon. President Johnson, in his State of the Union Message, emphasized this contradiction when he heralded the United States' "highest standard of living in the world", and *deplored* ② that it was accompanied by "dislocation; loss of jobs, and the specter of poverty in the midst of plenty".

2 So it is obvious that if man is to redeem his spiritual and moral "lag", he must go all out to bridge the social and economic gulf between the "haves" and the "have nots" of the world. Poverty is one of the most urgent items on the agenda of modern life.

3 There is nothing new about poverty. What is new, however, is that we have the resources to get rid of it. More than a century and a half ago people began to be disturbed about the twin problems of population and production. A thoughtful Englishman named Malthus wrote a book that set forth some rather frightening conclusions. He predicted that the human family was gradually moving toward global starvation

穷的孤岛上慢慢毁灭，而包围他们的却是繁荣的物质海洋。在他们居住的贫民窟里就可以看到光彩夺目的玻璃大厦和钢铁大楼几乎在一夜之间拔地而起。喷气式客机以每小时 600 英里的速度从他们的贫民窟上方飞过，卫星穿越外太空，详细揭示着月球的情况。约翰逊总统在他的国情咨文里强调美国的矛盾，一方面美国将拥有"世界上最高的生活水平"，但另一方面他哀叹伴随着这样的生活水平的是"无家可归、失业和夹在富裕中的贫困幽灵"。

2 所以，很显然，如果人类要挽回在精神和道德上的落后，就必须在社会和经济差距的鸿沟上架起桥梁，缩小世界上富人和穷人间的距离。贫困是现代生活中最亟待解决的事情之一。

3 贫困本身并不新鲜。新鲜的是我们有了摆脱贫困的资源。150 多年前，人们就已经开始被人口和产出两大密切相关的问题所困扰。一个有思想的英国人——马尔萨斯写了一本书，他在书中提出了一些相当惊人的结论。据他预测，人类将逐渐走向世界性的贫穷，因为人口增长速度远远超过生产食物和其他材料来供养他们

---

② deplore [dɪ'plɔː] *vt.* 哀叹

because the world was producing people faster than it was producing food and material to support them. Later scientists, however, disproved the conclusion of Malthus, and revealed that he had vastly underestimated the resources of the world and the resourcefulness of man.

4　Not too many years ago, Dr. Kirtley Mather, a Harvard geologist, wrote a book entitled *Enough and to Spare*. He set forth the basic theme that famine is wholly unnecessary in the modern world. Today, therefore, the question on the agenda must read: Why should there be hunger and privation in any land, in any city, at any table when man has the resources and the scientific know-how to provide all mankind with the basic necessities of life? Even deserts can be irrigated and top soil can be replaced. We cannot complain of a lack of land, for there are twenty-five million square miles of tillable land, of which we are using less than seven million. We have amazing knowledge of vitamins, nutrition, the chemistry of food, and the versatility of atoms. There is no deficit in human resources; the deficit is in human will. The well-off and the secure have too often become indifferent and *oblivious* ③ to the poverty and deprivation in their midst. The poor in our countries have been shut out of our minds, and driven from the mainstream of our societies, because we have allowed them to become invisible. Just as nonviolence exposed the ugliness of racial injustice, so must the infection

的速度。然而，后来科学家否定了马尔萨斯的结论，并称他极大地低估了世界的资源和人类的智慧与能力。

4　没几年前，哈佛大学地质学家科特利·马瑟博士写了一本名为《绰绰有余》的书，书中他提出了关于饥荒的基本主题——在现代社会饥荒是完全可以避免的。所以，今天的问题就变成了：人类有丰富的资源，懂得如何为全人类提供基本的生活必需品，但为什么那些土地上、城市里、餐桌上依然存在饥饿和贫困？就连沙漠都可灌溉，表层土也可以被代替。我们不能抱怨土地贫乏，因为我们有 2 500 万平方英里可耕土地，其中已经利用的还不到 700 万平方英里。我们掌握了大量惊人的知识，有关维生素、营养、食物的化学形成过程以及用途广泛的原子等。并非资源不足，不足的是人类的意愿。生活安乐无忧的富人常常冷漠看待或忽视他们周围尚在贫困中的人们。穷人被我们屏蔽在脑海之外，驱赶出主流社会，我们让他们成了隐形人。正如非暴力运动揭露了种族不平等的丑恶一样，贫困的疾病也必须得到揭露和治愈——不仅要治它的表面症状，还要查治它的根本病因。这也将是一场激

③ oblivious [ə'blɪvɪəs] *adj.* 不注意的，未察觉的　如：He drove off, oblivious of the damage he has caused. 他把车开走了，没有注意到他造成的伤害。

and sickness of poverty be exposed and healed—not only its symptoms but its basic causes. This, too, will be a fierce struggle, but we must not be afraid to pursue the remedy no matter how formidable the task.

5   The time has come for an all-out world war against poverty. The rich nations must use their vast resources of wealth to develop the underdeveloped, school the unschooled, and feed the unfed. Ultimately a great nation is a compassionate nation. No individual or nation can be great if it does not have a concern for "the least of these". Deeply etched in the fiber of our religious tradition is the conviction that men are made in the image of God and that they are souls of infinite metaphysical value, the heirs of a legacy of dignity and worth. If we feel this as a profound moral fact, we cannot be content to see men hungry, to see men victimized with starvation and ill health when we have the means to help them. The wealthy nations must go all out to bridge the gulf between the rich minority and the poor majority.

6   In the final analysis, the rich must not ignore the poor because both rich and poor are tied in a single garment of destiny. All life is interrelated, and all men are interdependent. The agony of the poor diminishes the rich, and the salvation of the poor enlarges the rich. We are inevitably our brothers' keeper because of the interrelated structure of reality. John Donne interpreted this truth in graphic terms when he

烈的斗争，但是无论任务多艰巨，我们都要毫不畏缩地去寻求良方。

5   需要全世界倾力对抗贫困的时候到了。富裕国家要用他们巨大的资源财富去帮助那些欠发达的地区，为那些未受教育的人提供教育，给那些饥饿的人提供食物。从根本上来说，一个伟大的民族应该是一个慈悲的民族。没有任何一个人或一个民族能够置卑微的人于不顾却仍然成其伟大。在我们的宗教传统里浸透着这样深刻的信仰：人类是根据上帝的形象被创造出来的，他们是无穷的超自然价值的灵魂，他们是尊严和价值遗产的继承者。如果我们还认为这是深刻的道德事实，我们就不会在有办法提供帮助的情况下还心安理得地看着人们挨饿，看着他们被饥饿和疾病伤害。富裕国家必须伸出援手，搭建起连接少数富裕国家和多数贫困国家的桥梁。

6   从根本上看，富人绝对不能忽视穷人，因为无论贫富，他们早已被命运捆绑在一起了。所有的生命都互相关联，所有人都相互依存。穷人的痛苦会使富人随之减少，穷人的获救也会扩大富人的数量。因为现实结构的相互关联，我们难免要成为其他兄弟的守护者。英国诗人约翰·邓恩用形象的语言解释和确认了这

affirmed:

No man is an Island, intire of its selfe: every man is a peece of the Continent, a part of the maine: if a Clod bee washed away by the Sea,

Europe is the lesse, as well as if a Promontorie

were, as well as if a Mannor of thy friends or of thine owne were: any mans death diminishes me, because I am involved in Mankinde: and therefore never send to know for whom the bell tolls: it tolls for thee.

7 A third great evil confronting our world is that of war. Recent events have vividly reminded us that nations are not reducing but rather increasing their arsenals of weapons of mass destruction. The best brains in the highly developed nations of the world are devoted to military technology. The proliferation of nuclear weapons has not been halted, in spite of the *Limited Test Ban Treaty*.

8 The fact that most of the time human beings put the truth about the nature and risks of the nuclear war out of their minds because it is too painful and therefore not "acceptable", does not alter the nature and risks of such war. The device of "rejection" may temporarily cover up anxiety, but it does not bestow peace of mind and emotional security.

9 So man's proneness to engage in war is still a fact. But wisdom born of experience should tell us that war is obsolete. There may have been

一点：

没有人能自全，没有人是孤岛，
每个人都是大陆的一片，要为本土应卯。
那便是一块土地，那便是一方海角，那便是一座庄园，
不论是你的，还是朋友的，
一旦海水冲走，欧洲就要变小。
任何人的死亡，都是我的减少，
作为人类的一员，我与生灵共老。
丧钟在为谁敲，我本茫然不晓，
不为幽明永隔，它正为你哀悼。

【李敖译】

7 世界面临的第三大不幸就是战争。最近发生的事件都生动地警示着我们，很多国家并没有减少，反而在扩张他们的大规模杀伤性武器。那些高度发达的国家里最聪明的人都在投身于军事科技的发展。尽管有《部分禁止核试验条约》的存在，核武器的扩散却并未停止。

8 大多数时候人类都将核武器的性质和危险抛诸脑后，因为那太过痛苦，无法接受。然而逃避并不能改变战争的性质和危险。表面的"拒绝"能一时掩盖焦虑，却并不能给予人们心灵的和平和情感的安全。

9 所以人类仍然趋向于战争，这是事实。但是来自于经验的智慧告诉我们，战争已经过时了。可能历史

a time when war served as a negative good by preventing the spread and growth of an evil force, but the destructive power of modern weapons eliminated even the possibility that war may serve as a negative good. If we assume that life is worth living and that man has a right to survive, then we must find an alternative to war. In a day when vehicles hurtle through outer space and guided ballistic missiles carve highways of death through the stratosphere, no nation can claim victory in war. A so-called limited war will leave little more than a calamitous legacy of human suffering, political turmoil, and spiritual disillusionment. A world war—God forbid!—will leave only smoldering ashes as a mute testimony of a human race whose folly led inexorably to ultimate death. So if modern man continues to flirt unhesitatingly with war, he will transform his earthly habitat into an inferno such as even the mind of Dante could not imagine.

10　Therefore, I venture to suggest to all of you and all who hear and may eventually read these words, that the philosophy and strategy of nonviolence become immediately a subject for study and for serious experimentation in every field of human conflict, by no means excluding the relations between nations. It is, after all, nation-states which make war, which have produced the weapons which threaten the survival of mankind, and which are both *genocidal* [④] and suicidal in character.

11　Here also we have ancient habits to deal

上某个时间战争可以带来消极利益，因为它能阻止恶势力的增长蔓延；但是如今现代武器的破坏力摧毁了这一可能性。如果我们觉得生命可贵，人类有权生存下去，那我们就必须找到战争的替代者。如果有一天，飞行器穿过外太空，指导着弹道导弹在平流层冲出一条死亡高速路，到那时没有任何国家可以宣称取得了战争的胜利。一场所谓的有所控制的战争只能给人类留下灾难性的遗产——痛苦、政治动乱和精神幻灭。一场世界战争——上帝决不允许！——只能带来燃烧的余烬，这灰烬见证了人类愚蠢造成的终极死亡。所以，如果现代人继续未假思索地发动战争，那么他在尘世的栖居地将变成连但丁都无法想象的人间地狱。

10　因此，我斗胆建议在场的各位以及所有能听到或读到我这些话的人们，希望你们能迅速将非暴力的哲学和策略在人类每个领域的冲突中，包括在国家关系上，都加以研究、严肃施行。毕竟是一个个国家制造了战争，制造了威胁人类生存，或毁灭他人或自我毁灭的武器。

11　我们有处理结构庞大的恶势

④ genocidal [ˌdʒenəʊˈsaɪdəl] *adj.* 种族灭绝的，集体屠杀的

with, vast structures of power, indescribably complicated problems to solve. But unless we *abdicate* ⑤ our humanity altogether and succumb to fear and impotence in the presence of the weapons we have ourselves created, it is as imperative and urgent to put an end to war and violence between nations as it is to put an end to racial injustice. Equality with whites will hardly solve the problems of either whites or Negroes if it means equality in a society under the spell of terror and a world doomed to extinction.

12 I do not wish to minimize the complexity of the problems that need to be faced in achieving disarmament and peace. But I think it is a fact that we shall not have the will, the courage, and the insight to deal with such matters unless in this field we are prepared to undergo a mental and spiritual reevaluation—a change of focus which will enable us to see that the things which seem most real and powerful are indeed now unreal and have come under the sentence of death. We need to make a supreme effort to generate the readiness, indeed the eagerness, to enter into the new world which is now possible, "the city which hath foundations, whose builder and maker is God".

13 We will not build a peaceful world by following a negative path. It is not enough to say "We must not wage war." It is necessary to love peace and sacrifice for it. We must concentrate not merely on the negative expulsion of war, but on the positive affirmation of peace. There is a fascinating little story that is preserved for us in

力的老习惯，也有解决极其复杂的问题的经验。但是如果我们不想放弃整个人类，不想在我们自己制造的武器面前畏缩屈服，我们就必须认识到结束战争暴力同结束种族不平等同样紧迫和重要。在恐怖笼罩下的社会里或注定要毁灭的世界里，即使达到了种族平等，也不能解决白人或黑人的问题。

12 我并不希望通过减少问题的复杂性来达到裁军与和平的目的。但事实是，如果我们没有做好准备经历心灵和精神的重新定位，我们就不会有解决这些问题的意愿、勇气和远见。而重新定位意味着改变我们的关注点，这样我们会看到原本好像最真实、最有利的，现在都被判了死刑，成了幻想。我们需要尽最大的努力为进入现已可能的新世界做好准备，"这是一座有根基的城市，它的建造者就是上帝"。

13 我们不可能通过一条消极的道路建造一个和平的世界。只说"我们一定不能发动战争"是不够的。我们要热爱和平，并且为它牺牲。我们不能只专注于消极地用战争驱逐邪恶，也要致力于肯定和平的积极性。希腊文学里有一个关于尤利西斯和塞

---

⑤ abdicate ['æbdɪkeɪt] *vt.* 放弃

Greek literature about Ulysses and the Sirens. The Sirens had the ability to sing so sweetly that sailors could not resist steering toward their island. Many ships were lured upon the rocks, and men forgot home, duty, and honor as they flung themselves into the sea to be embraced by arms that drew them down to death. Ulysses, determined not to be lured by the Sirens, first decided to tie himself tightly to the mast of his boat, and his crew stuffed their ears with wax. But finally he and his crew learned a better way to save themselves: they took on board the beautiful singer Orpheus whose melodies were sweeter than the music of the Sirens. When Orpheus sang, who bothered to listen to the Sirens?

14 So we must fix our vision not merely on the negative expulsion of war, but upon the positive affirmation of peace. We must see that peace represents a sweeter music, a cosmic melody that is far superior to the discords of war. Somehow we must transform the dynamics of the world power struggle from the negative nuclear arms race which no one can win to a positive contest to harness man's creative genius for the purpose of making peace and prosperity a reality for all of the nations of the world. In short, we must shift the arms race into a "peace race". If we have the will and determination to mount such a peace offensive, we will unlock hitherto tightly sealed doors of hope and transform our imminent cosmic elegy into a psalm of creative fulfillment.

壬的美丽故事。塞壬的歌声是那么美妙动听，水手们都忍不住将船驶向她们的岛屿。许多船只都被引诱到岛边的岩石上，人们忘记了家园、责任和荣耀。他们一个个纵身投进海中塞壬的怀抱，却被那些伸出的手臂拖向死亡。尤利西斯下决心一定不受塞壬的诱惑。他开始时将自己绑在船的桅杆上，船员们都用蜡将耳朵堵上。但是最后他和船员们找到了更好的办法：他们出海的时候戴上了俄尔普斯，他的歌声比塞壬的还要甜美。因此当俄尔普斯唱起歌的时候，谁还会去听那些塞壬海妖唱的歌呢？

14 所以我们不只要将目光放在消极的战争上，还要积极地关注和平。我们必须看到和平能唱出更美的音乐，这是比战争的不和谐之音更高级的宇宙之歌。不管通过什么方法，我们必须促使世界各国放弃没有谁能赢的消极核武器竞赛，转向为世界各国的和平与繁荣贡献智慧的积极竞赛中。总之，我们必须化军备竞赛为"和平竞赛"。如果我们愿意并且有决心展开这样一个和平角逐，我们就能够打开紧闭的希望之门，将我们即将成真的宇宙挽歌转化成一曲具有创造性成就的赞歌。

15 All that I have said *boils down to* [6] the point of affirming that mankind's survival is dependent upon man's ability to solve the problems of racial injustice, poverty, and war; the solution of these problems is in turn dependent upon man squaring his moral progress with his scientific progress, and learning the practical art of living in harmony. Some years ago a famous novelist died. Among his papers was found a list of suggested story plots for future stories, the most prominently underscored being this one: "A widely separated family inherits a house in which they have to live together." This is the great new problem of mankind. We have inherited a big house, a great "world house" in which we have to live together—black and white, Easterners and Westerners, Gentiles and Jews, Catholics and Protestants, Moslem and Hindu, a family unduly separated in ideas, culture, and interests who, because we can never again live without each other, must learn, somehow, in this one big world, to live with each other.

16 This means that more and more our loyalties must become ecumenical rather than sectional. We must now give an overriding loyalty to mankind as a whole in order to preserve the best in our individual societies.

17 This call for a worldwide fellowship that lifts neighborly concern beyond one's tribe, race, class, and nation is in reality a call for an all-embracing and unconditional love for all

15 我所说的这些都可以归结为，人类的生存要靠人们结束种族不平等、贫困和战争来实现；而这些问题的解决又要靠人们调整自己的道德和科学发展，使之互相适应，并学习和平共处的实用之道来实现。几年前一位著名的小说家去世了。在他的遗稿中人们发现了一系列未来故事的情节暗示，最为人强调的就是："一个广泛分散的大家庭继承了一座需大家共同居住的房子。"这就是人类的一大新问题。我们继承了一座大房子，"世界大房子"，我们——白人和黑人，东方人和西方人，非犹太人和犹太人，天主教徒和新教徒，穆斯林和印度教徒，要共同居住在这里。这是一个思想、文化、兴趣都极度分化的大家庭，但是由于我们不可能再离开彼此独自生存，所以在这个大世界里，我们必须想办法共同生活。

16 这意味着我们越来越多的忠诚必须是普遍联合的，而非部落的。为了保护我们人类社会里最优秀的财产，我们现在必须对全人类保持最高的忠诚。

17 我们呼吁这种超越了单个部落、种族、阶级和民族的世界性友谊和关怀，实际上也是呼吁一种对整个人类的无条件博爱。这个概念常被尼

---

⑥ boil down to 归结为……　如：In the end, what it all boils down to is money, or the lack of it. 问题的症结是钱，或者说缺钱。

men. This oft misunderstood and misinterpreted concept so readily dismissed by the Nietzsches of the world as a weak and cowardly force, has now become an absolute necessity for the survival of man. When I speak of love I am not speaking of some sentimental and weak response which is little more than emotional bosh. I am speaking of that force which all of the great religions have seen as the supreme unifying principle of life. Love is somehow the key that unlocks the door which leads to ultimate reality. This Hindu-Moslem-Christian-Jewish-Buddhist belief about ultimate reality is beautifully summed up in the *First Epistle of Saint John*:

Let us love one another: for love is of God; and everyone

that loveth is born of God, and knoweth God.

He that loveth not knoweth not God; for God is love.

If we love one another, God dwelleth in us, and His

love is perfected in us.

18 Let us hope that this spirit will become the order of the day. As Arnold Toynbee says: "Love is the ultimate force that makes for the saving choice of life and good against the damning choice of death and evil. Therefore the first hope in our inventory must be the hope that love is going to have the last word." We can no longer afford to worship the God of hate or bow before the altar of *retaliation* [7]. The oceans of history are made turbulent by the ever-rising tides

采的信奉者们排斥和误解为懦弱胆小的力量，但现在已经成了人类生存必需的理念。我所说的爱并非那些多愁善感、柔弱的情感碎片。我所说的是所有的伟大宗教都将其奉为生命统一原则的爱的力量。从某种程度上说，爱是打开天堂之门的钥匙。印度教、伊斯兰教、基督教、犹太教和佛教关于神的理念在《新约》的《约翰一书》中曾有概括：

让我们爱彼此：因为爱是上帝；

因为每个有爱的人都是上帝的子民，都懂得上帝。

不懂爱的人就不懂上帝，因为上帝就是爱。

如果我们彼此相爱，上帝就会降临伴随我们，

上帝之爱也会在我们身上实现。

18 希望这种精神能成为今天的世界秩序。就像阿诺德·汤因比说的："爱是拯救生命、对抗邪恶与死亡的终极力量。所以我们愿望清单上的第一个愿望必须是让爱掌握最终决定权。"我们再也承受不起崇拜仇恨或报复之神的代价了。历史已经被以往的仇恨搅得动荡不安。因为追求自我毁灭的仇恨之路，历史的长河里已经堆满了国家和人民的尸骸。爱才是

---

⑦ retaliation [rɪˌtælɪˈeɪʃən] *n.* 报复

of hate. History is cluttered with the wreckage of nations and individuals that pursued this self-defeating path of hate. Love is the key to the solution of the problems of the world.

19　Let me close by saying that I have the personal faith that mankind will somehow rise up to the occasion and give new directions to an age drifting rapidly to its doom. In spite of the tensions and uncertainties of this period something profoundly meaningful is taking place. Old systems of exploitation and oppression are passing away, and out of the womb of a frail world new systems of justice and equality are being born. Doors of opportunity are gradually being opened to those at the bottom of society. The shirtless and barefoot people of the land are developing a new sense of "some-bodiness" and carving a tunnel of hope through the dark mountain of despair. "The people who sat in darkness have seen a great light." Here and there an individual or group dares to love, and rises to the majestic heights of moral maturity. So in a real sense this is a great time to be alive. Therefore, I am not yet discouraged about the future.

20　Granted that the easygoing optimism of yesterday is impossible. Granted that those who pioneer in the struggle for peace and freedom will still face uncomfortable jail terms, painful threats of death; they will still be battered by the storms of persecution, leading them to the nagging feeling that they can no longer bear such a heavy burden, and the temptation of wanting to retreat to a more quiet and serene life. Granted that we face a world crisis

解决世界问题的关键。

19　最后我想说，我个人坚信人类会迎头而上，在厄运面前扭转乾坤，为人类开辟新的航向。尽管这期间仍会有紧张的事态和不确定性，但一定会有意义深刻的事情发生。剥削和压迫的旧制度正在消逝，世界正在孕育正义平等的新制度。机遇的大门逐渐向社会最底层的人们开启。那些衣不蔽体的人们对"人"的概念有了新的认识，他们正在开辟一条穿越绝望之山的希望之路。"黑暗中的人们已经看到了光亮。"世界各地的人们开始勇敢爱人，他们已经到了道德成熟的庄严高度。所以，事实上这是活着的最好时光。所以，我并没有对未来失去信心。

20　即使已经不再可能有昨天那悠闲的乐观主义，即使为和平自由奋斗的先驱们仍将面临痛苦的监禁、死亡的威胁，他们仍将遭受一连串的迫害，以至于他们自己都感觉承受不了了，还要受到安静平和的生活的诱惑。即使我们面临着一场时常将我们陷于动荡不安的世界危机。但是每一次危机都是既有危险也有机遇，既能

和平的使者：点燃和平希望的诺贝尔奖大师演讲

which leaves us standing so often amid the surging murmur of life's restless sea. But every crisis has both its dangers and its opportunities. It can spell either salvation or doom. In a dark confused world the kingdom of God may yet reign in the hearts of men.

带来拯救，也能招致毁灭。在一个充满困惑的世界，上帝的王国也还要靠人心来统治。

 ## 演讲关键词 Practical Expressions

1. undernourished 营养不良（的）
2. jet liner 喷气式客机
3. weapons of mass destruction 大规模杀伤性武器
4. the surging murmur of life's restless sea 动荡不安
5. world crisis 世界危机
6. nuclear arms race 核武器竞赛

1. In the final analysis, the rich must not ignore the poor because both rich and poor are tied in a single garment of destiny.

   从根本上看，富人绝对不能忽视穷人，因为无论贫富，他们早已被命运捆绑在一起了。

2. Equality with whites will hardly solve the problems of either whites or Negroes if it means equality in a society under the spell of terror and a world doomed to extinction.

   在恐怖笼罩下的社会里或注定要毁灭的世界里，即使达到了种族平等，也不能解决白人或黑人的问题。

 **诺贝尔奖背后的那些趣事**

"非诺贝尔奖"的"诺贝尔奖"

几乎所有人都知道诺贝尔奖是瑞典化学家诺贝尔先生创立的，但所有的奖项中，诺贝尔经济学奖是个例外——它并非诺贝尔遗嘱中提到的五大奖励项目之一。在 20 世纪 60 年代，瑞典中央银行捐款给诺贝尔基金，增设了"纪念阿尔弗雷德·诺贝尔瑞典银行经济学奖"。这个额外的奖项习惯上被称为诺贝尔经济学奖，这也是唯一由诺贝尔基金会官方颁发的"非诺贝尔奖"的"诺贝尔奖"。在评选步骤、授奖仪式方面，经济学奖与其他诺贝尔奖相似。奖项由瑞典皇家科学院每年颁发一次，遵循对人类利益做出最大贡献的原则给奖。1969 年（瑞典银行的 300 周年庆典）第一次颁发诺贝尔经济学奖，由挪威人拉格纳·弗里希和荷兰人简·丁伯根共同获得。

Speech 3
A Just and Lasting Peace（Excerpt）
守护正义而持久的和平（节选）

—Nobel Lecture by Barack Obama on December 10, 2009
——美国首位黑人总统巴拉克·奥巴马 2009 年 12 月 10 日诺贝尔和平奖获奖演讲

名家速览 About the Author

诺贝尔奖大师	巴拉克·奥巴马
奖 项 归 属	诺贝尔和平奖
获 奖 理 由	为增强国际外交及各国人民间的合作做出非同寻常的努力。
相关演讲链接	奥巴马于 2008 年 5 月 26 日在阵亡将士纪念日上的演讲（*Their Lives Are a Model for Us All*）

巴拉克·奥巴马（Barack Obama，1961 年 8 月 4 日—）是美国民主党派政治家，第 44 任美国总统，也是美国历史上第一位非洲裔总统；2007 年 2 月 10 日，宣布参加 2008 年美国总统选举；2008 年 11 月 4 日正式当选为美国总统；在第 57 届美国总统大选中，击败共和党候选人罗姆尼获得连任。奥巴马的父亲是肯尼亚来美国的留学生，母亲为白人，两人在大学相识，结婚。后来父母关系破裂，奥巴马跟随母亲和继父生活。母亲与继父的婚姻失败后，奥巴马长期同外祖父母生活在一起。外祖父对他的一生产生了极大的影响。由于多民族的血统，奥巴马年轻时也曾为身份问题焦虑苦恼，甚至自卑。他在哥伦比亚大学修习了国际关系学，又在哈佛大学获得了法学博士学位，并以"优等生"身份毕业。他在执政期间执行了一系列新政，带领美国人民应对金融危机。作为最强大的军队的领导者，他倡导无核化理念，为世界和平做出了很大贡献。本文是奥巴马在 2009 年获得诺贝尔和平奖时的演讲，在文中他指出在必要时可以使用武力打击恐怖主义，世界各国应该团结起来，追求正义持久的和平。

 **演讲现场**
Speech Script

 精美译文
Suggested Translation

1 I receive this honor with deep gratitude and great humility. It is an award that speaks to our highest aspirations—that for all the cruelty and hardship of our world, we are not mere prisoners of fate. Our actions matter, and can bend history in the direction of justice.

2 And yet I would be *remiss*① if I did not acknowledge the considerable controversy that your generous decision has generated. In part, this is because I am at the beginning, and not the end, of my labors on the world stage. Compared to some of the giants of history who've received this prize—Schweitzer and King; Marshall and Mandela—my accomplishments are slight. And then there are the men and women around the world who have been jailed and beaten in the pursuit of justice; those who toil in humanitarian organizations to relieve suffering; the unrecognized millions whose quiet acts of courage and compassion inspire even the most hardened cynics. I cannot argue with those who find these men and women—some known, some obscure to all but those they help—to be far more deserving of this honor than I.

3 But perhaps the most profound issue surrounding my receipt of this prize is the fact that I am the Commander-in-Chief of the military of a nation in the midst of two wars. One of these wars

1 我非常感激，也怀着无限谦卑之心来接受这项荣誉。它是对我们最高理想的奖励——不管这个世界有多少艰难残酷，我们并非只能做命运的囚徒。我们的行动不但会起作用，而且能让历史朝着正义的方向发展。

2 如果我没有认识到你们的慷慨决定带来的巨大争议，那只能说我太怠慢这个奖了。在某种程度上，争议之大是因为我对世界所做的只是一个开始，远非终点。同历史上曾获此荣誉的伟人们相比，如施伟策和马丁·路德·金，马歇尔和曼德拉，我的成绩微不足道。何况还有那些世界各地为了追求正义而忍受监禁、酷刑的人们，那些为人类缓解苦难，在人道主义组织辛苦工作的人们，以及数以百万计默默付出、不为人知的人们，他们的勇气和悲悯甚至感动着那些最顽固的犬儒主义者。有些人认为这些人——有知名的，也有除了受帮助者、几乎不为人知的——比我更应该获此荣誉，我对此无可反驳。

3 但是可能我接受这个奖项最深远的意义在于，我是一个深陷两场战争的国家军队的首领。其中一场战争已经结束了。另一场则并非美国所

---

① remiss [rɪ'mɪs] *adj.* 懈怠的，疏忽的，不负责任的   如：be remiss on one's duty 玩忽职守

is *winding down* [2]. The other is a conflict that America did not seek; one in which we are joined by 42 other countries—including Norway—in an effort to defend ourselves and all nations from further attacks.

4 Still, we are at war, and I'm responsible for the deployment of thousands of young Americans to battle in a distant land. Some will kill, and some will be killed. And so I come here with an acute sense of the costs of armed conflict—filled with difficult questions about the relationship between war and peace, and our effort to replace one with the other.

5 Now these questions are not new. War, in one form or another, appeared with the first man. At the dawn of history, its morality was not questioned; it was simply a fact, like drought or disease—the manner in which tribes and then civilizations sought power and settled their differences.

6 And over time, as codes of law sought to control violence within groups, so did philosophers and clerics and statesmen seek to regulate the destructive power of war. The concept of a "just war" emerged, suggesting that war is justified only when certain conditions were met: if it is waged as a last resort or in self-defense; if the force used is proportional; and if, whenever possible, civilians are *spared from* [3] violence.

7 Of course, we know that for most of

求，这是一次有另外 42 个国家，包括挪威，共同参与捍卫所有国家安全的自卫性冲突。

4 是的，我们还在打仗。而我还要为部署成千上万的年轻士兵远赴异国战斗而负责。有人会举起屠刀杀别人，有些人则会被别人杀害。因此，我怀着对武力冲突所付代价的强烈感受站在这里，满脑子都是关于战争与和平关系的难题，以及我们为此所做的努力。

5 这些在今天并不是什么新问题。不管以何种方式呈现，战争在人类出现伊始就已经存在了。在早期历史中，其道德性并未受到质疑；它只是一种事实，就像干旱或疾病一样——是不同部落或文明之间权力斗争和消除分歧的一种方式。

6 后来，正如法律规范企图将暴力控制在集团内部一样，哲学家、牧师和政治家也力图控制战争的破坏力。于是出现了"正义战争"的概念，表明战争只有满足了一定条件才具备合理性：比如，不得已或出于自卫而付诸战争；武力的使用控制在合适的范围内；尽可能地不殃及平民。

7 当然，历史上大多数时候，

---

② wind down 平复，逐步结束　如：The government is winding down its nuclear program. 政府正在逐步取消核计划。

③ spare sth. from... 使免于……

211

history, this concept of "just war" was rarely observed. The capacity of human beings to think up new ways to kill one another proved inexhaustible, as did our capacity to exempt from mercy those who look different or pray to a different God. Wars between armies gave way to wars between nations—total wars in which the distinction between combatant and civilian became blurred. In the span of 30 years, such *carnage* ④ would twice engulf this continent. And while it's hard to conceive of a cause more just than the defeat of the Third Reich and the Axis powers, World War II was a conflict in which the total number of civilians who died exceeded the number of soldiers who perished.

8 *In the wake of* ⑤ such destruction, and with the *advent* ⑥ of the nuclear age, it became clear to victor and vanquished alike that the world needed institutions to prevent another world war. And so, a quarter century after the United States Senate rejected the League of Nations—an idea for which Woodrow Wilson received this prize—America led the world in constructing an architecture to keep the peace: a Marshall Plan and a United Nations, mechanisms to govern the waging of war, treaties to protect human rights, prevent *genocide* ⑦, restrict the most dangerous weapons.

这个"正义战争"的概念都被忽略了。人类为战争倾尽其能、不遗余力，对那些持不同价值观和信仰的人毫无怜悯之心。民族战争超越了军队之间的战争，在所有的战争中，参战者和平民的区别变得模糊。30 年间，这样的大屠杀曾两度吞噬大陆。很难想象有比打败希特勒的第三帝国和轴心国更加正义的事业，第二次世界大战中平民的死亡数量超过了牺牲的士兵。

8 战争带来的破坏，以及战后核时代的到来，使胜利者和战败国清醒地认识到，需要共同的组织机构阻止世界大战的再次发生。所以，在美国参议院否决国际联盟（威尔逊总统因对建立国际联盟做出的卓越贡献获得诺贝尔和平奖）25 年之后，美国开始实施马歇尔计划，参与创建联合国，领导世界建立守护和平的大厦——通过机制和条约控制战争，保护人权，阻止种族杀戮，限制危险性武器。

④ carnage ['kɑːnɪdʒ] n. 大屠杀，残杀

⑤ in the wake of... 紧随其后的　如：There have been demonstrations on the streets in the wake of recent bomb attack. 在近来的炸弹袭击后，大街上随即出现了示威游行。

⑥ advent ['ædvənt] n.（不寻常的事）出现，到来　如：the advent of spring 春天的到来

⑦ genocide ['dʒenəˌsaɪd] n. 种族灭绝，种族屠杀

212

9 In many ways, these efforts succeeded. Yes, terrible wars have been fought, and *atrocities* [8] committed. But there has been no Third World War. The Cold War ended with jubilant crowds dismantling a wall. Commerce has stitched much of the world together. Billions have been lifted from poverty. The ideals of liberty and self-determination, equality and the rule of law have haltingly advanced. We are the heirs of the fortitude and foresight of generations past, and it is a legacy for which my own country is rightfully proud.

10 And yet, a decade into a new century, this old architecture is *buckling* [9] under the weight of new threats. The world may no longer shudder at the prospect of war between two nuclear superpowers, but proliferation may increase the risk of catastrophe. Terrorism has long been a tactic, but modern technology allows a few small men with outsized rage to murder innocents on a horrific scale.

11 Moreover, wars between nations have increasingly given way to wars within nations. The resurgence of ethnic or sectarian conflicts; the growth of *secessionist* [10] movements, insurgencies, and failed states—all these things have increasingly trapped civilians in unending chaos. In today's wars, many more civilians are killed than soldiers; the seeds of future conflict are sown, economies are wrecked, civil societies torn asunder, refugees amassed, children scarred.

9 这些努力在许多方面是成功的。诚然，恐怖战争和暴行时有发生，但好在没有发生第三次世界大战。冷战也伴随着人们拆毁柏林墙时的呼唤声结束了。商业贸易将世界连在了一起，数以十亿计的人已经摆脱贫穷。自由民主、平等法治的观念也在艰难中逐渐深入民心。我们继承了祖先的刚毅和远见，在这一点上，我的祖国足以引以为豪。

10 然而，在新世纪的头十年，这已经构筑的古老大厦在新的威胁下出现了扭曲。世界可能不再恐惧两个核大国之间爆发战争，但是灾难的危险性却可能随着核扩散而日益增加。恐怖主义策略由来已久，现代科技更是能使一小部分愤怒的人以惊人的规模杀害无辜民众。

11 此外，国家内部战争也已经超越了国家间的战争。民族和宗教冲突再现，分离主义运动、暴乱和"国中国"此起彼伏——所有这些都将民众陷于无止境的混乱之中。今天的战争，平民的牺牲要比士兵大得多，还往往埋下未来冲突的种子，经济遭到破坏，公民社会分崩离析，难民集聚，儿童惨遭荼毒。

---

⑧ atrocity [əˈtrɒsɪtɪ] *n.* 残酷，暴行

⑨ buckle [ˈbʌkl] *vt.* 压弯，压垮

⑩ secessionist [sɪˈseʃənɪst] *n.* 分离主义者

12 I do not bring with me today a definitive solution to the problems of war. What I do know is that meeting these challenges will require the same vision, hard work, and persistence of those men and women who acted so boldly decades ago. And it will require us to think in new ways about the notions of just war and the imperatives of a just peace.

13 We must begin by acknowledging the hard truth: We will not eradicate violent conflict in our lifetimes. There will be times when nations—acting individually or in concert—will find the use of force not only necessary but morally justified.

14 I make this statement mindful of what Martin Luther King Jr. said in this same ceremony years ago: "Violence never brings permanent peace. It solves no social problem: it merely creates new and more complicated ones." As someone who stands here as a direct consequence of Dr. King's life work, I am living testimony to the moral force of non-violence. I know there's nothing weak—nothing passive—nothing naive—in the creed and lives of Gandhi and King.

15 But as a head of state sworn to protect and defend my nation, I cannot be guided by their examples alone. I face the world as it is, and cannot *stand idle* [11] in the face of threats to the American people. For make no mistake: Evil does exist in the world. A non-violent movement could not have halted Hitler's armies. Negotiations cannot convince al Qaeda's leaders to lay down their arms. To say that force may sometimes

12 我今天并没有带来一个一定能解决战争问题的办法。但我知道，面对这些挑战我们要像几十年前勇敢行动的人们那样有远见、兢兢业业、坚持不懈。我们也需要用新的方式去思考正义战争，以及要守护正义的和平我们需要做些什么。

13 首先我们要承认一个残酷的现实：在我们的有生之年，暴力冲突不会完全消失。终有一天，很多国家，或众或独，都会发现武力不仅必要，在道德上也是合理的。

14 我说这些的时候，想起了马丁·路德·金数年前在这个典礼上的讲话："暴力不可能带来永久和平。它不仅解决不了社会问题，还会带来更多更复杂的问题。"作为马丁·路德·金毕生事业的直接受益者，我才能站在这里，见证非暴力运动的道德力量。我知道甘地和路德的信仰和生命中没有怯懦、消极和幼稚。

15 但是我作为一国的元首，曾宣誓要保护和捍卫我的国家，我不能仅仅用他们的例子作指导。我面对的世界就是这个样子，我不能看着美国人民受到威胁还袖手旁观。这个世界上确实有邪恶存在，这一点不会有错。非暴力运动不能制止希特勒的军队，谈判也不能说服"基地"组织的领导人放下武器。武力有时是必要

⑪ stand idle 袖手旁观

be necessary is not a call to cynicism—it is a recognition of history; the imperfections of man and the limits of reason.

16 I raise this point, I begin with this point because in many countries there is a deep *ambivalence* [12] about military action today, no matter what the cause. And at times, this is joined by a reflexive suspicion of America, the world's sole military superpower.

17 But the world must remember that it was not simply international institutions—not just treaties and declarations—that brought stability to a post-World War II world. Whatever mistakes we have made, the plain fact is this: The United States of America has helped underwrite global security for more than six decades with the blood of our citizens and the strength of our arms. The service and sacrifice of our men and women in uniform has promoted peace and prosperity from Germany to Korea, and enabled democracy to take hold in places like the Balkans. We have borne this burden not because we seek to impose our will. We have done so out of enlightened self-interest—because we seek a better future for our children and grandchildren, and we believe that their lives will be better if others' children and grandchildren can live in freedom and prosperity.

18 So yes, the instruments of war do have a role to play in preserving the peace. And yet this truth must coexist with another—that no matter how justified, war promises human tragedy. The soldier's courage and sacrifice is full of glory,

的，这并不是犬儒主义的说法——这是对历史、对人性缺陷和对有限的理性的审视和认知。

16 我持此观点，并以此开始演讲，是因为不管军事行动的原因是什么，今天许多国家都对其怀着一种矛盾情绪。有时，因为这种矛盾情绪，他们也会下意识地怀疑美国，这个世界上唯一的军事大国。

17 但是世界各国必须牢记，第二次世界大战后的世界和平并不是只靠国际组织、条约和宣言就能带来的。不管我们曾犯下什么过错，有一点是肯定的：60多年来，美利坚合众国用它自己国民的鲜血和军事力量给世界安全上了一道保险。我们穿着制服的国民通过自己的奉献和牺牲确保了从德国到朝鲜的和平与繁荣，使得民主在像巴尔干半岛这样的地方生根发芽。我们主动承担这个任务，不是企图强加我们的意志，而是为了文明时代自己的利益——因为我们想为子孙后代寻求一个更好的未来，我们相信如果其他人的后代也能生活在民主自由的社会，那我们自己孩子的生活将会更美好。

18 因此，战争在保护世界和平方面的确能发挥作用。但是伴随这个事实存在的还有，不管战争有多正义，它对人类来说都是一场悲剧。士兵的勇气和牺牲是光荣的，他们表现

---

[12] ambivalence [æmˈbɪvələns] *n.* 矛盾心理

expressing devotion to country, to cause, to comrades in arms. But war itself is never glorious, and we must never trumpet it as such.

19 So part of our challenge is reconciling these two seemingly inreconcilable truths—that war is sometimes necessary, and war at some level is an expression of human folly. Concretely, we must direct our effort to the task that President Kennedy called for long ago. "Let us focus," he said, "on a more practical, more attainable peace, based not on a sudden revolution in human nature but on a gradual evolution in human institutions."

20 What might this evolution look like? What might these practical steps be?

21 To begin with, I believe that all nations—strong and weak alike—must adhere to standards that govern the use of force. I—like any head of state—reserve the right to act unilaterally if necessary to defend my nation. Nevertheless, I am convinced that adhering to standards, international standards, strengthens those who do, and isolates and weakens those who don't.

22 The world rallied around America after the 9/11 attacks, and continues to support our efforts in Afghanistan, because of the horror of those senseless attacks and the recognized principle of self-defense. Likewise, the world recognized the need to confront Saddam Hussein when he invaded Kuwait—a consensus that sent a clear message to all about the cost of aggression.

23 Furthermore, America—in fact, no nation—can insist that others follow the rules of the road if we refuse to follow them ourselves. For

着对国家、事业和战友的忠诚。但是战争本身却一点也不光荣，我们绝不可能以此吹嘘。

19 所以我们的挑战之一就是要协调两个看似不可协调的事实——战争有时是必要的，同时战争在某种程度上是人类愚蠢的象征。具体来说就是，我们要努力完成很久以前肯尼迪总统号召的任务。他说道："让我们专注在更实际、更易实现的和平上吧，不希冀人性会有突然的进步，而是依靠人类机构的逐渐完善。"

20 这个演化的过程究竟是怎样的？要采取哪些实际的措施？

21 首先，我认为所有的国家，不论强弱，都应该遵循管制武力的规则。但是我和其他任何国家的元首，出于捍卫本国的需要，都有权利单方面采取行动。尽管如此，我仍相信，遵守这些国际规则能使一个国家更强，否则就会被孤立和削弱。

22 9·11事件之后，出于对毫无理由的恐怖袭击的恐惧和对自卫原则的认可，世界团结在了美国周围，继续支持我们在阿富汗的努力。同样地，世界许多国家也意识到了同侵略科威特的萨达姆·侯赛因对抗的必要性，这给所有国家发出了一个信号：侵略是要付出代价的。

23 除此之外，美国——事实上，任何一个国家——都不能在自己都还没有遵守规则的前提下要求其他

when we don't, our actions appear arbitrary and undercut the legitimacy of future interventions, no matter how justified.

24 And this becomes particularly important when the purpose of military action extends beyond self-defense or the defense of one nation against an aggressor. More and more, we all confront difficult questions about how to prevent the slaughter of civilians by their own government, or to stop a civil war whose violence and suffering can engulf an entire region.

25 I believe that force can be justified on humanitarian grounds, as it was in the Balkans, or in other places that have been scarred by war. Inaction tears at our conscience and can lead to more costly intervention later. That's why all responsible nations must embrace the role that militaries with a clear mandate can play to keep the peace.

26 America's commitment to global security will never waver. But in a world in which threats are more diffuse, and missions more complex, America cannot act alone. America alone cannot secure the peace. This is true in Afghanistan. This is true in failed states like Somalia, where terrorism and piracy is joined by famine and human suffering. And sadly, it will continue to be true in unstable regions for years to come.

27 The leaders and soldiers of NATO countries, and other friends and allies, demonstrate this truth through the capacity and courage they've shown in Afghanistan. But in

国家这样做。因为如果我们不遵守这些规则，我们的行动就是专制，不管有多正义，这就等于放弃了未来干预的合法性。

24 当我们的军事行动目的超出了自卫或者抵抗侵略的范畴时，这就变得极为重要了。何况我们越来越多地面对这样的难题：如何通过当事国自己的政府阻止对平民的屠杀？或者如何阻止一场其暴力和苦难足以吞没整个地区的内战？

25 我相信，武力可以基于人道的理由显示其正当性，比如在巴尔干半岛或其他受过战争创伤的地方。不行动只能使我们的良心受到谴责，并且可能导致后期不得不以更大的代价去干预。这就是为什么所有负责任的国家都应该主动演好通过有明确指令的军事行动保护和平的角色。

26 美国对全球安全的投入不会动摇。但是在一个威胁越发扩散、任务更加复杂的世界里，美国不可能单独行动。只有美国自己也不可能保证和平。这在阿富汗已经得到证实。在恐怖主义、海盗、饥荒和人民苦难遍布的索马里等国家也已得到证实。可悲的是，接下来的几年，在一些动乱的地区同样的事情也将上演。

27 北约国家的领导人和士兵，以及其他友国和同盟，已经通过他们在阿富汗的勇气和能力印证了这一真理。但是在许多国家，为此付出的人

many countries, there is a disconnect between the efforts of those who serve and the ambivalence of the broader public. I understand why war is not popular, but I also know this: The belief that peace is desirable is rarely enough to achieve it. Peace requires responsibility. Peace *entails* [13] sacrifice. That's why NATO continues to be indispensable. That's why we must strengthen UN and regional peacekeeping, and not leave the task to a few countries. That's why we honor those who return home from peacekeeping and training abroad to Oslo and Rome; to Ottawa and Sydney; to Dhaka and Kigali—we honor them not as makers of war, but of wagers—but as wagers of peace.

28 Let me make one final point about the use of force. Even as we make difficult decisions about going to war, we must also think clearly about how we fight it. The Nobel Committee recognized this truth in awarding its first prize for peace to Henry Dunant—the founder of the Red Cross, and a driving force behind the *Geneva Conventions*.

29 Where force is necessary, we have a moral and strategic interest in binding ourselves to certain rules of conduct. And even as we confront a vicious adversary that abides by no rules, I believe the United States of America must remain a standard bearer in the conduct of war. That is what makes us different from those whom we fight. That is a source of our strength. That is why I prohibited torture. That is why I ordered

们与怀着矛盾心理的更广大民众之间则出现了裂痕。我能理解为什么战争不受欢迎，但是我也知道：要得到和平，只凭和平可贵的信念是远远不够的。和平需要责任意识，还需要牺牲。这就是北约继续存在且必不可少的原因。正因为如此，我们必须加强联合国的地位和地区性维和，不能把任务留给少数几个国家。正因为如此，我们尊敬那些执行维和任务和训练归来的人们，他们到奥斯陆和罗马，到渥太华和悉尼，到达卡和基加利，我们以他们为荣不是因为他们制造战争，而是因为他们下的赌注，关于和平的赌注。

28 关于武力的作用，我再讲一点。即使我们做出艰难的决定去参与战争，我们也必须考虑清楚要如何作战。诺贝尔奖委员会将第一个和平奖授予亨利·杜南（红十字会的创始人，《日内瓦公约》的推动者）的时候就已经认识到了这一点。

29 当有必要使用武力时，我们无论是出于道德还是策略，都会很乐意遵守行动准则。即便我们的对手恶贯满盈，从不遵守任何规则，我认为美国也必须在战争中保持一个规则倡导者的姿态。因为这正是我们区别于对手的地方。这是我们力量的源泉，是我禁止酷刑的原因，是我关停关塔那摩湾监狱的原因，也是我重申美国

⑬ entail [ɪnˈteɪl] *vt.* 需要　如：The work entails precision. 这项工作要做到精细精准。

the prison at Guantanamo Bay closed. And that is why I have reaffirmed America's commitment to abide by the *Geneva Conventions*. We lose ourselves when we compromise the very ideals that we fight to defend. And we honor—we honor those ideals by upholding them not when it's easy, but when it is hard.

30 I have spoken at some length to the question that must weigh on our minds and our hearts as we choose to wage war. But let me now turn to our effort to avoid such tragic choices, and speak of three ways that we can build a just and lasting peace.

31 First, in dealing with those nations that break rules and laws, I believe that we must develop alternatives to violence that are tough enough to actually change behavior—for if we want a lasting peace, then the words of the international community must mean something. Those regimes that break the rules must be held accountable. Sanctions must exact a real price. Intransigence must be met with increased pressure—and such pressure exists only when the world stands together as one.

32 One urgent example is the effort to prevent the spread of nuclear weapons, and to seek a world without them. In the middle of the last century, nations agreed to be bound by a treaty whose bargain is clear: All will have access to peaceful nuclear power; those without nuclear weapons will forsake them; and those with nuclear weapons will work towards disarmament. I am committed to upholding this treaty. It is

将不遗余力地遵守《日内瓦公约》的原因。如果我们在最初为之战斗的理想上让步，我们就会迷失自我。我们以那些理性为荣，在艰难而非容易的时候为之奋斗。

30 我已经相当详细地阐述了选择发动战争时在我们心中举足轻重的系列问题。现在我要转向为避免这类悲剧而选择我们要付出的努力，我们可以通过三种方式建立正义而持久的和平。

31 首先，在同那些违反规则的国家打交道时，除了武力，我们必须有其他后果足够严重的选择能改变他们的行为——因为要想有持久和平，国际组织的话语就必须管用。那些违反规则的政权必须对此负责任。必须严格执行制裁。如果不妥协就必须继续施加压力，而这些压力只有在整个世界站在同一边时才能实施。

32 一个当务之急的例子就是阻止核武器的扩散，寻求一个没有核武器的世界。20 世纪中期，各个国家对一个内容明确的条款表示赞同：所有国家都可以和平利用核能；那些没有核武器的国家要放弃拥有核武器的想法；拥有核武器的国家则要裁军。我一直致力于维护这项条约，这也是我对外政策的核心。我和梅德韦杰夫

a centerpiece of my foreign policy. And I'm working with President Medvedev to reduce America and Russia's nuclear stockpiles.

33　But it is also *incumbent* ⑭ upon all of us to insist that nations like Iran and North Korea do not game the system. Those who claim to respect international law cannot avert their eyes when those laws are *flouted* ⑮. Those who care for their own security cannot ignore the danger of an arms race in the Middle East or East Asia. Those who seek peace cannot stand idly by as nations arm themselves for nuclear war.

34　The same principle applies to those who violate international laws by brutalizing their own people. When there is genocide in Darfur, systematic rape in Congo, repression in Burma— there must be consequences. Yes, there will be engagement; yes, there will be diplomacy—but there must be consequences when those things fail. And the closer we stand together, the less likely we will be faced with the choice between armed intervention and complicity in oppression.

35　This brings me to a second point—the nature of the peace that we seek. For peace is not merely the absence of visible conflict. Only a just peace based on the inherent rights and dignity of every individual can truly be lasting.

36　It was this insight that drove drafters of the *Universal Declaration of Human Rights* after the Second World War. In the wake of devastation,

总统正在致力于减少各自的核武器储存。

33　同时，坚持使伊朗、朝鲜这样的国家严格遵守规则也是我们义不容辞的责任。那些宣称尊重国际规则的国家不能无视别国蔑视这些规则。那些关心本国安全的国家也不能忽视中东或东亚地区搞军备竞赛带来的危险。而那些追求和平的国家也不能看着别国发展核武器而袖手旁观。

34　对那些违反国际规则，践踏本国人民的行为，这些原则同样适用。无论是达富尔发生种族屠杀，刚果发生有组织的强奸，还是缅甸的镇压，都应该得到相应的惩罚。是的，会有承诺，有外交，但是当这些失败的时候他们必须要承担后果。我们越团结，面对在武力干预和共谋施加压力之间抉择的可能性就越小。

35　这让我想到了第二点——我们追求的和平本质是什么。因为和平并非仅仅是暂时看不到冲突。只有保证了每个人固有的权力和尊严的和平，才能真正持久。

36　正是洞察了这样的真理，才驱使人们在第二次世界大战后起草了《世界人权宣言》。在大规模的破

⑭　incumbent [ɪnˈkʌmbənt] *adj.* 义不容辞的，职责所在的　如：It was incumbent on them to attend. 他们的出席是职责所在。

⑮　flout [flaʊt] *vt.* 轻视，蔑视

220

they recognized that if human rights are not protected, peace is a hollow promise.

37 And yet too often, these words are ignored. For some countries, the failure to uphold human rights is excused by the false suggestion that these are somehow Western principles, foreign to local cultures or stages of a nation's development. And within America, there has long been a tension between those who describe themselves as realists or idealists—a tension that suggests a stark choice between the narrow pursuit of interests or an endless campaign to impose our values around the world.

38 I reject these choices. I believe that peace is unstable where citizens are denied the right to speak freely or worship as they please; choose their own leaders or assemble without fear. Pent-up grievances fester, and the suppression of tribal and religious identity can lead to violence. We also know that the opposite is true. Only when Europe became free did it finally find peace. America has never fought a war against a democracy, and our closest friends are governments that protect the rights of their citizens. No matter how callously defined, neither America's interests—nor the world's—are served by the denial of human aspirations.

39 So even as we respect the unique culture and traditions of different countries, America will always be a voice for those aspirations that are universal. We will bear witness to the quiet dignity of reformers like Aung Sang Suu Kyi; to the bravery of Zimbabweans who cast their

坏之后，他们认识到如果人权没有保障，和平将只能是空谈。

37 然而，这些宣言却经常被忽略。对于有些国家，他们侵犯人权的借口就是，种种迹象表明这些规则是定给西方国家的，与他们当地文化冲突，不适合他们国家的发展阶段。而且长期以来美国内部那些标榜现实主义和理想主义的势力关系都很紧张，这反映出在狭隘的利益追求和无休止地强加于我们的价值观之间的抉择。

38 我拒绝做这种选择。我认为在人民没有言论自由和信仰自由，不能毫无畏惧地集会、选举自己的领导人的情况下，和平是不会稳定的。压抑的愤怒终会爆发，对种族和宗教身份的压迫可能导致暴力。而且我们知道反之亦然。欧洲只有自由了，才能找到最终的和平。美国从未对民主国家发起过战争，我们最亲近的朋友是那些保障民权的政府。不管如何无情地定义，美国的利益和世界利益都不是靠否定人类愿望来谋取的。

39 所以即使要尊重不同国家独特的文化传统，美国也会为人类共同的愿望而呼喊。我们会见证像昂山素季这样的改革者的无声的尊严；见证津巴布韦的人们面对暴行依然投下选票的勇敢；也会见证成千上万的民众

ballots in the face of beatings; to the hundreds of thousands who have marched silently through the streets of Iran. It is telling that the leaders of these governments fear the aspirations of their own people more than the power of any other nation. And it is the responsibility of all free people and free nations to make clear that these movements— these movements of hope and history—they have us on their side.

40 Let me also say this: The promotion of human rights cannot be about exhortation alone. At times, it must be coupled with painstaking diplomacy. I know that engagement with repressive regimes lacks the satisfying purity of indignation. But I also know that sanctions without outreach—condemnation without discussion—can carry forward only a crippling status quo. No repressive regime can move down a new path unless it has the choice of an open door.

41 ...

42 Third, a just peace includes not only civil and political rights—it must encompass economic security and opportunity. For true peace is not just freedom from fear, but freedom from want.

43 It is undoubtedly true that development rarely takes root without security; it is also true that security does not exist where human beings do not have access to enough food, or clean water, or the medicine and shelter they need to survive. It does not exist where children can't aspire to a decent education or a job that supports a family. The absence of hope can rot a society from

沉默着游行在伊朗的街道上。这些都说明这些国家的领导人害怕自己人民的愿望远超过害怕别国的力量。因此所有自由的国家和人民都有责任明确一点——这些事关希望与历史的运动，我们站在他们这边。

40 我还要说，提升人权不只是只靠在这儿劝诫。有时，也需要艰苦的外交努力。我知道同专制政权交往缺乏令人满意的纯洁的尊严，但我也知道没有广度的制裁，没有讨论的谴责只能使现状更严重。如果没有一扇开着的门可供选择，没有任何专制政权能够走上一条新道路。

41 ……

42 第三，正义的和平不只包括民权和政治权利——还必须包括经济贸易安全和机遇。因为真正的和平不只是远离恐惧，还要远离贫乏。

43 毋庸置疑，没有安全保障，发展就得不到巩固；而没有基本的生存必需品，食物缺乏，饮用水不洁净，医药短缺，安全也就没有保障。在儿童得不到良好教育，人们找不到一份工作维持家庭的情况下，安全也不可能存在。希望的缺乏会从内部腐蚀一个社会。

within.

44 And that's why helping farmers feed their own people—or nations educate their children and care for the sick—is not mere charity. It's also why the world must come together to confront climate change. There is little scientific dispute that if we do nothing, we will face more drought, more famine, more mass displacement—all of which will fuel more conflict for decades. For this reason, it is not merely scientists and environmental activists who call for swift and forceful action—it's military leaders in my own country and others who understand our common security hangs in the balance.

45 Agreements among nations. Strong institutions. Support for human rights. Investments in development. All these are vital ingredients in bringing about the evolution that President Kennedy spoke about. And yet, I do not believe that we will have the will, the determination, the staying power, to complete this work without something more—and that's the continued expansion of our moral imagination; an insistence that there's something irreducible that we all share.

46 As the world grows smaller, you might think it would be easier for human beings to recognize how similar we are; to understand that we're all basically seeking the same things; that we all hope for the chance to live out our lives with some measure of happiness and fulfillment for ourselves and our families.

47 And yet somehow, given the dizzying

44 这就是为什么帮助别国的农业、教育和医疗并不仅仅是在做慈善。这也是为什么世界各国必须一起面对气候变化。如果我们什么都不做，将会面临更多的干旱、饥荒和流离失所，而这些会在几十年内引发更多的冲突。对此几乎没有什么科学争议。也正是因为如此，不只是科学家和环境保护学家们在号召快速有力的行动，美国和其他国家的军事领导人也都能理解我们共同的安全岌岌可危。

45 国家间的协定，强有力的机制，支持保障人权，投资发展，所有这些都是促进肯尼迪总统所说的演变必不可少的因素。然而，如果缺少某些更重要的东西——我们持续扩大的道德想象，以及对于我们共同拥有的必不可少的东西的坚持，我不相信我们还有意愿、有决心、有耐力去完成这项工作。

46 随着世界变得越来越小，你会觉得人类更容易认识到我们彼此是多么相似；从根本上来看，我们有着同样的追求；我们都希望有机会快乐地生活，实现自我和家庭的价值。

47 但是，某种程度上，面对

pace of globalization, the cultural leveling of modernity, it perhaps comes as no surprise that people fear the loss of what they cherish in their particular identities—their race, their tribe, and perhaps most powerfully their religion. In some places, this fear has led to conflict. At times, it even feels like we're moving backwards. We see it in the Middle East, as the conflict between Arabs and Jews seems to harden. We see it in nations that are torn asunder by tribal lines.

48 And most dangerously, we see it in the way that religion is used to justify the murder of innocents by those who have distorted and defiled the great religion of Islam, and who attacked my country from Afghanistan. These extremists are not the first to kill in the name of God; the cruelties of the Crusades are amply recorded. But they remind us that no Holy War can ever be a just war. For if you truly believe that you are carrying out divine will, then there is no need for restraint—no need to spare the pregnant mother, or the medic, or the Red Cross worker, or even a person of one's own faith. Such a warped view of religion is not just incompatible with the concept of peace, but I believe it's incompatible with the very purpose of faith—for the one rule that lies at the heart of every major religion is that we do unto others as we would have them do unto us.

49 Adhering to this law of love has always been the core struggle of human nature. For we are fallible. We make mistakes, and fall victim to the temptations of pride, and power, and sometimes evil. Even those of us with the best of intentions will at times fail to right the wrongs

令人眩晕的全球化节奏和现代文化水平，人们惧怕他们珍视的特殊身份——种族、群体，甚至最有影响力的宗教，会丢失。这令人感到惊奇。有些地方，这种恐惧已经引发了战争。有时，感觉好像我们在倒退一样。比如在中东，阿拉伯民族和犹太人之间的冲突似乎有加深的迹象。有些国家因为种族裂痕而分崩离析。

48 最危险的是，他们拿宗教当借口为滥杀无辜辩护，他们曲解和玷污伟大的伊斯兰教，从阿富汗来袭击我的国家。这些极端组织并不是最先以上帝的名义杀人的；在这之前，十字军的残酷行为在历史上的记载并不少。这些提醒我们，没有任何一场圣战是正义的战争。因为如果你真的认为你在进行一场正义的战争，那就没有必要克制——没有必要在杀戮时避开孕妇、医生或红十字会的工作人员，甚至一个有着自己信仰的人。这种扭曲的宗教观不仅与和平的概念不相容，也与信仰的初衷不相容——因为所有主要宗教的核心就是希望别人以我们对待他们的方式对待我们自己。

49 遵守这种爱的法则一直是人性斗争的核心。因为我们容易犯错误。我们会受骄傲、权利，有时甚至是邪恶的诱惑而沦为受害者。即使是那些有最好的动机的人们有时也难免犯错，且无法改正。

before us.

50 But we do not have to think that human nature is perfect for us to still believe that the human condition can be perfected. We do not have to live in an idealized world to still reach for those ideals that will make it a better place. The non-violence practiced by men like Gandhi and King may not have been practical or possible in every circumstance, but the love that they preached—their fundamental faith in human progress—that must always be the North Star that guides us on our journey.

51 For if we lose that faith—if we dismiss it as silly or naïve; if we divorce it from the decisions that we make on issues of war and peace—then we lose what's best about humanity. We lose our sense of possibility. We lose our moral compass.

52 Like generations have before us, we must reject that future. As Dr. King said at this occasion so many years ago, "I refuse to accept despair as the final response to the ambiguities of history. I refuse to accept the idea that the 'isness' of man's present condition makes him morally incapable of reaching up for the eternal 'oughtness' that forever confronts him."

53 Let us reach for the world that ought to be—that spark of the divine that still stirs within each of our souls.

54 Somewhere today, in the here and now, in the world as it is, a soldier sees he's outgunned, but stands firm to keep the peace. Somewhere today, in this world, a young protester awaits the brutality of her government, but has the courage

50 我们没必要认为人性完美到让我们相信人类境况可以达到完美。我们无须生活在一个理想世界却还在追寻能让它变得更美好的理想。圣雄甘地和马丁·路德·金的非暴力运动也不是在所有情况下都可能或适用，但是他们宣传的爱——这一人类进步最基础的信念——必须成为路途中永远引领我们的北极星。

51 因为如果我们失去信念——将其置之不顾或认为它愚蠢幼稚，在做战争与和平等决定时将其排除在外——我们就失去了人性中最美好的部分，失去了可能性，也失去了道德标准。

52 就像我们之前的数代人一样，我们必须拒绝那样的将来。就像马丁·路德·金许多年前在此说过的一样："我拒绝将绝望作为历史歧义的最终回答。我拒绝接受所谓反映人类现实状况的'实然'使其无法从道义上达到永远需要面对的终极'应然'。"

53 让我们去追求世界应该有的样子，这是我们每个人灵魂深处还在迸射的火花。

54 今天，就在此时此刻，在这样一个世界里，某个地方的一位士兵看到自己已经在武器上失去优势了，但他还在坚持守卫着和平；在另一个地方，等待着一个抗议者的是政府的

to march on. Somewhere today, <u>a mother facing punishing poverty still takes the time to teach her child, scrapes together what few coins she has to send that child to school—because she believes that a cruel world still has a place for that child's dreams.</u>

55　Let us live by their example. We can acknowledge that oppression will always be with us, and still strive for justice. We can admit the intractability of depravation, and still strive for dignity. Clear-eyed, we can understand that there will be war, and still strive for peace. We can do that—for that is the story of human progress; that's the hope of all the world; and at this moment of challenge, that must be our work here on Earth.

56　Thank you very much.

残酷镇压，但他依然勇敢前行着；今天，在某处，<u>有一位母亲面对赤贫依然坚持花时间去教育她的孩子，搜刮齐仅有的几枚硬币也要把孩子送到学校——因为她相信世界虽残酷，但终有一个地方盛放孩子的梦想。</u>

55　让我们以他们为榜样生活吧。我们承认压迫始终存在，而我们也会继续为公平正义奋斗。我们承认堕落很难对付，但仍为尊严奋斗。睁大眼睛，我们就能理解还会有战争，但我们仍会为和平奋斗。我们能做到这些——因为这就是人类进步的故事，是整个世界的希望所在；而在此面临挑战的时刻，这些也必须成为我们在地球上为之奋斗的事业。

56　非常感谢大家！

演讲关键词 Practical Expressions

1. armed conflict 武装冲突
2. settle differences 消除分歧
3. codes of law 法律规范
4. Axis powers 轴心国
5. United States Senate 美国参议院
6. the League of Nations 国际联盟
7. Marshall Plan 马歇尔计划
8. the rule of law 法治
9. violent conflict 暴力冲突
10. NATO（全称：North Atlantic Treaty Organization）北大西洋公约组织
11. foreign policy 对外政策
12. arms race 军备竞赛
13. armed intervention 武装干预

1. And even as we confront a vicious adversary that abides by no rules, I believe the United States of America must remain a standard bearer in the conduct of war.

即便我们的对手恶贯满盈，从不遵守任何规则，我认为美国也必须在战争中保持一个规则倡导者的姿态。

2. A mother facing punishing poverty still takes the time to teach her child, scrapes together what few coins she has to send that child to school——because she believes that a cruel world still has a place for that child's dreams.

有一位母亲面对赤贫依然坚持花时间去教育她的孩子，搜刮齐仅有的几枚硬币也要把孩子送到学校——因为她相信世界虽残酷，但终有一个地方盛放孩子的梦想。

诺贝尔奖背后的那些趣事

发明武器也能得奖?

1918 年诺贝尔化学奖授予德国化学家弗里茨·哈伯。1914 年第一次世界大战开始，哈伯所在的厂子在战争期间为德国提供了世界少有的氮化合物。在民族沙文主义和盲目爱国热情的刺激下，昏了头的哈伯把自己的实验室变成了为战争服务的军事机构，并担任德国毒气战的科学负责人。在哈伯的建议下，德军开始在战场上使用毒气。3 个多月后，"毒气战"在伊普雷战役中正式诞生，造成英法联军约 15 000 人中毒，残害了 5 000 多人的性命。1918 年，哈伯因研制合成氨做出的重大贡献而获得诺贝尔化学奖，但是由于第一次世界大战中哈伯为德国军方研制杀人化学武器，他也被战胜国列入战犯名单。哈伯本人在战后感到罪孽深重，他因害怕被人认出而故意蓄须，甚至跑到外国躲起来。这件事顿时在整个科学界闹得沸沸扬扬。

Speech 4

Democracy and Human Rights, a Less Lonely Path to Follow

民主和人权，不再孤单的征程

—Speech by Aung San Suu Kyi for the Nobel Peace Prize in 2012

——缅甸的自由女神昂山素季 2012 年发表的诺贝尔和平奖获奖演讲

名家速览 About the Author

诺贝尔奖大师	昂山素季
奖 项 归 属	1991 年诺贝尔和平奖
获 奖 理 由	因为她为争取民主与人权所做的非暴力斗争。
相关演讲链接	结束软禁后，2010 年 11 月 14 日昂山素季在缅甸仰光发表演讲

　　昂山素季（Aung San Suu Kyi, 1945 年 6 月 19 日—）出生于缅甸仰光，其父亲昂山将军是缅甸民族独立的英雄，但在昂山素季 2 岁的时候被英国支持的缅甸爱国党人杀害。1963 年，18 岁的昂山素季被送往英国读书，在英国牛津大学攻读哲学、政治学和经济学，并在 1967 年获得学士学位。她是提倡民主和非暴力的著名政治家，1990 年带领全国民主联盟赢得大选的胜利，但选举结果被军政府作废。其后 21 年间，她被军政府断断续续软禁于其寓所中长达 15 年，期间她于 1990 年获得萨哈罗夫奖，于 1991 年获诺贝尔和平奖。在 2010 年 11 月 13 日她终于获释。昂山素季一生致力于缅甸的民主与人权斗争，与缅甸军政府进行非暴力的对抗和交涉，多次被当局软禁。期间有两次被释放，她本可以去英国探望自己的家人，但她清楚，这一去就不可能再返回缅甸，于是她放弃了。连丈夫患癌症去世，她都没能回去探望照料。本文本应是 1991 年她在获诺贝尔和平奖时的演讲，但当时她正在软禁期间，于是 2012 年才于挪威发表了这迟到 21 年的演讲。文中她讲述了诺贝尔和平奖对她本人和对世界的意义，号召世界人民携手共创民主和平的美好社会。

和平的使者：点燃和平希望的诺贝尔奖大师演讲

演讲现场
Speech Script

精美译文
Suggested Translation

1　Excellencies, Distinguished members of the Norwegian Nobel Committee, Dear Friends,

2　Long years ago, sometimes it seems many lives ago, I was at Oxford listening to the radio programme *Desert Island Discs* with my young son Alexander. It was a well-known programme (for all I know it still continues) on which famous people from all walks of life were invited to talk about the eight discs, the one book beside the *Bible* and the *Complete Works of Shakespeare*, and the one luxury item they would wish to have with them were they to be **marooned**① on a desert island. At the end of the programme, which we had both enjoyed, Alexander asked me if I thought I might ever be invited to speak on *Desert Island Discs*. "Why not?" I responded lightly. Since he knew that in general only celebrities took part in the programme he proceeded to ask, with genuine interest, for what reason I thought I might be invited. I considered this for a moment and then answered: "Perhaps because I'd have won the Nobel Prize for literature," and we both laughed. The prospect seemed pleasant but hardly probable.

3　(I cannot now remember why I gave that answer, perhaps because I had recently read a book by a Nobel Laureate or perhaps because the *Desert Island Disc* celebrity of that day had been a famous writer.)

1　尊敬的殿下，尊敬的挪威诺贝尔奖委员会的成员们，亲爱的朋友们：

2　多年前，有时回想起来像是几生几世以前了，我和我的儿子亚历山大在牛津听广播节目《荒岛唱片》。这个节目非常有名（据我所知，现在还在播），它邀请各行各业的著名人士来节目做访谈，谈论如果被置于无人荒岛，他们希望带哪八张唱片，以及除了《圣经》和《莎士比亚全集》外的哪本书，另外，他们还可以选择额外带一件物品。我和儿子都很享受这个节目，在节目结尾的时候，他问我是否想过会被这个节目邀请做嘉宾。"怎么没想过，我当然想过，"我轻声回答。他继续问，那会以什么理由邀请我呢，因为他知道通常只有名人才能上这个节目。我想了一会儿说道："可能我获得了诺贝尔文学奖吧。"于是我们都笑了。这个设想很美好，但却不大可能。

3　（我现在已经记不起我为什么会那么回答了，可能因为我当时读了一本诺贝尔奖得主的书，也可能因为那天《荒岛唱片》的嘉宾刚好是一位著名作家。）

---

① maroon [məˈruːn] *vt.* 使孤立，被放逐到无人荒岛上

4 In 1989, when my late husband Michael Aris came to see me during my first term of house arrest, he told me that a friend, John Finnis, had nominated me for the Nobel Peace Prize. This time also I laughed. For an instant Michael looked amazed, then he realized why I was amused. The Nobel Peace Prize? A pleasant prospect, but quite improbable! So how did I feel when I was actually awarded the Nobel Prize for Peace? The question has been put to me many times and this is surely the most appropriate occasion on which to examine what the Nobel Prize means to me and what peace means to me.

5 As I have said repeatedly in many an interview, I heard the news that I had been awarded the Nobel Peace Prize on the radio one evening. It did not altogether come as a surprise because I had been mentioned as one of the frontrunners for the prize in a number of broadcasts during the previous week. While drafting this lecture, I have tried very hard to remember what my immediate reaction to the announcement of the award had been. I think, I can no longer be sure, it was something like: "Oh, so they've decided to give it to me." It did not seem quite real because in a sense I did not feel myself to be quite real at that time.

6 Often during my days of house arrest it felt as though I were no longer a part of the real world. There was the house which was my world, there was the world of others who also were not free but who were together in prison as a community, and there was the world of the free; each was a

4 1989 年，我第一次被软禁在家的时候我丈夫迈克尔·阿里斯（现已去世）来看我。他告诉我，一位叫约翰·菲尼斯的朋友提名我为诺贝尔奖候选人。这次我又笑了。当时迈克尔很惊讶，后来他意识到我为什么笑了。诺贝尔和平奖？这又是多么美好的设想，可是根本不可能发生！所以当我真的被授予诺贝尔和平奖的时候，我做何感想呢？这个问题我想过很多次了，而现在肯定是最适合我思考诺贝尔奖对我的意义以及和平对我的意义的时候了。

5 就像我在很多采访中说过的一样，我是有一天晚上听广播的时候得知我荣获诺贝尔奖的。对此我并没有太惊讶，因为之前的几周很多广播都已经在报道我有望获奖了。在写这份演讲草稿的时候，我还在努力回忆自己得知获奖时的第一反应是什么。我想我已经不太确定，大概就是："噢，所以他们决定把奖颁给我了。"这可能听起来不大真实，因为在那一刻我确实很恍惚。

6 我在被软禁在家的日子里，常常觉得自己已经不是这个世界的一部分了。我自己的房子就是我的世界；在这个世界之外是一个像监狱一样集体不自由的世界；在那个世界之外才是自由世界。每个世界都是一个

different planet pursuing its own separate course in an indifferent universe. What the Nobel Peace Prize did was to draw me once again into the world of other human beings outside the isolated area in which I lived, to restore a sense of reality to me. This did not happen instantly, of course, but as the days and months went by and news of reactions to the award came over the airwaves, I began to understand the significance of the Nobel Prize. It had made me real once again; it had drawn me back into the wider human community. And what was more important, the Nobel Prize had drawn the attention of the world to the struggle for democracy and human rights in Burma. We were not going to be forgotten.

7 To be forgotten. The French say that to part is to die a little. To be forgotten too is to die a little. It is to lose some of the links that anchor us to the rest of humanity. When I met Burmese migrant workers and refugees during my recent visit to Thailand, many cried out: "Don't forget us!" They meant: "don't forget our *plight* ②, don't forget to do what you can to help us, don't forget we also belong to your world." When the Nobel Committee awarded the Peace Prize to me they were recognizing that the oppressed and the isolated in Burma were also a part of the world, they were recognizing the oneness of humanity. So for me receiving the Nobel Peace Prize means personally extending my concerns for democracy and human rights beyond national borders. The Nobel Peace Prize opened up a door in my heart.

不同的星球，都在属于自己的宇宙里上下求索。诺贝尔奖带给我的就是，将我从自己被隔离的世界拖出来，带我重回其他人类的世界，还我真实感。这当然不是瞬间发生的。经过这些天新闻对获奖事件的连续报道，我才开始渐渐明白诺贝尔奖的意义。它让我自己又真实起来，重回更广阔的人类社会。更重要的是，诺贝尔奖使世界开始关注缅甸的民主和人权斗争。我们不会被遗忘。

7 法国人说，离别就是某种程度上的死亡，而遗忘在某种程度上也是死亡。遗忘意味着失去我们与世界的联系。我最近访问泰国时见到了很多缅甸的农民工和难民，他们都哭诉着："请不要忘记我们！"他们是想说："不要忘记我们的困境，不要忘了尽你所能帮助我们，不要忘了我们也属于你们的世界。"诺贝尔奖委员会将奖项授予我，实际上是肯定了缅甸受压迫和被隔离的人们也是这个世界的一部分，也是在肯定这个世界的统一性。对我个人来说，获诺贝尔奖意味着将我对民主和人权的担忧超越国界。诺贝尔和平奖打开了我心中的一扇门。

---

② plight [plaɪt] *n.* 困境

8 The Burmese concept of peace can be explained as the happiness arising from the cessation of factors that *militate* ③ against the harmonious and the *wholesome* ④. The word nyein-chan translates literally as the beneficial coolness that comes when a fire is extinguished. Fires of suffering and strife are raging around the world. In my own country, *hostilities* ⑤ have not ceased in the far north; to the west, communal violence resulting in arson and murder were taking place just several days before I started out on the journey that has brought me here today. News of atrocities in other reaches of the earth abound. Reports of hunger, disease, displacement, joblessness, poverty, injustice, discrimination, prejudice, *bigotry* ⑥; these are our daily fare. Everywhere there are negative forces eating away at the foundations of peace. Everywhere can be found thoughtless *dissipation* ⑦ of material and human resources that are necessary for the conservation of harmony and happiness in our world.

9 The First World War represented a terrifying waste of youth and potential, a cruel squandering of the positive forces of our planet.

8 缅甸人的和平观是通过终止那些妨碍和谐与福祉的因素而提升幸福感。"nyein-chan"这个词，按字面意义可译作"大火熄灭之后的凉爽"。苦难和冲突的大火正在世界上蔓延。在我自己的国家，北方的战争并未停止；就在我开始自己此次旅程前的几天，缅甸西部地区群体暴力导致的纵火和谋杀还在发生。新闻里世界其他地方也还有暴力横行。关于饥饿、疾病、流离失所、失业、贫困、非正义、歧视、偏见和偏执的报道构成了我们每天的生活。世界各地都有恶势力在侵蚀着和平的根基。保护世界和谐幸福需要大量人力物力，然而对这些资源的浪费却随处可见。

9 第一次世界大战即是对青春和潜力的可怕浪费，是对地球上积极力量的极大浪费。那个时代的诗歌对

---

③ militate ['mɪlɪteɪt] *vt.* 产生作用和（坏的）影响　如：militate against... 阻碍，防止（某事的发生或存在）

④ wholesome ['həʊlsəm] *adj.* 有益健康的，健全的　如：a wholesome climate 有益健康的气候

⑤ hostility [hɒs'tɪləti] *n.* 战争，敌对行为（常为复数）　如：the outbreak of hostilities between the two sides 双方之间爆发敌对行为

⑥ bigotry ['bɪɡətri] *n.* 顽固，固执，偏执

⑦ dissipation [ˌdɪsɪ'peɪʃən] *n.* 浪费　如：great dissipation of time 极其浪费时间

The poetry of that era has a special significance for me because I first read it at a time when I was the same age as many of those young men who had to face the prospect of withering before they had barely blossomed. A young American fighting with the French Foreign Legion wrote before he was killed in action in 1916 that he would meet his death: "at some disputed barricade;" "on some scarred slope of battered hill;" "at midnight in some flaming town." Youth and love and life perishing forever in senseless attempts to capture nameless, unremembered places. And for what? Nearly a century on, we have yet to find a satisfactory answer.

10 Are we not still guilty, if to a less violent degree, of recklessness, of improvidence with regard to our future and our humanity? War is not the only arena where peace is done to death. Wherever suffering is ignored, there will be the seeds of conflict, for suffering degrades and embitters and enrages.

11 A positive aspect of living in isolation was that I had ample time in which to *ruminate* [8] over the meaning of words and precepts that I had known and accepted all my life. As a Buddhist, I had heard about dukha, generally translated as suffering, since I was a small child. Almost on a daily basis elderly, and sometimes not so elderly, people around me would murmur "dukha, dukha" when they suffered from aches and pains or when they met with some small, annoying mishaps. However, it was only during my years of house

我有很大影响，因为我在和那些年轻人相仿的年纪里第一次读到那些诗，他们却成了还没盛开就要凋谢的花朵。法国外籍兵团的一位美国年轻人在 1916 年一次行动前预见了他的死亡，他写道："在争执的障碍前"，"在破败不堪的山丘上"，"在小镇上火光冲天的午夜里。"为了试图占领那些毫无意义的无名或记不住名字的地方，那些年轻人、爱和生命永远地消逝了。这究竟是为了什么呢？一个世纪都过去了，我们还没找到一个满意的答案。

10 面对人类社会的未来，如果暴力程度轻一些，只是鲁莽无知，没有远见，我们就能够脱罪吗？战争并不是争取和平的唯一办法，和平并不取决于死亡。无论何时，苦难若被忽略就会引起冲突，因为苦难会恶化，会引发怨恨和愤怒。

11 离群索居的一个好处就是，我有大量时间反复体会我一生奉为格言的话语。作为一名佛教徒，我从小就知道"苦谛"的意义。我周围上了年纪的人，有时也没有多大年纪，当他们遭受苦难或一些小祸端的时候就会默念"苦谛，苦谛"。然而，只有在我被软禁的日子里，我才有时间去探索六大苦谛的意义：生、老、病、死、爱别离、怨相会。不是以宗教的立场，而是从我们普通人每天的生活

---

⑧ ruminate ['ruːmɪneɪt] *vi.* 反思　如：ruminate over sth. 反思某事

arrest that I got around to investigating the nature of the six great dukha. These are: to be conceived, to age, to sicken, to die, to be parted from those one loves, to be forced to live in *propinquity* ⑨ with those one does not love. I examined each of the six great sufferings, not in a religious context but in the context of our ordinary, everyday lives. <u>If suffering were an unavoidable part of our existence, we should try to alleviate it as far as possible in practical, earthly ways.</u> I mulled over the effectiveness of ante- and post-natal programmes and mother and childcare; of adequate facilities for the aging population; of comprehensive health services; of compassionate nursing and hospices. I was particularly intrigued by the last two kinds of suffering: to be parted from those one loves and to be forced to live in propinquity with those one does not love. What experiences might our Lord Buddha have undergone in his own life that he had included these two states among the great sufferings? I thought of prisoners and refugees, of migrant workers and victims of human trafficking, of that great mass of the uprooted of the earth who have been torn away from their homes, parted from families and friends, forced to live out their lives among strangers who are not always welcoming.

12 We are fortunate to be living in an age when social welfare and humanitarian assistance are recognized not only as desirable but necessary. I am fortunate to be living in an age when the fate of prisoners of conscience anywhere has become

的角度，我一一品味这六大苦谛。<u>如果生而为人，苦谛难免的话，我们应该尽可能地通过实际办法来缓解苦痛。</u>我认真考虑过母子产前产后护理项目，为老龄人群提供充足的设备，提供综合健康服务，以及慈善护理和救济。我对后面两种苦谛尤为感兴趣：爱别离和怨相会。我们伟大的如来佛祖一生究竟经历了什么，让他将这两项列为人生的大苦难？我想到了政治犯和难民，想到了流动工人和非法贩卖人口的受害者，想到了那些远离家园，亲友离散，漂泊无依，被迫在并不友善的异国他乡过活的人们。

12 我们很幸运地生活在一个承认社会福利和人道主义援助有帮助而且有必要的时代。我也倍感幸运能生活在一个政治犯开始受到关心的时代，一个民主和人权已经被广泛地、

⑨ propinquity [prəˈpɪŋkwɪtɪ] *n.* 接近

the concern of peoples everywhere, an age when democracy and human rights are widely, even if not universally, accepted as the birthright of all. How often during my years under house arrest have I drawn strength from my favourite passages in the preamble to the *Universal Declaration of Human Rights:*

13 *... disregard and contempt for human rights have resulted in barbarous acts which have outraged the conscience of mankind, and the advent of a world in which human beings shall enjoy freedom of speech and belief and freedom from fear and want has been proclaimed as the highest aspirations of the common people.*

14 *... it is essential, if man is not to be compelled to have recourse, as a last resort, to rebellion against tyranny and oppression, that human rights should be protected by the rule of law...*

15 If I am asked why I am fighting for human rights in Burma the above passages will provide the answer. If I am asked why I am fighting for democracy in Burma, it is because I believe that democratic institutions and practices are necessary for the guarantee of human rights.

16 Over the past year there have been signs that the endeavours of those who believe in democracy and human rights are beginning to bear fruit in Burma. There have been changes in a positive direction; steps towards democratization have been taken. If I advocate cautious optimism it is not because I do not have faith in the future but because I do not want to encourage blind faith.

虽然不是普遍地接受的时代。在我被软禁的岁月里，曾有多少次我从《世界人权宣言》我最喜欢的序文里汲取力量：

13 ……对人权的无视和蔑视已发展为野蛮暴行，这些暴行玷污了人类的良心，而一个人人享有言论和信仰自由并免予恐惧和匮乏的世界的来临，已被宣布为普通人民的最高愿望。

14 ……为使人类不致迫不得已铤而走险对暴政和压迫进行反叛，有必要使人权受法治的保护……

15 如果有人问我为什么要为缅甸的人权做斗争，那么上面的话就是我的答案。如果问我，为什么要为缅甸的民主斗争，那是因为我相信民主机构和实践是对人权的必要保证。

16 在过去一年中，已经有迹象表明，那些为坚持民主与人权所做的努力在缅甸已经初见成效。有很多改变在朝着积极的方向发展，人们正在踏步走向民主。我不提倡过早的乐观，不是因为我对未来没有信心，而是因为我不鼓励盲目自信。如果对未来没有信心，不相信民主观念和基本

Without faith in the future, without the conviction that democratic values and fundamental human rights are not only necessary but possible for our society, our movement could not have been sustained throughout the destroying years. Some of our warriors fell at their post, some deserted us, but a dedicated core remained strong and committed. At times when I think of the years that have passed, I am amazed that so many remained staunch under the most trying circumstances. Their faith in our cause is not blind; it is based on a clear-eyed assessment of their own powers of endurance and a profound respect for the aspirations of our people.

17 It is because of recent changes in my country that I am with you today; and these changes have come about because of you and other lovers of freedom and justice who contributed towards a global awareness of our situation. Before continuing to speak of my country, may I speak out for our prisoners of conscience. There still remain such prisoners in Burma. It is to be feared that because the best known detainees have been released, the remainder, the unknown ones, will be forgotten. I am standing here because I was once a prisoner of conscience. As you look at me and listen to me, please remember the often repeated truth that one prisoner of conscience is one too many. Those who have not yet been freed, those who have not yet been given access to the benefits of justice in my country number much more than one. Please remember them and do whatever is possible to

的人权对人类社会不仅必要而且可能实现，那我们的运动就不可能在这些年的艰难岁月里持续下来。我们有些战士在他们的岗位上倒下了，而有些抛弃了我们，但是我们还有一个愿为之献身的强有力的核心。有时，想想过去的那些年我不仅感到惊讶，在最折磨人的情况下，有那么多人依然坚定如初。他们对我们事业的信念不是盲目的，而是基于对他们自身承受力的清晰判断和对人民愿望的深切尊重。

17 我今天能站在这里，是因为我的国家已经发生了变化，而这些变化之所以能发生，是因为你们和其他热爱自由与正义的人们使世界人民看到了我们的处境。在继续谈论我的国家之前，我想为政治犯说几句话。今天的缅甸依然有这样的犯人。如果最有名的被释放了，而剩下的却因此被遗忘，那是很可怕的。我站在这里，因为我曾经是一名政治犯。在你们看着我、听我讲话的时候，请别忘记并经常重复这样的事实：即使是一名政治犯也嫌多。而在我国没有被释放的、无法享受正义的好处的政治犯还有很多。请记住他们，尽可能地做些事情，让他们能及早得到无条件释放。

effect their earliest, unconditional release.

18　Burma is a country of many ethnic nationalities and faith in its future can be founded only on a true spirit of union. Since we achieved independence in 1948, there never has been a time when we could claim the whole country was at peace. We have not been able to develop the trust and understanding necessary to remove causes of conflict. Hopes were raised by ceasefires that were maintained from the early 1990s until 2010 when these broke down over the course of a few months. One unconsidered move can be enough to remove long-standing ceasefires. In recent months, negotiations between the government and ethnic nationality forces have been making progress. We hope that ceasefire agreements will lead to political settlements founded on the aspirations of the peoples, and the spirit of union.

19　My party, the National League for Democracy, and I stand ready and willing to play any role in the process of national reconciliation. The reform measures that were put into motion by President U Thein Sein's government can be sustained only with the intelligent cooperation of all internal forces: the military, our ethnic nationalities, political parties, the media, civil society organizations, the business community and, most important of all, the general public. We can say that reform is effective only if the lives of the people are improved and in this regard, the international community has a vital role to play. Development and humanitarian aid, bi-lateral agreements and investments should be

18　缅甸是一个多民族国家，相信它的未来只能建立在依靠团结统一的精神之上。从 1948 年独立以来，我们就没有过整个国家一片和平的时候。我们不能建立起必要的信任和理解来摧毁冲突的根源。20 世纪 90 年代到 2010 年间停战曾带来了短暂的和平，然而几个月前这种局面又被打破了。一个鲁莽的举动就足以毁掉停战以来的长久和平。最近几个月，政府和少数民族武装力量间的谈判已经取得进展。我们希望停战协议能带来基于人民意愿的政治稳定和统一。

19　我和我的政党都愿意也随时准备着达成国内和解。总统吴登盛实行的改革措施只有国内各领域的有才之士合作才能贯彻下去，这包括：军方、少数民族、各政党、媒体、民间组织、商业团体以及最重要的人民大众。可以说，只有人民生活水平得到改善，改革才能说有效，在这一点上，国际社会要扮演关键的角色。整合发展、人道主义援助、双边协议和投资等资源来保证社会、政治和经济的平衡和可持续增长。我们国家潜力巨大。我们应该充分发展利用这些潜力，创造一个不仅更加繁荣，而且更加和谐、民主，人民享受充分的和

coordinated and calibrated to ensure that these will promote social, political and economic growth that is balanced and sustainable. The potential of our country is enormous. This should be nurtured and developed to create not just a more prosperous but also a more harmonious, democratic society where our people can live in peace, security and freedom.

20　The peace of our world is indivisible. As long as negative forces are getting the better of positive forces anywhere, we are all at risk. It may be questioned whether all negative forces could ever be removed. The simple answer is: "No!" It is in human nature to contain both the positive and the negative. However, it is also within human capability to work to reinforce the positive and to minimize or neutralize the negative. Absolute peace in our world is an unattainable goal. But it is one towards which we must continue to journey, our eyes fixed on it as a traveller in a desert fixes his eyes on the one guiding star that will lead him to salvation. Even if we do not achieve perfect peace on earth, because perfect peace is not of this earth, common endeavours to gain peace will unite individuals and nations in trust and friendship and help to make our human community safer and kinder.

21　I used the word "kinder" after careful deliberation; I might say the careful deliberation of many years. Of the sweets of adversity, and let me say that these are not numerous, I have found the sweetest, the most precious of all, is the lesson I learnt on the value of kindness. Every kindness

平、安全和自由的社会。

20　世界的和平是不可分割的。任何地方的恶势力超越了积极力量，那我们就都要遭殃。也许有人要质疑能否消灭所有的恶势力。答案很简单，是"不能"。善恶原本就在人性中共存。但是，加强积极力量，削弱或中和消极力量同样是人性的一部分。绝对和平是不可能达到的。但是我们仍要紧盯着这个目标，向它前进，就像沙漠中的旅行者跟定那颗可以带他走出沙漠的星星一样。即使不能达到绝对和平——因为绝对和平根本不存在——我们也要团结一切个人和国家，彼此信任，共同努力，互帮互助使人类社会更加安全和仁爱。

21　我是在认真考虑之后才用了"仁爱"这个词的，应该说仔细推敲了好多年。苦难中的欢乐可以说屈指可数，但是所有的乐趣中最珍贵的就是我在仁慈上领悟到的东西。我经历过的所有的仁爱行为，或大或小，都

I received, small or big, convinced me that there could never be enough of it in our world. To be kind is to respond with sensitivity and human warmth to the hopes and needs of others. Even the briefest touch of kindness can lighten a heavy heart. Kindness can change the lives of people. Norway has shown exemplary kindness in providing a home for the displaced of the earth, offering *sanctuary* [10] to those who have been cut loose from the moorings of security and freedom in their native lands.

22　There are refugees in all parts of the world. When I was at the Maela refugee camp in Thailand recently, I met dedicated people who were striving daily to make the lives of the inmates as free from hardship as possible. They spoke of their concern over "donor fatigue", which could also translate as "compassion fatigue". "Donor fatigue" expresses itself precisely in the reduction of funding. "Compassion fatigue" expresses itself less obviously in the reduction of concern. One is the consequence of the other. Can we afford to indulge in compassion fatigue? Is the cost of meeting the needs of refugees greater than the cost that would be consequent on turning an indifferent, if not a blind, eye on their suffering? I appeal to donors the world over to fulfill the needs of these people who are in search, often it must seem to them a vain search, of refuge.

23　At Maela, I had valuable discussions with Thai officials responsible for the administration of Tak Province where this and several other camps

使我相信仁爱对我们的世界来说永远不够。仁爱就是对他人的希望和需要保持敏感和人性的温暖。即使是一点点仁爱之行也可以舒展一颗沉重的心。仁爱可以改变人们的生活。在施行仁爱方面，挪威人是我们的榜样。他们为世界上失去家园的人提供住所，为那些在自己国家无法保障安全与自由的人提供避难所。

22　难民遍布世界各地。最近我探访泰国的米拉难民营的时候，见到许多为使被收容者尽可能远离艰难困苦而奋力投身于营救事业的人们。他们谈到了"捐助疲劳"的问题，也可以说成"同情疲劳"。"捐助疲劳"的实际表现就是经费短缺。"同情疲劳"则没有那么明显，它主要表现在对苦难的关注不够。这两者互为因果。我们能否沉溺在"同情疲劳"中呢？满足难民需要的是否比对难民冷眼相向——如果不是视而不见的话——要付出更大的代价呢？我呼吁世界倾力帮助那些苦苦寻觅避难所的人们，因为他们往往找不到这样的避难处。

23　在米拉的时候，我同泰国达府省的领导人有过珍贵的会谈，在这个省份还有好几个这样的难民营。他

---

⑩ sanctuary ['sæŋktʃuərɪ] *n.* 避难所

are situated. They acquainted me with some of the more serious problems related to refugee camps: violation of forestry laws, illegal drug use, home brewed spirits, the problems of controlling malaria, tuberculosis, dengue fever and cholera. The concerns of the administration are as legitimate as the concerns of the refugees. Host countries also deserve consideration and practical help in coping with the difficulties related to their responsibilities.

24 Ultimately our aim should be to create a world free from the displaced, the homeless and the hopeless, a world of which each and every corner is a true sanctuary where the inhabitants will have the freedom and the capacity to live in peace. Every thought, every word, and every action that adds to the positive and the wholesome is a contribution to peace. Each and every one of us is capable of making such a contribution. Let us join hands to try to create a peaceful world where we can sleep in security and wake in happiness.

25 The Nobel Committee concluded its statement of October 14, 1991 with the words: "In awarding the Nobel Peace Prize... to Aung San Suu Kyi, the Norwegian Nobel Committee wishes to honour this woman for her unflagging efforts and to show its support for the many people throughout the world who are striving to attain democracy, human rights and ethnic conciliation by peaceful means." When I joined the democracy movement in Burma it never occurred to me that I might ever be the recipient of any prize or honour.

们向我讲述了难民营一些更严重的问题：违反林业法，非法使用毒品，自酿烈酒，疟疾、肺结核、登革热和霍乱的蔓延。政府当局的焦虑同难民的焦虑一样合情合理。东道国在解决这些职责所在的问题时也应该得到国际社会的关注和支援。

24 我们最终的目标是创建一个没有流离失所、充满希望的世界，这个世界的每一个角落都是真正的避难所，人民可以自由地享受和平与生活。每一种思想、每一句话、每一次行动，只要是积极健康的，就都是对和平的贡献。我们每一个人都有能力做出这样的贡献。让我们携手共建一个可以伴着安全入睡、拥着幸福醒来的和谐世界吧。

25 1991年10月4日，诺贝尔奖委员会总结陈述道："委员会将诺贝尔和平奖……授予昂山素季，以此向她毫不动摇的努力表示敬意，也向这个世界上以和平方式寻求民主、人权的人们表示支持。"我加入缅甸的民主运动时，从未想过有一天我会因此得什么奖项或荣誉。我们为之奋斗的奖项是一个自由、安全、公平正义、人们可以充分发挥他们潜力的社会。荣誉就在我们的努力之中。历史给了

The prize we were working for was a free, secure and just society where our people might be able to realize their full potential. The honour lay in our endeavour. History had given us the opportunity to give of our best for a cause in which we believed. When the Nobel Committee chose to honour me, the road I had chosen of my own free will became a less lonely path to follow. For this I thank the Committee, the people of Norway and peoples all over the world whose support has strengthened my faith in the common quest for peace. Thank you.

我们为自己信仰的事业全力奋斗的机会。当诺贝尔奖委员会选择授予我此项荣誉的时候，我自愿选择的这条路走起来就没有那么孤单了。为此，我感谢诺贝尔奖委员会，感谢挪威人民和世界上所有人，你们的支持使我和世界人民追求和平的信念更加坚定。感谢大家。

演讲关键词 Practical Expressions

1. migrant workers 流动工人，农民工
2. communal violence 地区暴力冲突
3. social welfare 社会福利
4. humanitarian assistance 人道主义援助
5. bilateral agreement 双边协议
6. the displaced and the homeless 流离失所、无家可归的人们
7. house arrest 软禁

 精华佳句

1. When the Nobel Committee awarded the Peace Prize to me they were recognizing that the oppressed and the isolated in Burma were also a part of the world, they were recognizing the oneness of humanity.

诺贝尔奖委员会将奖项授予我，实际上是肯定了缅甸受压迫和被隔离的人们也是这个世界的一部分，也是在肯定这个世界的统一性。

2. If suffering were an unavoidable part of our existence, we should try to alleviate it as far as possible in practical, earthly ways.

如果生而为人，苦谛难免的话，我们应该尽可能地通过实际办法来缓解苦痛。

诺贝尔奖背后的那些趣事

提名真假 50 年后方可验证

诺贝尔物理学奖、化学奖以及经济学奖由瑞典皇家科学院评定，生理学或医学奖则由瑞典卡罗琳斯卡医学院评定，文学奖由瑞典文学院评定，而和平奖由挪威议会选出。每个授奖单位的委员会由 5 人组成，委员任期三年。诺贝尔奖得主的名字只有在揭晓那一刻才会宣布，然后及时致电通知这些获奖者。而诺贝尔奖候选人的名字在 50 年内都不会对外公开。所以每年大家都会听到或看到关于某人获得诺贝尔奖提名，成为诺贝尔奖候选人的新闻，然而其真实性还得等 50 年后才能得到验证。